Angela Merkel

Angela Merkel

*A Chancellorship
Forged in Crisis*

Alan Crawford
and Tony Czuczka

WILEY | Bloomberg PRESS

This edition first published 2013
© 2013 Alan Crawford and Tony Czuczka

Registered office

John Wiley & Sons Ltd, The Atrium, Southern Gate, Chichester, West Sussex, PO19 8SQ, United Kingdom

For details of our global editorial offices, for customer services and for information about how to apply for permission to reuse the copyright material in this book please see our website at www.wiley.com.

Reprinted July 2013, October 2013

Wiley publishes in a variety of print and electronic formats and by print-on-demand. Some material included with standard print versions of this book may not be included in e-books or in print-on-demand. If this book refers to media such as a CD or DVD that is not included in the version you purchased, you may download this material at http://booksupport.wiley.com. For more information about Wiley products, visit www.wiley.com.

Designations used by companies to distinguish their products are often claimed as trademarks. All brand names and product names used in this book are trade names, service marks, trademarks or registered trademarks of their respective owners. The publisher is not associated with any product or vendor mentioned in this book.

Limit of Liability/Disclaimer of Warranty: While the publisher and author have used their best efforts in preparing this book, they make no representations or warranties with the respect to the accuracy or completeness of the contents of this book and specifically disclaim any implied warranties of merchantability or fitness for a particular purpose. It is sold on the understanding that the publisher is not engaged in rendering professional services and neither the publisher nor the author shall be liable for damages arising herefrom. If professional advice or other expert assistance is required, the services of a competent professional should be sought.

Library of Congress Cataloging-in-Publication Data
Crawford, Alan.
    Angela Merkel: a chancellorship forged in crisis / Alan Crawford and Tony Czuczka.
      pages   cm
    Includes index.
    ISBN 978-1-118-64110-1 (cloth)
      1. Financial crises—Germany—History—21st century.   2. Germany—Economic policy—1990-   3. Merkel, Angela, 1954-   4. Heads of state—Germany.   I. Czuczka, Tony, 1959-   II. Title.
    HB3789.C73   2013
    943.088'3092—dc23
    [B]   2013011633

A catalogue record for this book is available from the British Library.

ISBN 978-1-118-64110-1 (hardback)   ISBN 978-1-118-64107-1 (ebk)
ISBN 978-1-118-64109-5 (ebk)   ISBN 978-1-118-64108-8 (ebk)

Set in 11.5/14pt Bembo Std by MPS Limited, Chennai, India
Printed in Great Britain by TJ International Ltd, Padstow, Cornwall, UK

MIX
Paper from
responsible sources
FSC
www.fsc.org   FSC® C013056

Contents

Acknowledgements

The idea for this book was hatched during a European Union summit in Brussels, but it was in a bar adjacent to the former U.S. Embassy building in Berlin that the opportunity to write it first became reality. After nearly three years of turmoil, the story of Angela Merkel and Europe's debt crisis had reached critical mass. As our colleague John Fraher, one of Bloomberg's managing editors, put it: The planets had aligned and now was the time to grasp our chance. Within two days we were at our writing desks, suddenly realizing the magnitude of the project.

We set about it armed with our own reporting from across Europe before and during the crisis; we re-examined speeches, trawled through public comments, mined archives and interviewed key participants in Berlin, Paris, Athens, Washington and elsewhere. The nature of any book examining the most powerful political figure in Europe, a serving leader, means that many of those who know the most are reluctant to speak openly. As a result, this work is based partly on discussions with European and U.S. officials who declined to be named, yet were important to portraying their side's version of events. Though we agreed not to identify them by name, we wish to thank them for their contribution.

First and foremost, we would like to thank Bloomberg's editor in chief, Matt Winkler, who approved our project and whose interest in the German chancellor was indispensable to making it happen. This book is a collaborative effort, which means it's also a tribute to the depth of knowledge and reporting by Bloomberg journalists world-wide. We had access to the expertise and articles of colleagues in the government and economy teams, but also in bonds, finance and currencies, in Europe and in the U.S., in print, television and the pictures department. Our thanks goes to them all. Notably, we wish to thank the government team in Berlin – Leon Mangasarian, Brian Parkin, Rainer Buergin and Patrick Donahue – who covered for our three-month absence without complaint during a time of crisis, literally. Leon and Stefan Nicola conducted interviews of two German officials that we gratefully included. Special thanks go to Maria Petrakis, Simon Kennedy, Jana Randow and Helene Fouquet for their help in providing contacts. We would never have gotten to that stage had it not been for the backing of Reto Gregori, Bloomberg's chief of staff, who provided the initial encouragement. John Fraher and Dan Moss fixed it for us to embark on the project, providing us with the time and travel needed. Our thanks also to Jim Hertling, whose spirited leadership of European government news and enthusiasm for the German story kept pushing Bloomberg to stay ahead of the pack.

Having the Bloomberg name behind the project opened doors. Many of those we spoke to did so because they trusted Bloomberg to paint an accurate picture of what happened during the crisis that almost brought the euro area to its knees. We hope that we measure up to those standards. We would like to single out Xavier Musca and Angel Gurria in Paris, who gave us the confidence at the outset that we were on the right track, and George Papaconstantinou, who graciously invited us into his home in Athens. Holger Schmieding and Carsten Brzeski gave us valuable feedback on substance and style. Our Bloomberg Muse team colleague Catherine Hickley offered key advice that greatly helped us to fashion the end product. Finally, we wish to thank our families – Judith, Freya and Magnus; Barbara and Adrian – for their resilience in the face of often absent and regularly moody husbands and fathers all through the tumultuous times of crisis culminating in the writing of this book. Judith Crawford, a political scientist and artist who grew up in East Germany, taught her husband about the true resonance of Europe. Barbara Kramžar, Tony's wife and inspiration, spurred him with her energy, understanding of the euro's significance and feel for the nexus between politics and human nature. We dedicate this book to them.

Chapter 1

Exodus
(Merkel's Journey)

*A*s a young woman, Angela Kasner would set out from East Berlin each summer on a pilgrimage to the furthermost reaches of where it was permitted to go. While others left to tend the fruit trees and berry bushes of their countryside dachas, Angela traveled south through Dresden, where the wartime remains of the Baroque Frauenkirche were visible from the railway station, on to the faded capital of the Czechoslovak Republic, where the Prague Spring had long since reverted to winter. From there, she went to Bratislava on the Danube river, which formed the border with Austria and the unattainable West, then on to Budapest, where she occasionally mingled with the few Western visitors who visited; some told her the city's parliament building and river setting reminded them of far-off London.

From Hungary it was across Romania on the long stretch east and then south to Bucharest, where Nicolae Ceauşescu was pursuing a policy of openness toward the West, a course that he would later reverse with brutal effect. She recrossed the Danube at Ruse on the Bulgarian border before arriving at Pirin in Bulgaria's southwestern corner, the end of the road. This was as far as she was able to travel. There, in a mountainous region known for its brown bears and wolves, the pastor's daughter who would become German chancellor looked longingly from the heights across the border toward Greece just a few kilometers distant. Greece, she thought; I'd like to go there, if even just once in my life.[1]

1

Angela Merkel's political journey took her to become Germany's first woman chancellor and its first from the former communist East. As she was sworn in on November 22, 2005, she could not have imagined the role that Greece would play during her time in office, nor the significance that her eventual trip to Athens in the fall of 2012 would assume.

Greece and its aftermath were to mark the evolution of her chancellorship, forcing her transition from one of many political leaders in Europe to the region's pre-eminent crisis handler. Faced with economic and financial turmoil stemming from Greece that threatened the euro, the singular achievement of the unprecedented period of post-World War II peace and unity, Merkel was forced to evolve and adapt in ways that tested her ability to balance external demands for greater action with domestic political constraints on doing so. For Merkel, Greece was the pivotal challenge of a chancellorship forged in crisis.

Barring an 18-month honeymoon period, Merkel's time in office came to be defined by a continuous thread of unprecedented turmoil not of her making but which required her to act nonetheless. Her first term was dominated by the U.S. subprime-led banking meltdown and subsequent global recession, which led straight into the crisis in the euro area spreading from Greece that rocked her second term.

Greece was admitted to the euro in 2000, the same year that Merkel became the leader of her party, swapping the untested European currency for the drachma which had been in use since long before the age of Homer or Alexander the Great conquered the known world. Once inside the euro club, from January 1, 2001, the country went on a spending spree it could not afford. State outlays on infrastructure soared in the run-up to the 2004 Olympic Games in Athens, matched by a record surge in consumer spending, and by late 2009, as a new Greek government was elected and Merkel began her second term, the bill was overdue. What came to be known as the sovereign debt crisis erupted, rippling out from Greece across the 17-country euro area. Financial markets took fright at the state of the region's finances and started to push up the rates governments paid to borrow to unbearable levels, forcing Greece, Ireland, Portugal, Spain and Cyprus to seek international bailouts and bringing down governments across Europe as voters protested spending cuts and tax increases.

Investors betting on the euro's demise were pitted against politicians determined to stop it from happening, chief among them Merkel.

A scientist by training whose defining trait is caution, Merkel was forced to look beyond just Germany's interests and to assume leadership in Europe. Thrust to the fore of policy making, she stepped up, slowly but with growing determination, to defend the euro she saw as the glue holding together the European Union (EU) that had been forged out of the ashes of war to stop the continent ever again descending into conflict. But how did the chancellor who came to office pledging to govern by means of many "small steps" come to take on the role of European savior? And what would the rest of Europe make of her prescription for Europe's ills?

When she assumed the German chancellorship, Merkel took the helm of Europe's biggest economy when it was struggling to adapt to the challenges of globalization. Unemployment had reached a postwar record of 12.1 percent eight months previously, in March 2005, growth was an anemic 0.7 percent compared with an average 1.7 percent for the euro area – Greece recorded 2.3 percent – and Germany's budget deficit was poised to breach EU limits for the third straight year.[2] The EU's biggest wave of enlargement to date had brought 10 countries predominantly from the East into the bloc the previous year, including economically dynamic entrants such as the Baltic States and the regional powerhouse, Poland. Far from being Europe's dominant player, a decade and a half after German reunification in 1990 the continent's most populous country was playing catch up.

Germany was riven politically as well as economically after Merkel's predecessor, Gerhard Schröder, had split with the U.S. over his refusal to join the 2003 invasion of Iraq. His program of far-reaching labor-market and welfare reforms had prompted street protests and divided his Social Democratic Party, even if Merkel had aligned her Christian Democratic bloc behind the measures. Yet Merkel was unable to capitalize on the situation and beat Schröder by a single percentage point in the 2005 election, limping into power at the head of an unwanted grand coalition with his party as governing partner.

As she prepared to contest elections in the fall of 2013, Merkel presided over Europe's predominant country, with unemployment near a two-decade low and a budget close to balanced. Courted by prime ministers and presidents from across Europe who sought to win her over to their side, her policy stances were those that mattered most, her example the line hard to ignore. She had become Europe's indispensable leader. So how did Merkel turn the continent's most populous country around? What qualities did she bring to the post of chancellor that united a majority of Germans behind her? More than that, how did she position Germany as Europe's foremost country, so much so that traditional allies including France, Italy, and Spain grew resentful of her methods and some in Greece, Ireland, and Portugal even questioned her motives?

The answer lies in large part with the evolution of the crisis and how Merkel brought the rigor of scientific analysis she'd learned in the physics laboratories of East Berlin and Leipzig to problem-solving of an economic and financial nature. Through trial and error, she edged her way forward, often to the dismay of her European peers and the exasperation of global partners. The German public, however, liked what they saw; polls consistently showed that they overwhelmingly backed her cautious stance, toward aiding banks in 2008, on measures to kick-start the economy in 2009 and above all on her handling of the debt crisis from 2010 onward. Throughout, she refused to be Europe's unconditional paymaster.

Merkel's response was to impose limits on aid and demand strict conditions in return, foremost among them budget cuts and deficit reduction to tackle what she saw as the root causes of the debt crisis. As she pushed a wary Europe to adopt the ways of Germany's highly competitive economy, Merkel stirred up old enmities and became the fulcrum in a clash between European and U.S. economic values. Her prescription exposed a fault line with U.S. officials who urged the deployment of more firepower to fight the crisis and greater burden sharing by Germany, while the austerity she advocated exacerbated a surge in unemployment to record levels in countries such as Greece and Spain and risked deepening the economic slump. Standing out in front as those who challenged her answers fell by the wayside, Merkel's means of defeating the crisis brought Europe to a crossroads. She was demonized in the Greek press as a jackboot-wearing Nazi hell-bent on reducing Greece, suffering the worst economic downturn since the war, to the status of a German colony.

Dispensing with caution for once, Merkel's visit to Athens in October 2012 was intended as a riposte and a tangible show of solidarity for the Greek people. The German government insisted it was a "normal visit," but it was clear she was entering the lion's den. The *New York Times* called Athens "the most hostile territory in Europe" for the chancellor.[3] Police were drafted from across Greece as some 40,000 protesters gathered on the streets to show their rejection of the European leader they regarded as the chief cause of their misery. Merkel, heavily guarded, came with no promises of additional aid, no pledge to ease the terms of Greece's bailout loans, nothing other than a message of support. "I believe that we will see light at the end of the tunnel," she said beside Prime Minister Antonis Samaras. "I want Greece to stay in the euro."[4]

After assessing the alternatives, Merkel took the political gamble of her life and decided to stand by Greece and save the euro – but on her terms. In doing so, she garnered plaudits and criticism for her path to resolving the turmoil. As the biggest paymaster, her status as de-facto leader of Europe was undisputed, yet with resentment of her newly assertive Germany growing, it was far from clear whether the rest of Europe was prepared to share the journey to her final destination. Merkel acknowledged that her recipe for addressing the problems of the euro region through austerity and painful reform could raise hackles in other countries. But she saw that as one of many climbs to be surmounted on the way to a fitter Europe better able to compete on the global stage. "We have to be a bit strict with each other at the moment so that in the end we are all successful together," Merkel said in November 2012. "I think it's better to try and tell the truth among friends and then continue to show solidarity with one another."[5]

As she concentrated on Europe, Merkel's domestic agenda was swept away by crisis. From March 2010, when she delivered her first speech to the Bundestag on Greece, through the end of 2012, Merkel addressed the full plenary session 24 times: two of her speeches focused on energy and the decision to abandon nuclear power in favor of renewables, and one on Germany's contribution to the military mission in Afghanistan; the other 21 dealt with aspects of the euro crisis and its ramifications for Germany and Europe.

Investors, economists, and political analysts hung on her every speech and policy twist as she honed her strategy to defend Europe and save the euro. Yet the chancellor has remained an enigma to many, her driving forces often misunderstood both in and outside Germany. A political outsider because of her roots, Merkel and her decision making remains opaque because of her Eastern habits such as a preference for doing her negotiating behind closed doors, turns of phrase that even Germans find hard to decipher and a dislike of sound bites. For Merkel, the European debt crisis centered on Greece became the crucible of her chancellorship, dominating her second term and helping to determine whether she served a third. Going forward, her choices will decide the success of Europe's experiment to leave war behind, preserve its welfare states, and become the world's most competitive economy. Where is she going? If she wants to, using Germany's returned strength, Merkel has unprecedented leverage to take Europe in whichever direction she chooses.

Notes

1. Merkel speech on EU Danube strategy, Regensburg, November 28, 2012: http://www.bundeskanzlerin.de/Content/DE/Rede/2012/11/2012-11-28-merkel-donau.html.
2. Eurostat table of EU country GDP: http://epp.eurostat.ec.europa.eu/tgm/table.do?tab=table&init=1&plugin=1&language=en&pcode=tec01115.
3. http://www.nytimes.com/2012/10/10/world/europe/angela-merkel-greece-visit.html.
4. Brian Parkin and Marcus Bensasson, "Merkel Urges Greece to Maintain Austerity to Stay in Euro," *Bloomberg News*: October 9, 2012: http://www.bloomberg.com/news/2012-10-09/merkel-s-athens-message-seen-directed-at-german-greek-audiences.html.
5. RTL interview, November 10, 2012: http://www.bundeskanzlerin.de/Content/DE/Interview/2012/12/2012-12-11-bkin-n-tv.html.

Chapter 2

Revelation (Five Minutes to Midnight)

A ngela Merkel stepped out of her Audi A8 and on to the red carpet at the Cannes conference center to be greeted by Nicolas Sarkozy flanked by French Republican Guards in white breeches and ceremonial plumed helmets, their sabres held aloft in salute. For all the pomp, the mood on the French Riviera in November 2011 was far from celebratory: Merkel shook her head and Sarkozy raised his hands in a gesture of exasperation as they met. It was Greece again.

Europe was two years into the sovereign debt crisis that had emerged in Greece and was rippling through the euro area. Governments were toppling as borrowing costs soared, dividing the region into a relatively healthy northern core anchored by Germany and a weaker periphery that ran in an arc from Ireland to Spain and Portugal, through Italy to its focal point, Greece. Each step of the fight to beat back the contagion only ever calmed financial markets for a matter of weeks or less before the flames reappeared somewhere else. Two bailouts worth 240 billion euros for Greece alone, almost the equivalent of its entire annual gross domestic product, the promise of debt relief, enrolling the expertise of the International Monetary Fund (IMF) alongside a 440 billion euro European rescue fund had failed to stop the crisis in its tracks. Now Greece's Prime Minister George Papandreou had given a televised address in Athens announcing his intention to hold a referendum on the latest round of measures approved by European governments to aid his country. A "No" vote would unravel what progress had been made and cause fresh waves of uncertainty to crash over the euro area, throwing the future of the single currency further into doubt. Merkel, as the leader of Europe's dominant economy, was first in line to stop that from happening.

She and Sarkozy met in Cannes on the eve of a Group of 20 summit of world leaders to decide the next move in their campaign to save the euro and defend European unity. Over two days in the Cannes conference center at one end of the palm-lined Boulevard de la Croisette, Merkel joined with Sarkozy to threaten Greece with defenestration from the euro and browbeat Italian Prime Minister Silvio Berlusconi into the humiliation of allowing outside monitoring of his country's economy. Within a week of being publicly cut loose, the Greek and Italian leaders lost what residual support they had and stood down, twin victims of the crisis. It was regime change by alternative means. Cannes, the Riviera town that hosts the eponymous film festival, was the moment that all strands came together in the crisis, and Merkel was the principal actor.

The Greek economy was on a life support system, dependent upon international aid as it faced a fifth straight year of recession. Public backing for Papandreou's government had collapsed as jobs and spending were slashed in a bid to wrestle down the biggest debt load per capita in the 27-nation European Union,[1] measures that were demanded in return for financial help under the terms of Greece's rescue deal. Papandreou's way out was to call a referendum in a bid to lance the boil and win some space to press on in the hope that signs of progress would emerge to alleviate the anger at home. His problem was that he failed to inform either his European partners or his own ministers before he made the announcement. "His behavior was disloyal," said Luxembourg's Prime Minister Jean-Claude Juncker, who also headed meetings of finance ministers of the euro countries, a role that gained in importance the longer the crisis persisted. "We would like to have been told."[2] Le Monde reported that Sarkozy was dismayed by the revelation. The G-20 summit hosted by France was meant to set the stage for his campaign for a second term. Sarkozy planned to show a united European front and win agreement from world leaders for a global effort to restore confidence to financial markets that were losing faith in Europe's ability to tackle the malaise at its heart. He was going to be photographed with Chinese President Hu Jintao and sign autographs with U.S. President Barack Obama as the crowds cheered. "History is being written in Cannes," read the G-20 banners going up around the town. Now his plans were threatened by Greece, and it wasn't even a member of the G-20 club.

In Berlin, Chancellor Merkel learned of the referendum at 7:20 p.m. on October 31 and took a moment to consider her response. She called Sarkozy and the two decided to summon Papandreou to Cannes to explain himself. They also agreed to halt the next aid payment to Greece until the referendum was cleared up, money that Greece desperately needed to pay its bills. At 7:15 a.m. on Tuesday morning, German Finance Minister Wolfgang Schäuble called his Greek counterpart, Evangelos Venizelos, in the Athens hospital where he was undergoing treatment for stomach pains and told him of the decision. Finance ministers from the other euro countries rubber stamped the suspension of aid within 90 minutes. Greece was effectively in limbo until Merkel and Sarkozy decided what to do with Papandreou. "Merkel and Sarkozy were upset because they felt they were betrayed," said Xavier Musca, Sarkozy's chief economic adviser and G-20 coordinator at the time. "They also felt Papandreou was not reliable, because they had spent one night with him discussing everything, and then he decides to do something he never talked about."[3]

The night in question was a 10-hour crisis session of European leaders in Brussels the previous week on October 26–27 again dominated by Greece. Papandreou's maneuvering was particularly galling for Merkel and Sarkozy because they had sat up half the night to negotiate a deal aimed at saving Greece, the second in almost 18 months. Their backing had secured agreement on a 130 billion-euro bailout for Greece crafted with the IMF on top of a 110 billion-euro rescue agreed in May 2010. They had personally intervened with the banks' representative, Charles Dallara of the International Institute of Finance, summoning him from his hotel that night to accept losses of 50 percent on Greek government debt held in private hands. When he resisted, he was told the alternative was to allow Greece to go bankrupt, after which the banks would in all likelihood receive nothing back on their investments.[4] The same summit also forged a plan to increase Europe's rescue fund for any future countries that went the way of Greece to 1 trillion euros, as well as compelling banks to raise the amount of money they held in store to absorb financial shocks. Taken together, it was a package that promised to finally snuff out the flames of financial contagion that were spreading across Europe while putting a lid on the source of the conflagration: Greece. At the summit's close, Papandreou personally thanked Merkel and Sarkozy for their efforts. "This agreement gives us time," he said. "Tens of billions of euros have been lifted from the backs of the Greek people." Even Merkel departed from her characteristically restrained rhetoric. "I am very aware that the world's attention was on these talks," she said at a press conference after 4 a.m. as the summit ended. "We Europeans showed tonight that we reached the right conclusions." It took one weekend for Europe to demonstrate its inherent capacity to shoot itself in the foot. Greeks were in open rebellion and opposed putting their country any more at the mercy of its international creditors. They wanted nothing do with a policy that promised to inflict yet more deprivation on a population already on its knees. Papandreou, having successfully negotiated for the debt burden to be eased, returned home to be greeted as a traitor.

A snap poll in Greece taken after the EU summit floated the idea that the measures agreed should be put to a referendum, with 46 percent saying they would vote against. More than seven in 10 still said they wanted to stay in the euro. With his majority whittled down to 153 seats in the 300-member parliament, Papandreou felt he needed to resolve that contradiction and regain democratic legitimacy. A plebiscite fit the bill, even if for Greece as well as for the rest of Europe the prospect of a referendum created a whole new set of unknown factors. International financial markets, already highly strung after months of bombardment by the crisis centered on Greece, were quick to offer their verdict. On Tuesday, November 1, the day after the referendum plan was announced, Germany's DAX lost 5 percent, France's CAC 40 Index dropped 5.4 percent and Italy's FTSE MIB Index sank 6.8 percent. U.S. stocks were hit and shares in Asia tumbled. National Bank of Greece plunged 15 percent, sending its share price to its lowest since 1992.[5] Fitch Ratings said the referendum "dramatically raises the stakes for Greece and the eurozone," increasing the risks of a "forced and disorderly" default. What that meant for the rest of the eurozone was incalculable, but the implications were dire. According to an estimate by Natixis, if Greece left the euro it could cause an additional 16.4 billion euros in net losses to French banks alone, with Sarkozy's government left to fill the hole.[6]

Papandreou's proposal "surprised all of Europe," the French president said on November 1. "The plan adopted unanimously by the 17 members of the euro area last Thursday is the only possible way to resolve the problem of Greek debt." In a joint statement issued the same day, he and Merkel said the package of measures agreed in Brussels was "more necessary than ever today." EU President Herman Van Rompuy and EU Commission President José Barroso raised the pressure on Papandreou to stop the deal from unraveling. "We fully trust that Greece will honor the commitments undertaken in relations to the euro area and the international community," they said. Italy, the euro area's third largest economy, was meanwhile coming under threat. That night in Rome, on the eve of the G-20 summit and after a day in which Italy's government borrowing costs climbed to the highest relative to Germany since before the advent of the euro, Prime Minister Berlusconi called an emergency meeting of his Cabinet.

With the stage set for Cannes, Merkel and Sarkozy arranged to meet Papandreou at the film festival center facing the harbor filled with extravagant super-yachts. The Greek premier arrived a few hours after Merkel. This time there was no guard of honor. The EU's Barroso and Van Rompuy attended the November 2 meeting along with the eurogroup head Juncker, IMF chief Christine Lagarde and the finance ministers of France, Germany and Greece. Papandreou arrived in Cannes bolstered by his Cabinet's unanimous endorsement for his referendum plan, for all the residual doubts. There was still no word on the question to be put to the people. "The referendum will be a clear mandate and strong message within and outside Greece on our European course and our participation in the euro," Papandreou told his ministers that morning before leaving for France. Already having to fend off calls for new elections from the opposition New Democracy party led by Antonis Samaras, the Greek premier said the question was not one of his government or another government: "The dilemma is yes or no to the loan accord, yes or no to Europe, yes or no to the euro."

Merkel and Sarkozy wouldn't allow Papandreou the luxury of choice. The meeting, in one of the many rooms off the main conference hall, was explosive. Merkel, who was visibly "very upset," according to Musca, saw it as time to face up to some unpleasant truths that had been avoided for too long. She and Sarkozy confronted Papandreou and berated him for presenting them with a fait accompli. Yes, the Greek people had made sacrifices, but the country as a whole was not an innocent party in the crisis of confidence sweeping the eurozone. They told him his planned ballot had placed the entire euro area at risk, and Europe's biggest powers could not let the single currency be wrecked by one country. Suspecting him of trying to wriggle out of the commitments he made one week previously in Brussels, they handed him an ultimatum: hold to the agreement or wave goodbye to 8 billion euros in international rescue funds he needed to pay Greece's bills. If he must hold a referendum on the outcome of what was decided, then it could be about one thing only: Greece's future membership of the euro; in or out, they were prepared to let Greece go and risk the consequences. Sarkozy and Merkel dictated the timing and the content of Papandreou's referendum, and spelled out the consequences of its outcome. The vote had to be brought forward to December to get it out of the way, removing a source of uncertainty as soon as possible. It could address Greece's future in the euro only and not any aspect of the country's bailout terms. Furthermore, there would be no money for Greece until the result was known. Sarkozy held a press conference after the meeting and said that not one cent would flow to Greece in the event of a "No" vote. It was all or nothing. Papandreou, presented with no alternative and his referendum eviscerated, accepted their terms. Publicly humiliated, he returned to Athens to face a confidence vote in parliament.

The G-20 started the next day, Thursday November 3, with a discussion of Greece. Underscoring the global ramifications of one small country's travails, a television set was brought into the main meeting room to allow leaders to watch the debate in the Greek parliament broadcast live on BBC World. As he addressed the main chamber in Athens, world leaders and the assembled press of more than 20 nations gathered around television screens to watch Papandreou. His majority dwindling further to two, the prime minister made a plea for a government of national unity to overcome the country's epic problems. Political consensus, with the opposition coming on board to secure outside aid and help the transition through this unprecedented situation, would remove the need to ask the public's backing for the deal struck in Brussels, he said. Venizelos, his finance minister, was more direct: Greece wasn't going to hold a referendum. The vote scrapped and his attempt to seek legitimacy for the deal in tatters, Papandreou offered to stand aside to help the formation of a national unity government. He went on to win the confidence ballot by 153 votes to 145 votes after promising his own parliamentary group that he would go. His last-ditch gamble had failed. Politically he was a spent force and he resigned the following week on November 11, nine days after Merkel and Sarkozy lost patience with him. Papandreou, who compared Greece's path out of the crisis to Homer's classic tale of Odysseus's 10-year journey back to Ithaca, foundered at sea without reaching home. Merkel, acting with Sarkozy, helped seal his fate.

If Greece could trigger the biggest two-day decline in global stocks in almost three years, as Papandreou's referendum flip-flop had done, then events in Italy had the potential to cause even more carnage. Italy, the third biggest economy in the euro, with domestic output almost 10 times that of Greece, was becoming a worry to Merkel and Sarkozy alike. They'd already confronted Berlusconi on October 23 at a previous EU summit and told him to follow through on his commitments. Asked at a joint press conference what they'd said to Berlusconi then, Merkel and Sarkozy looked at each other for a moment, then laughed. Trust can only be regained by Italy assuming its responsibilities and taking credible steps for the future, Merkel said, dictating to Berlusconi what must be done. "Italy has great strengths but Italy also has a very high overall debt level, and that has to be credibly reduced," she said. "That, I think, is the expectation on Italy."[7] On the eve of traveling to Cannes, with Italian government borrowing costs soaring, Berlusconi had promised to enact emergency measures in a budget bill to be passed that month including raising the retirement age, easing rules on firing workers, and accelerating state asset sales. Yet having given the wrong signals to markets in the past, Berlusconi was unable to give investors the assurances they wanted on Italy's policy direction to merit an easing of the government's costs of borrowing. Germany and France were pressing the Italians in private to announce budgetary measures before it was too late. Powerless to change his course and unable to have him fail to meet his commitments, the French and German leaders summoned Berlusconi to a room in the conference center on Thursday morning. As with Papandreou, they gave him an ultimatum: this was not a discussion about voluntary measures. Sarkozy and Merkel told Berlusconi that solving Greece was one thing, dealing with Italy a problem of a different magnitude. Unless he gave an immediate signal demonstrating that he was aware of the gravity of the situation, he was lost. Now that the fire of contagion was in Italy, the whole eurozone was at risk of implosion, they said: Do something about it. When Berlusconi said that he had always done the right thing by Italy, Merkel and Sarkozy told him markets didn't share that faith. He needed to do something quickly to regain market confidence if he was to give Italy a chance of surviving the crisis. Boxed in, Berlusconi agreed to have the IMF send outside monitors to assess Italy's budget. In a statement issued the following day at the close of the G-20, Christine Lagarde welcomed "Italy's decision to invite the IMF to intensify our surveillance and monitoring work, to help support the major steps being taken by the government on both fiscal adjustment and structural reforms." It was too little too late. Battered by the markets that drove Italy's borrowing costs to fresh records, Berlusconi announced his resignation on November 10.

For Merkel, whose position as Europe's principal decision maker was cemented six months later when she lost her ally Sarkozy in France's presidential election, the moment of truth for the euro area was the latest incarnation of financial crisis that had rocked her chancellorship almost since the beginning. Merkel was just 18 months into office when she was confronted with the worst global financial meltdown in living memory. She set about resolving each stage of crisis for which there was no playbook – in the banks, the economy, and as a result of euro countries' debt loads – and she learned along the way. Catapulted to the forefront of European policy making during the euro trauma, it came to define Merkel's chancellorship even as she struggled for a solution. Some leaders, like Papandreou and Berlusconi, collapse and fall victim to crisis; others like Merkel flourish. Lambasted for delaying, for backtracking, and for refusing to commit more resources to the crisis fight, Merkel showed at Cannes that she can suddenly be decisive, brutally so.

The source of her resoluteness lay four months previously in the summer of 2011. Markets were plunging globally with the realization that Europe's common efforts to help Greece had failed and the bailout program wasn't working, spelling trouble for the rest of the euro area. An EU summit on July 21 had agreed on the second Greek bailout of 130 billion euros among a package of steps that included expanding the powers of the European rescue fund and easing the terms of emergency bailout loans awarded to Portugal and Ireland. Merkel also quietly dropped plans to enlist banks and other investors in helping to pay for the fallout of crises once a permanent rescue fund was set up in 2013, after criticism from the European Central Bank (ECB) and the U.S. that forcing the private sector to accept losses on their investments would worsen the situation and could tip the euro area over the edge. However, the summit still backed a German-led push for a restructuring of Greek debt, without shoring up Spain and Italy against contagion, sowing the seeds of the next bout of trouble. As early as April 2011, Germany had signaled its willingness to impose losses on Greece bondholders in the face of pledges by Papandreou to avoid such a situation. Werner Hoyer, Germany's minister for European affairs, said that a so-called haircut on the debt held by investors "would not be a disaster."[8] By broaching a previously taboo subject, Germany was setting itself up for a widening of the crisis for political reasons. The market response was swift: the turmoil spread and started to infect core euro countries, with the interest rates paid by the Spanish, Italian, and even French governments climbing steeply. ECB President Jean-Claude Trichet instructed the central bank to step in and start buying Spanish and Italian government bonds in a bid to impose some calm and stop the situation from spiraling out of control.

Until that summer, Europe's leaders had focused on tackling small, peripheral countries: Greece, Ireland and Portugal, together worth some 6 percent of euro area gross domestic product (GDP). The meltdown showed the crisis had moved to the core, marauding Italy and Spain, jointly representing more than 25 percent of the euro area's output, and lapping at the doors of the region's linchpin, Germany. Forced to confront the evidence that the entire region was facing an existential threat, Merkel shifted her focus: she decided she had to save the euro and to take Europe with her. As early as May 2010, she had expressed her conviction that "our Europe will overcome the present crisis of our common currency." Now it was time to act. Up to that point, Merkel insisted there were no innocent victims of the crisis, that countries had brought the market reaction upon themselves, whether through greed, corruption, or ineptitude. As Italy was sucked into the maelstrom despite a budget deficit of 3.9 percent in 2011 – just 0.9 percentage points outside EU limits and lower than France's[9] – she had to question that assessment. Markets were starting to price in a 98 percent chance of a Greek default, yet Merkel concluded it was impossible to calculate the impact of a "disorderly insolvency" on the wider euro area. Merkel told a closed meeting of leaders of her parliamentary group as they gathered in the Reichstag on the last day of August after the summer break that she would not go down in history as the person who wrecked the euro.[10] With a lack of drama typical of the chancellor, she announced her decision to the world two weeks later on a regional radio station serving the greater Berlin area. "The top priority is to avoid an uncontrolled insolvency because that wouldn't just hit Greece," Merkel said in an rbb Inforadio interview on September 13. "Everything must be done to keep the euro area together politically, because we would very quickly face a domino effect" otherwise.[11]

The U.S. was quick to recognize the shift in Merkel's thinking as a turning point for the global economy. Treasury Secretary Timothy Geithner appeared on CNBC the following day and praised Merkel's comments as an acknowledgment that Europe's crisis response to date had been "behind the curve" and that more had to be done. "And I think it's important that you saw the Chancellor of Germany say yesterday – Angela Merkel say yesterday they are absolutely committed, and they have the financial capacity and the economic capacity to do what it takes to hold this thing together," Geithner said.[12]

Merkel had until then been prepared to make it easy for Greece to leave the euro, perhaps offering guarantees of an early return to the currency under certain conditions, but the decision had to come from Greece. There was no mechanism to expel a country, however wayward, and to do so without the Greek government's agreement would have spelled meltdown. With the realization that this was a place she could not go, Merkel swung behind Greece. Gone was the chastising language threatening sanctions on deficit "sinners" and in its place was encouragement to meet targets on the road to recovery. "We want a strong Greece in the euro area and Germany is ready to offer all kinds of help that is needed," Merkel said after meeting with Papandreou in Berlin two weeks later, on September 27, 2011. Having finally acknowledged the stakes, Merkel made a choice to hold the eurozone together. That was why Papandreou's referendum so incensed her. It also explained Merkel's reconciliation with his successor, Antonis Samaras, after snubbing him for more than a year and a half. As the fall of 2011 drew closer, she had to rebalance German interests against Europe's future, pitting her domestic reality against the wider effort to save Europe's postwar unity. For a chancellor known for her love of weighing the evidence before settling upon her preferred option, it was decision time.

French philosopher Bernard-Henri Lévy, interviewed in the German newspaper *Frankfurter Allgemeine Zeitung* in November 2012, said the fact that Greece and Italy – the cradles of European civilization – were among the countries worst affected by the crisis showed how it had reached "to the very fundament of European existence." The crisis had overcome Europe's "memory, everything that makes up its basis and origins, its soul, its grammar," he said.[13] Lévy's assessment of the debt crisis was dramatic. Yet the fact he pronounced on it at all underscored the extent to which the saga of Greece and its sequels had gone mainstream. As the impact began to be felt by every taxpayer, it went from back page business news to the front pages of the tabloids. The lexicon of the crisis began to seep into the popular culture, with bond yields and spreads used to denote how bad things were. Dispatches from Greece or details of the latest EU summit agreement were top-of-the-hour news across Europe, raising the pressure on Merkel, who was cast as making or breaking deals. If the chancellor glanced at *Bild*, Germany's biggest-selling daily, she saw headlines such as "So the

Greeks DO want our money," or "The Iron Chancellor," an epithet first attached to Bismarck, the first chancellor of a united Germany. *Bild* regularly featured the crisis on its front page alongside pictures of topless women, criticizing Greece or railing against joint sales of government bonds across the euro region – a proposal known as euro bonds that would mean Germany underwriting the debts of weaker states.

While Germany obsessed about how much it was having to pay for euro rescues, others were preoccupied with how much their governments were paying to service debts. The higher the rate charged by markets, the riskier lending to the government was seen to be. Greece, Portugal, and Ireland were unable to keep functioning as their respective costs breached 7 percent, forcing them to seek outside help. The spread, or divergence from the German bonds that serve as the benchmark, showed how far from the path of fiscal rectitude a country had strayed. In France, "les spreads" became a national obsession; in Italy they echoed political turmoil that helped bring down governments. Italy's top-selling *Corriere della Sera* ran a headline on its front page on November 9, 2011, proclaiming "Spread a 500," as the spread over Germany reached 500 basis points, or 5 percentage points.[14] Berlusconi announced his intention to step down as premier the next day. Pope Benedict XVI, a German, used one of his final speeches as pontiff, at the Vatican in January 2013, to urge European leaders to devote the same energy to tackling the growing divergence in wealth as the spread in borrowing costs.

With euro countries locked into a single exchange rate, the hitherto obscure business of buying and selling government bonds became both an indicator of the relative economic performance of the 17 countries belonging to the euro and a sign of how imbalanced market perceptions of them had become. Merkel's response was to call for all euro countries to undertake measures aimed at reducing debt and making Europe more economically competitive; though she never said it in such plain terms, they should become a lot more like Germany.

With Europe split into those countries in need of help and those in a position to provide it, Merkel's combination of austerity and structural reforms gained Germany enemies as the economic mood darkened. Economists such as Nobel Prize winner Paul Krugman held

Germany to blame for exacerbating the crisis by enforcing budget cuts at a time of recession. In his *New York Times* blog, Krugman compared the process to the medieval practice of bleeding a patient to make them well. Billionaire investor George Soros said Merkel risked generating a revolt across Europe. The Obama administration clashed with Merkel over her refusal to deploy Germany's economic might to do more to stop the crisis from proliferating. Europeans haven't responded "as effectively as they needed to," Obama said during a roundtable discussion at the White House on September 28, 2011. U.S. officials have been more scathing in private, applying constant pressure for Germany to take the lead and calm the crisis, just as they badgered Germany to step up domestic consumption and increase the size of its economic stimulus measures in 2009. They acknowledge that Merkel has been pivotal throughout, however. One senior U.S. official said that Merkel has been the key decision maker at all turning points in the crisis.

What anyone attempting to coerce Merkel into more action had to learn to appreciate was the domestic balancing act she had to perform, not only between the public and her three-party coalition, but also taking into account the responses of Germany's constitutional court and the powerful voice of the central bank, the Bundesbank. The day after Obama's public comment on the inadequacy of Europe's crisis response, Merkel faced down her coalition critics to win passage in the lower house, the Bundestag, of a bill allowing an expansion of the euro area rescue fund's firepower, raising Germany's share of guarantees to a maximum 211 billion euros from 123 billion euros. She had paved the way for it the previous month by allowing the German parliament veto right over future rescue measures, thus satisfying potential rebels as well as settling any legal doubts of the constitutional court in Karlsruhe. She also used the opportunity to stamp her authority on the coalition, telling dissenters to stop talking down Greece. "What we don't need is unrest in the financial markets," she said. "The uncertainties are big enough as it is." But the domestic concerns remained.

The raising of Germany's guarantees meant that Merkel was unable to agree to a Sarkozy proposal at Cannes to enlist the rest of the world to help Europe's crisis-fighting efforts. The French had brokered a tentative deal with G-20 nations including China and the U.K. to provide funds that would enable the euro rescue fund to be leveraged to increase its size. To go along, Merkel had to win the support of the Bundesbank. Although by then run by Merkel's former chief economic adviser, Jens Weidmann, the German central bank refused. The French suggested using a credit from the state-owned KfW development bank, but that too was out of the question as parliament would have to vote on any attempt to use the KfW. Coming so soon after lawmakers agreed to raise German liabilities to 211 billion euros, that route too was politically impossible. The French plan was thwarted by Merkel's unwillingness to risk a domestic defeat and it came to nothing. Where outside observers saw German obstructionism during the crisis, Merkel's government saw the pressure placed on them to agree to measures that were domestically impossible as posing a threat to the most stable economy in Europe. Political instability in Germany would not help the crisis fight, in the Merkel administration's view. Nevertheless, as the turmoil spread, Europe's epiphany was overdue and it fell to Merkel, the pastor's daughter from the provincial East German town of Templin, to act.

Notes

1. European Commission Autumn projections, November 7, 2012: http://ec.europa.eu/economy_finance/eu/forecasts/2012_autumn_forecast_en.htm.
2. Juncker interview with Germany's ZDF television, November 3, 2011, on Luxembourg government website: http://www.gouvernement.lu/salle_presse/interviews/2011/11-novembre/03-pm/index.html.
3. Interview in Paris, November 30, 2012.
4. "Sarkozy Temper Boils, Banks Yield in Six-Day War Saving the Euro," *Bloomberg News*, November 2, 2011: http://www.businessweek.com/news/2011–11–02/sarkozy-temper-boils-banks-yield-in-six-day-war-saving-the-euro.html.
5. "Papandreou Grip on Power Weakens," *Bloomberg News*, November 14, 2011: http://www.businessweek.com/news/2011–11–14/papandreou-grip-on-power-weakens-as-lawmakers-rebel-on-vote.html.
6. James Amott, "Agricole May Lose EU10.4b on Greek Euro Exit, Natixis Says," *Bloomberg News*, November 2, 2011: (not on web).
7. Merkel–Sarkozy press conference: https://www.youtube.com/watch?v=D8NtEXnc4jY.
8. "Germany Would Back Greece Debt Restructuring, Hoyer Says," *Bloomberg News*, April 15, 2011: http://www.bloomberg.com/news/2011–04–15/germany-would-back-greece-if-it-sought-debt-restructuring-minister-says.html.

9. Kristian Siedenberg, "EU commission autumn forecasts," Bloomberg table.
10. "Angela Merkel: A Rational European," *Frankfurter Allgemeine Zeitung*, October 13, 2012: http://www.faz.net/aktuell/politik/europaeische-union/angela-merkel-europaeerin-aus-vernunft-11924570.html.
11. rbb Inforadio interview, September 13, 2011: http://www.bundeskanzlerin.de/Content/DE/Artikel/2011/09/2011–09–13-merkel-rbb-euro.html.
12. Transcript of Geithner interview with CNBC's Jim Cramer: http://www.cnbc.com/id/44487020/.
13. *Frankfurter Allgemeine Zeitung*, November 20, 2012: http://www.faz.net/aktuell/feuilleton/debatten/bernard-henri-levy-im-gespraech-reformen-reichen-nicht-aus-um-europa-zu-retten-11965397.html.
14. Dan Liefgreen and Armorel Kenna, "Italians Obsessed by 'Lo Spread' as Advance in Bond Yields Makes Headlines," *Bloomberg News*, November 14, 2011: http://www.bloomberg.com/news/2011–11–14/italians-obsessed-by-lo-spread-as-advance-in-bond-yields-makes-headlines.html.

Chapter 3

Genesis (Eastern Roots)

Angela Merkel is more than just Germany's first female chancellor, the first from the formerly communist East and the first born after World War II. She is the first true postwar chancellor. Brought up behind the Iron Curtain as the future European Union took shape, she was little burdened by 40 years of West German politics and ideology when the Berlin Wall fell in 1989. Cautious by nature, she exploited freedom gradually, driven by a will to succeed honed since her sheltered childhood in small-town East Germany. She had grown up the daughter of a Lutheran minister and chosen an academic profession, making her an outsider in a communist state that worshipped workers and peasants. That meant she had to work harder than others to get ahead. Over time, she realized that the German Democratic Republic was an inefficient, hemmed-in place where striving for excellence wasn't rewarded. Living in a police state that snooped on its own people – and shot them if they tried to flee to West Germany – taught her to be careful about whom to trust and what to say. Merkel explained some of her other "cultural values" in a speech to delegates of her Christian Democratic Union party in 1991, less than a year after the two Germanys reunited. West Germans might find it strange, but an "ability to read between the lines" had been crucial in the East. Also, people were attuned to reaching "satisfaction in life with modest means" and to "holding your ground if you're in the minority."[1] Merkel is unusual in another way: she came to politics from the physics lab, not a law practice or the shop floor. More than 20 years later in the midst of the debt crisis, she reflected on the mental adjustment. Politicians, she said, are expected to "repeat the same things pretty often. In my previous job as a physicist, that was a mortal sin. In science, the task is never to tell the same thing twice" because it would indicate "that you haven't done anything all day."[2]

Angela Kasner was born July 17, 1954, in Hamburg, the cosmopolitan port city that was devastated by Allied bombs during World War II and would help launch the Beatles about six years later. Her father Horst Kasner, son of a Berlin police officer, had finished studying theology and was needed by the church. Bucking the exodus of East Germans fleeing to West Germany's reviving economy, he and his wife put their infant first-born into a basket and headed the other way. The first stop was a parish house in Quitzow, a farming village outside a former Prussian garrison town only 20 kilometers (12 miles) east of the intra-German border. Merkel said her father always intended to return to his native eastern Germany after studying in the western cities of Heidelberg and Hamburg.[3] Merkel's mother, Herlind, an English teacher who had grown up and met her husband in Hamburg, went along "out of love."[4] Suspect to the regime because the family wasn't part of the "workers' class," the pastor's wife was barred from teaching, so she became a stay-at-home mother. In 1957, the family moved to Templin, a market town of fewer than 20,000 inhabitants some 80 kilometers (50 miles) northeast of Berlin, where church authorities asked Horst Kasner to set up a theological seminary. Angela Merkel grew up in the "Waldhof" complex on the edge of town, perched on a bluff above the Templin canal and bounded on two sides by pine forests. The house still stands and a church-run center for the disabled and mentally ill that she remembers from her childhood continues to serve a similar function today. This is where the future chancellor comes from – a provincial, sparsely populated rural area of lakes, fields, and forests, closer to the Polish border than to Berlin's city limits. Merkel, born in the West, raised in the East and now chancellor of both, calls the region home. The weekend house she shares with her second husband, Berlin chemistry professor Joachim Sauer, is even more remote in the tiny hamlet of Hohenwalde. In keeping with the cordon of privacy surrounding Merkel, her husband, a fellow physicist, strenuously avoids the public eye. So do her brother, Marcus, born in 1957, and her sister Irene, who is 10 years her junior. Her brother is a university lecturer in physics at Frankfurt am Main and her sister has a physiotherapy practice in Berlin.

Getting from Berlin to Merkel's homeland in the Uckermark region takes little more than an hour, but it is a journey from the reconstructed capital of Europe's biggest economy to the rural backwaters of the east. The Brandenburg state road cuts through a patchwork of villages and small towns carved out of the forest, skirts lakes and passes fields laced with pine and birch woods. It is a typically Central European landscape that could easily be in Poland or the Czech Republic. Lining the route to Templin are East German-era concrete-panel housing projects, each apartment adorned with a rusting balcony; crumbling red-brick barns; the occasional industrial site; and renovated family homes, many with their own woodpile, shed and small fruit orchard. Occasional signposts point to a country manor, or Schloss, some of which date from the times of Prussia's King Frederick the Great. The road passes a sprawling abandoned Soviet Army barracks that Moscow used as a secret nuclear-missile base in the late 1950s, even before the Cuban missile crisis. A mural of a peasant woman bearing sheaves of wheat still decorates the entrance.[5] Like other towns and cities across the eastern German states, Templin has a war memorial dedicated to the Soviet soldiers who lost their lives on the final march for Berlin in 1945. The area was enticing enough for Hermann Goering, the morphine-addicted head of the Luftwaffe, Nazi Germany's air force, to build his country estate, Carinhall, a few miles to the east. It was blown up in 1945 on Goering's orders as the Soviet Army advanced. Soviet troops remained in eastern Germany until 1994, first as an occupying force and later as a bulwark against the West.

The layers of history go deeper still in Templin, where walls dating back to the 14th century encircle the old town. First mentioned in records in 1270, Templin was located on the site of an older Slavic settlement built on raised land at the crossroads of trading routes from Magdeburg northeast to the Hanseatic city of Szczecin, in present-day Poland, and northwest toward Hamburg. Towers still crown the three gates that admitted access to the town: the Mill Gate, the Prenzlau Gate, and the Berlin Gate. Merkel's first wedding was held beside the Berlin Gate in the tiny 14th-century St. George's Chapel, Templin's oldest church. A plaque on the red-brick wall says the building "survived all town fires and wars." Half-timbered medieval houses renovated since German reunification line the street. On the corner, aphorisms painted in Gothic script on the outside of a former bank exhort Templin's citizens to manage their money prudently. "The saver of today is the winner of tomorrow," reads one. "Whoever saves fulfills a great public service," says another, while a third assures Templiners: "He who practices thriftiness early on gets twice as far in life."

Templin was bombed by Allied aircraft on March 6, 1944, and by the end of World War II, after Soviet troops took the town, two-thirds of the center lay in ruins. By the late 1950s, when Merkel's parents arrived with their newborn baby, rebuilding was very much still underway: the historic town hall was only completed in 1965. The picturesque Templin of today was still bomb-scarred in Merkel's youth. The commerce that had made the town and helped it to flourish for centuries was long gone. In its place East German authorities encouraged small trades alongside the mainstays of forestry, farming, and the timber industry. By the mid-1960s there were about 100 small businesses involved in trades and crafts, while a clothing plant provided work for many of the town's women. One modest claim to fame was that the communist-era textile conglomerate that made East German blue jeans was headquartered in Templin. Easterners never much liked them, and longed for their more stylish Western counterparts, which were less liable to chafe. Helped by its rail link with Berlin, the town became a vacation destination in the 1970s, with complexes built for the state-controlled FDGB labor federation to allow workers to enjoy the lakes and forests.

Merkel's weekend house is 20 kilometers (12 miles) from Templin on a cobbled road through a forest that ends in a fork, one lane ending in a farmyard and the other leading down a muddy grass track. Only the solid wood fence with a base of red brick and concealed cameras at its corners are a giveaway. It's her favorite place to recover from international trips and domestic politics; she relaxes by gardening and cooking with her husband. Home for the German chancellor is not the Rhineland of Helmut Kohl, the industrial cityscape of Helmut Schmidt's Hamburg nor the Westphalian fields of Gerhard Schröder, but that doesn't make it any less German. Asked by the eastern German magazine *SUPERillu* about her concept of "Heimat," or homeland, Merkel replied that it was "the landscape of the Uckermark, with all its lakes and forests," the scent of lilac blossom in springtime and the aromatic smell of the pine forest in summer.

When East Germany's communist regime buckled in the face of pro-democracy protests and opened the Berlin Wall on November 9, 1989, Merkel was a 35-year-old divorcee working in quantum chemistry at the Academy of Sciences in East Berlin, and a stranger to political activism. "The way I lived my life, I truly wasn't an active resistance fighter," she recalls.[6] She had been best in her class in high school, excelling at math and Russian. At university in the 1970s, she delved into physics because she relished the challenge of "something that didn't come easy." It was also the only subject she ever failed in school, a field that produces results by scientific method and experimentation, rather than gut instinct. While Merkel wasn't handy with a soldering iron in the physics lab, "theory was tangible" for her.[7] Her church background limited her choice of fields, though studying the natural sciences may have shielded her from the worst pressures of the police state. What she liked about physics was that "the truth couldn't be distorted so easily" as elsewhere in the communist state.[8] Growing up this way made Merkel a fighter. "Everything was always a struggle: to avoid attracting attention at all costs, to always be a little bit better than the others."[9]

For West German Chancellor Helmut Kohl, the fall of the Berlin Wall signaled restoration: a return to Germany's natural status and an end to 40 years as a divided nation under the sway of the World War II Allies that defeated Nazi Germany. For Merkel, a generation younger, it was a time for experiments. Caught up in the whirl of the peaceful democratic revolution, she shopped around for a political home. She hints at her ambition to prove that easterners – and she in particular – were achievers, not "second-class Germans."[10] The Social Democrats were too egalitarian for her and she also had "a certain mistrust" of democracy activists and their grass-roots politics.[11] "I'm a bourgeois person," Merkel said. "It just wasn't my style to stay up and have debates for nights at a time in a smoke-filled dump. I'm conservative in that way."[12] Breaking with her father's politics, she also rejected the "Third Way" of reformed socialism as a romantic notion. Merkel joined Democratic Awakening, a small independent party

with links to the Lutheran church that soon allied with Kohl and his
Christian Democratic Union. It was her ticket to politics, and her start
came on the spur of the moment: having hung around and hooked up
Western-donated computers in the party's East Berlin office, she suddenly
found herself appointed press spokeswoman. East Germany's first and only
free election in March 1990 was fast approaching, the party was chaotic
and Merkel, after initial hesitation, jumped in. It didn't hurt that she soon
aligned with Kohl's push for quick reunification. Looking back, she says
it was inevitable given the East's economic decay. "When it became clear
how much money would have to flow into the second German state so
it could survive even for an interim period, one did realize that there was
no way around reunification."[13] Europe's new order came on October 3,
1990, when East Germany ceased to exist and its 16 million citizens in
effect joined West Germany on West German terms. Three days before
reunification, Merkel had arranged an introduction to Kohl at a CDU
convention in Hamburg, city of her birth.[14] She had moved up and
served for seven months as deputy press secretary to East German premier
Lothar de Maizière, witnessing first-hand the reunification diplomacy
involving the two German states and the former occupying powers – the
U.S., the Soviet Union, the U.K. and France. She made the cut and Kohl
named her minister for women's affairs in his first post-unity Cabinet in
January 1991. At age 36, she was postwar Germany's youngest Cabinet
minister and on the path to power.

By her own account, Merkel's parents loom large in her life. Her
father, whose position soon made him an influential and busy clergy-
man, taught her "clarity of argument" and "logical rigor." Her mother
was the one for emotional warmth. It was from Horst Kasner, not at
school, that Merkel learned the difference between telling a story and
constructing an argument.[15] This dialectical task, known as "Erörterung,"
which can be translated as "determining a position," is still part of the
German school curriculum. It starts with defining one's terms, ascer-
taining the facts and outlining the arguments in favor and those against,
followed by a presentation of the opposing viewpoint. Only then is
one's opinion revealed, along with the possible implications. Young
Angela Kasner displayed other qualities she would later bring to the
world stage and the debt crisis. Wolf Donath, her high-school math
teacher, says she had an excellent memory and was always well prepared.

Yet she "never boasted" and showed solidarity with struggling classmates by helping them with homework.[16] "School presented absolutely no difficulties," she says. "Learning really was fun for me." Her favorite subjects were English and Russian.[17] She was so fascinated with physics that even at school she wanted to understand Einstein's theory of relativity.[18] Her great childhood idol was Polish-born Marie Curie, who "toughed it out in Paris" and won two Nobel prizes, one in physics and the second in chemistry – the fields Merkel would pursue.[19] Had the family stayed in West Germany, Merkel says she probably would have emulated her mother and become a teacher. Other traits emerged: she was cautious and cerebral. In a country fixated on winning Olympic medals for the glory of communism, Angela Kasner struggled with fear in gym class. "I didn't like high speeds," she says.[20] As a nine-year-old, she famously stood atop the three-meter diving board at the Templin pool and waited 45 minutes before screwing up the courage to jump just as the period was ending – an image cited repeatedly in media reports on Merkel's handling of the debt crisis. She was methodical, collecting modern-art postcards and planning Christmas presents two months in advance. "I always wanted to know what I'd face next, even though that was maybe a bit detrimental to spontaneity," she says. "Structuring my life and avoiding chaos was more important."[21]

Politics interested Merkel early on, though she looked outside East Germany for inspiration. As a 14-year-old, she hid in the school lavatory to listen to the radio broadcast of a West German presidential election. While others might have tuned in to rock music that day in 1969, Angela Kasner was captivated by the assembly of delegates that appointed Gustav Heinemann, a 69-year-old Social Democrat, to the largely ceremonial post in the other part of Germany.[22] It was a small act of rebellion that kept her connected with the West. Later that year, Willy Brandt became West German chancellor on a platform of closer ties with the Soviet bloc including East Germany. In France, Charles de Gaulle resigned as president after strikes and protests by workers and students. The U.S., stuck in the Vietnam War, was nearing the end of a tumultuous decade of change that culminated in the Woodstock rock festival that summer. Politics were never far below the surface in the seminary her father led at Waldhof, where young trainee pastors came and went, exchanging ideas. Church faith ran counter to the state's communist ideology, and the Stasi secret police infiltrated congregations and church groups as they did every other aspect of life in the GDR. Yet there was also a recognition of the welfare work the church performed in places such as Waldhof. By remaining deliberately open in the certainty that everything was being monitored, the church became the one sphere of East German life where alternative viewpoints could be expressed, a counterweight to the regime rather than a rival power base. It made the Protestant church the natural focal point for peaceful demonstrations against the regime in 1989, fostering the pro-democracy movement that helped bring down the Wall.

In the 1950s, the East–West link was still intact. Merkel's maternal grandmother and cousins occasionally visited from Hamburg. Merkel, like many East Germans, could also follow events by watching West German television. Many East Germans, however, simply left. By 1961, some 2.7 million had fled to freedom in West Germany, many of them workers in their prime who were needed for the state-run economy.[23] That summer, with Cold War tensions near a peak, Merkel's family and her grandmother traveled to West Germany for a month-long vacation to Bavaria. The Kasner family and Merkel's grandmother squeezed into a Volkswagen Beetle to take in the land of beer and lederhosen. The Alpine landscape of cows and green pastures made a lasting impression on seven-year-old Angela.[24] Days after the Kasners returned home, East Germany built the Berlin Wall, sealing off the 43-kilometer (26-mile) inner-city border with West Berlin that was the last escape route. With the U.S. and other Western powers standing by rather than risking nuclear war, East German workers were ordered to erect barbed wire and fences during the early hours of August 13, 1961. Back in Templin, Merkel's mother cried in church while her father held the Sunday sermon that day. "Everybody was stunned," Merkel says. "That was my first memory of political events."[25] *Time* magazine's cover the next week showed Walter Ulbricht, East Germany's Moscow-trained leader, with a chain and padlock.[26] Nine days after the Wall went up, Ida Siekmann, 58, became the first person to die while trying to escape. Living in a building that straddled Berlin's dividing line, she jumped from the window of her fourth-floor apartment to the western side, suffering fatal injuries. East Germany imposed a shoot-to-kill order for the entire East–West border, which gradually expanded into a heavily fortified barrier. For the next 28 years, free travel to the West was impossible for East Germans.

Even so, some rituals of teenage life weren't fundamentally different. Angela Kasner tried her first cigarette at age 14 and didn't like it, only to "really start smoking" after graduating from university in the late 1970s. (She isn't known to smoke anymore.) In the summer, she went swimming with friends.[27] When she was 15, her studiousness won her a trip to Moscow for a Russian-language competition. She came back with her first Beatles album, bringing the sounds of "Yellow Submarine" to the Waldhof, the cluster of buildings where the family lived and her father worked.[28] She wore clothes shipped by relatives in West Germany – not primarily to flaunt fashion, she says, but because her father didn't earn much. After graduating from high school in 1973, she wanted to make a break from her parents and strike out on her own. Even before graduation, she had traveled with friends to Prague and points further east, just to get away. Now, she moved to Leipzig, 270 kilometers (170 miles) to the south, to study at Germany's second-oldest university, whose past luminaries included quantum physics pioneer Werner Heisenberg. Outside the classroom, Merkel worked as a barmaid, mixing drinks at weekly disco parties in the physics building. She proudly recalls that the students played mostly Western music, defying a rule that called for a 40 percent share of home-grown tunes.[29]

Angela Kasner's first marriage illustrated her ability to make a sudden break and move on if something doesn't work. She and fellow physics student Ulrich Merkel first met as students in 1974. They were married three years later at the Templin church. Merkel, who was 23, says one reason was that the regime allowed only married couples to share an apartment and work in the same city. At first, that meant a 10-square-meter (100-square-foot) room with a shared bath and toilet. "Sounds spartan, but it was enough for us," Ulrich Merkel said in a 2005 magazine interview. He liked Angela "because she was a very friendly, open and natural girl." She also had "a very sharp intellect, unbelievable energy and was always very ambitious." When the marriage fell apart in 1981, it was she who walked out. "One day, she packed her bags and moved out of our apartment. She had sorted it out for herself and drawn her conclusions," her first husband recalled.

"She took the washer; I kept the furniture."[30] She also kept his name, even after marrying her second husband.

Another crucial decision Angela Merkel took during those years was to turn down the Stasi. While finishing her studies at the end of the 1970s, she applied for an assistant professor's post at an engineering school. Stasi officers demanded she sign up to inform on her co-workers to get the job. She says she refused, feeding the recruiters a line suggested by her parents: she wouldn't make a good spy because she couldn't keep her mouth shut. Turning down the feared secret police ended Merkel's bid for the professorship; the regime wouldn't let a person who was ideologically suspect due to her church background teach students. She took a post at the East German Academy of Sciences in Berlin, spending years in research and completing her Ph.D. in quantum chemistry in 1986. At the academy, she met Joachim Sauer, a quantum chemist five years her senior who became her second husband. Any work for the Stasi would have made a political career in reunited Germany impossible. Merkel found that out first-hand when Wolfgang Schnur, the head of Democratic Awakening, was exposed as an informer two weeks before East Germany's 1990 election and quit in disgrace.

While Merkel wasn't a dissident, she rebelled against her father's political views. Initially critical of the East German regime, Horst Kasner increasingly reached an accommodation with East Germany's rulers − for the sake of the church and, perhaps, his family.[31] Merkel says her father, who died in 2011, was captivated by the ideas of "socialism with a human face" − the slogan associated with the Prague Spring reforms that ended with a Soviet-led invasion of Czechoslovakia in 1968 − and "liberation theology," the Roman Catholic movement for social justice in Latin America. Those political directions were anathema to Merkel, who says she had concluded that East Germany was stifling and dysfunctional. Her father had a "milder" view of the communist state and, after reunification freed him to speak his mind publicly, criticized consumerism and the power games of politicians, just as his daughter was starting to rise in the system.[32] Her father could be a taskmaster. When Merkel and her first husband separated in then-East Berlin, she needed a new place and came up against the city's housing shortage. Friends from the science academy forced open an old apartment near the Friedrichstrasse train station and helped refurbish it, using bureaucratic tricks to defeat the authorities. Lacking a state permit for the run-down place, Merkel was living like a squatter. When her father visited her there on her 30th birthday, he wasn't impressed. "You haven't gotten very far," he said.[33] That would change as East Germany and its outdated economy headed toward oblivion.

Merkel moved cautiously the night the Berlin Wall opened. She saw the bumbling official announcement of free travel on television and called her mother to say she thought they could soon travel to West Berlin. Then she went for her regular Thursday evening sauna. Excitement did get the better of her when she came out. A few blocks away, the Bornholmer Strasse road crossing to West Berlin was the first to open that night. Faced with a swelling crowd shouting "Open the gate, open the gate," the border guards, unsure about what exactly the regime had ordered, gave up without firing a shot and let the jostling crowds through. Merkel skipped her post-sauna beer, joined the throng, and wound up celebrating with strangers in a West Berlin apartment. Dutifully, she put off visiting the Kurfürstendamm shopping boulevard, went home to sleep and took the train to work as usual the next morning. "I didn't want my head to sag to my desk," she said. Only later that day did she and her sister visit the boulevard, West Berlin's showcase of consumer culture.[34] As Soviet leader Mikhail Gorbachev decided to let events in East Germany run their course, the communist regime was doomed. Three weeks after the Wall's opening, Kohl presented a 10-point plan for German unification that called for free elections and a market economy in East Germany. Its people should "reap the fruits of their labor and achieve greater prosperity," he said.

Angela Merkel learned the contradictions of the East German economy from picking blueberries as a child. She brought part of the haul home to her mother and sold the rest to boost her allowance. That was where the planned economy and price controls came in. The state bought blueberries for four East German marks per kilo, then subsidized them to keep prices artificially low. The system wasn't hard to figure out. "One of us sold them. Another one of us went to the store an hour later and asked if they had blueberries. At that point he could buy a kilo for two marks."[35] When the Berlin Wall fell, tough economic questions loomed immediately behind the euphoria of reunited families and the end of the Stalinist dictatorship. East Germany's economy was dead in the water after decades of neglected investment and failure to innovate. East Germans wanted the deutsche mark – the currency that underpinned West Germany's postwar "economic miracle" and symbolized the country's global success – or they would head west en masse to get it. (East Germans were automatically eligible for West German citizenship.) West German policy makers scrambled to draw up plans to introduce the deutsche mark in the East. A decade before the euro's arrival, it was Merkel's first experience with a currency union, and it wasn't pleasant. Defying the economic gap between the two countries and warnings by the Bundesbank, Kohl's government decided on a one-to-one swap for East German marks. Karl Otto Pöhl, who quit as the central bank's president after reunification, says the conversion, on July 1, 1990, made East German companies "insolvent overnight" by forcing them to pay wages and bills in deutsche marks they didn't have and couldn't earn.[36] Anyone with debts woke up to find them halved, while the cost of everyday items soared as state subsidies were removed and price controls lifted. As her country headed toward its demise, Merkel moved up. Lothar de Maizière, a viola-playing lawyer of Huguenot descent, became East German premier after winning March 1990 elections at the head of a party alliance that included Democratic Awakening. He chose Merkel as his deputy press secretary at the suggestion of CDU envoys who had organized the alliance. She had her first post with the responsibilities of government, only to get a front-row seat for East Germany's collapse. Those months in 1990, when euphoria over Germany's internal currency union turned sour, shaped Merkel's response to the debt crisis, her prescription of budget austerity, and her notion of aid. "I come from a country in which I experienced economic collapse," she said in September 2012, drawing attention to a part of her past she rarely expands on publicly. "At German unification, we were lucky to get so much help from West Germany. Now, we have the good fortune of being able to help each other in Europe." Yet if debt reduction isn't done "sustainably and with a view to the long term, Europe simply will no longer be the prosperous continent that the world listens to and that gets people's attention."[37] Giving aid to euro countries struggling with debt only makes sense "if things are better afterwards, not even more difficult."

Hans-Christian Maass was sent by Kohl's government to help organize the Christian Democratic Union's East German sister party for the 1990 election. Maass knew East Germany: he was imprisoned by the regime in 1972 after being caught fleeing across the Baltic toward Denmark in an inflatable boat. The West German government bought his freedom in 1974, a common practice used by East Germany to get rid of unwanted citizens and make hard currency in the process. Maass wound up as a spokesman for government ministries in Bonn and was a logical choice to build ties in newly open East Germany. He was the one who picked up Merkel at her apartment in Berlin's gritty Prenzlauer Berg neighborhood, now an area of gentrified apartments, boutiques and organic food stores, for her appointment with Lothar de Maizière. Maass says "it was clear to all of us" that the East German economy was in bad shape. "What we couldn't have imagined, all of us, was the speed of the collapse. This whole system, from the security apparatus to the economy, came down like a house of cards."[38] Bad news came in every day from around the failing country – companies closing with workers losing their jobs, hospitals hamstrung because doctors and nurses had left, assembly lines stopped because the supply chain had broken down with other communist countries in transition such as Hungary, Czechoslovakia and Poland. "We thought the Soviet Union and the economic ties between the East Bloc countries would continue to function," de Maizière said.[39] Merkel was the spokeswoman of a country that had just held its first free election, yet was at the mercy of uncontrollable events. Fueled by Eastern dreams of freedom and a Western lifestyle, reunification was an unequal merger that led to the collapse of the East's uncompetitive industry, followed by mass joblessness after decades of enforced full employment. "This feeling of powerlessness, of no longer having control over your decisions, of having to submit as if it were an earthquake – we all found that very hard to take, her included," Maass said. Merkel evokes this strand of her past when she calls for stronger regulation of financial markets and portrays the debt crisis as a battle between speculators and governments. Starting in May 2010, when tension over the first European effort to save Greece was peaking, she has used the imagery repeatedly to justify her austerity policy. "We have to win back our inner freedom so we are not dependent on actors who can dictate what we do," she said in September 2012.[40] Merkel says what fascinated her about politics in the heady days of 1989 was the chance "to work freely with people [and] to speak openly." She found those opportunities depressingly absent in East Germany, where "everybody worked hard all day and had nothing to show for it."[41] With East Germany gone on October 3, 1990, she faced choices of her own. As 1 million freshly reunited Germans celebrated at Berlin's Brandenburg Gate, Merkel's government job disappeared and the writing was on the wall for her state-funded research establishment. Her next benefactor was Günther Krause, East Germany's chief negotiator of the unification treaty signed in August 1990. With post-unity national elections scheduled on December 2, Krause helped find an electoral district for Merkel in Mecklenburg-Western Pomerania, an eastern state bordering the Baltic that lies north of Merkel's home region. Her first campaign for public office yielded a memorable image of Merkel in a denim skirt meeting fishers in their hut on the island of Rügen. Merkel "drank a shot with them and smoked a cigarette," says Michael Ebner, the photographer.[42]

She took the seat, her first foothold in national politics, and Kohl's coalition of Christian Democrats and Free Democrats won the election with 47.7 percent of the vote. A few weeks later, Kohl took her aside during a reception for newly-minted Eastern lawmakers. Seeking to bring in women and East Germans, he asked her if she "gets along with women." Merkel said yes and became German minister for women and youth on January 18, 1991. West German politicians and journalists mocked the pastor's daughter who wore bulky dresses, eschewed makeup, and smoked cigarettes as "Kohl's girl." Merkel resented the put-downs and resolved to prove her detractors that she was not just her mentor's puppet. At the end of 1991, the CDU elected her deputy party chairwoman after de Maizière bowed out of politics. Merkel took over as party head of Mecklenburg-Western Pomerania in 1993 after Krause resigned, giving her a political power base for the first time. After Kohl won another term in 1994, he made Merkel environment minister. In her biggest leadership test until then, she led a U.N. climate summit in Berlin in 1995 that produced an agreement on reducing greenhouse gas emissions. She calls it one of her proudest achievements.[43]

When Germans voted out Kohl's coalition after 16 years in 1998, Merkel once again faced a crossroads. She had defended her seat in parliament and found herself in opposition. Her break came in late 1999 when Kohl, the "unity chancellor" for the history books, admitted he had received illegal campaign donations while chancellor. The scandal engulfed the CDU, forcing Kohl's successor as party chief, Wolfgang Schäuble, to resign. (He would later return as a member of Merkel's Cabinet, first as interior minister, then in the key post of finance minister.) Merkel, who was the party's secretary-general, stunned everyone by seizing the moment. She published an open letter in the *Frankfurter Allgemeine Zeitung* newspaper that criticized Kohl for refusing to reveal who was behind the campaign donations and urged the party to move out of her mentor's shadow. She had seen the crisis, weighed the options, and decided it was time to try a new approach. She had experienced powerlessness when East Germany fell apart; now she hated trying to fight the financing scandal from party headquarters while most of the information was coming from news leaks, not her own people. A decimated, scandal-scarred CDU elected Merkel as party chairwoman on April 10, 2000. When the Christian Democrat bloc chose its chancellor candidate to challenge incumbent Gerhard Schröder in September 2002, she stood aside and let her Bavarian rival Edmund Stoiber run. He lost, clearing another rival out of the way. Two days after the September 22 election, Merkel snared the post of Christian Democratic opposition leader in parliament. She was set to reach for Germany's biggest political prize.

As chancellor, Merkel's message of austerity for the euro area meshes with her no-frills lifestyle, a contrast with the back-slapping charm of her predecessor Gerhard Schröder. Attending the annual Richard Wagner Festival in Bayreuth with her husband, a long-standing opera fan, is about as extravagant as Germany's political power couple gets. They reject the post-modern halls of the Chancellery and live in her 19th-century apartment building in central Berlin. Merkel touts her potato soup and fruit-topped cakes, likes to shop at the neighborhood supermarket with her security detail in tow, and does her own laundry when time permits. That said, she tends to send out her husband on Friday to buy the weekend groceries. Merkel doesn't wear feminism on her sleeve. Still, in a 1993 article for *Emma*, a women's magazine, she talked about overcoming gender stereotyping and the value of "the man who washes the dishes and cleans the toilet."[44] Her recipe for stress relief is "simply to laugh once in a while. After all, nobody forced me to become chancellor."[45] When it comes to soccer, Merkel supports the overachievers of Bayern Munich, the club from the rich south that has won a record number of German championships. When the Bavarian team faced London club Chelsea in the 2012 European Champions League final, Merkel and her advisers took time out at the Group of Eight summit in Camp David to watch the game with British Prime Minister David Cameron and U.S. President Barack Obama. Merkel also attends national team games when she can, jumping up and pumping her fist in the air in the VIP box when Germany scores. In the buildup to the 2006 World Cup staged in Germany, Merkel called then-coach Jürgen Klinsmann to the Chancellery for a serious talk when the national team floundered in warmup matches.

In the debt crisis, Merkel is seen as the hard-bitten, humorless, austerity-enforcing "Madame Non" who refuses to underwrite the rest of the euro area's debt. Rudolf Zahradník, a Prague physics professor with whom Merkel did research in the late 1970s and early 1980s, knows a different Angela Merkel. "She was a hard worker, but also enjoyed good cuisine and a glass of beer or wine," he told Radio Prague in April 2012. "She has remained the same person as she was 20 or 25 years ago – a very modest human being who always defends her ideas."[46]

Notes

1. Speech by Merkel to CDU party convention in Dresden, December 15–17, 1991. Official minutes: "Protokoll des 2. Parteitags der CDU Deutschlands," p. 105. http://www.kas.de/upload/ACDP/CDU/Protokolle_Parteitage/1991-12-15-17_Protokoll_02.Parteitag_Dresden.pdf.
2. Speech by Merkel to mark start of International Year of Chemistry, Berlin, September 2, 2011: http://www.bundesregierung.de/Content/DE/Rede/2011/02/2011-02-09-bkin-jahr-der-chemie.html.
3. Speech to 1991 CDU convention in Dresden, p. 104 (referenced in Note 1).
4. Interview with Merkel in Bild, November 16, 2009.
5. Wolfgang Bayer, "Geheimoperation Fürstenberg," Der Spiegel, January 17, 2000: http://www.spiegel.de/spiegel/print/d-15433373.html.
6. Gerd Langguth, Interview with Merkel, February 5, 2005, as posted on Prof. Langguth's website: http://www.gerd-langguth.de/MerkelRezensionen/Merkel_Interview.pdf.

7. Angela Merkel, *Mein Weg: Ein Gespräch mit Hugo Müller-Vogg*, p. 55 (Hoffmann und Campe Verlag, Hamburg, 2005).
8. Merkel quoted in ARD television interview, *Bild*, July 17, 2009: http://www.bild.de/politik/2009/tv/zu-geschwaetzig-fuer-die-stasi-8415974.bild.html.
9. *Mein Weg*, p. 47.
10. *Mein Weg*, p. 69.
11. Merkel interview with Langguth (referenced in Note 6).
12. Merkel quoted in Jürgen Leinemann, "Ich muss härter werden," *Der Spiegel*, January 3, 1994, p. 34.
13. *Mein Weg*, p. 82.
14. Gerd Langguth, *Angela Merkel: Aufstieg zur Macht*, pp. 157–8 (Deutscher Taschenbuch Verlag, Munich, 2005).
15. *Mein Weg*, p. 37.
16. Donath quoted in *Neue Post* magazine, September 12, 2012.
17. Langguth, *Aufstieg zur Macht*, p. 53.
18. *Mein Weg*, pp. 49–50.
19. Speech by Merkel on September 2, 2011 (referenced in Note 2).
20. *Mein Weg*, p. 39.
21. *Mein Weg*, p. 51.
22. Leinemann, p. 33 (referenced in Note 12).
23. German Historical Museum website: http://www.hdg.de/lemo/html/Das GeteilteDeutschland/DieZuspitzungDesKaltenKrieges/DieMauer/abgeriegelt.html.
24. Merkel interview, "Die CSU fasziniert mich immer wieder," *Münchner Merkur*, September 22, 2008: http://www.merkur-online.de/nachrichten/politik/interview-csu-merkel-10305.html.
25. *Mein Weg*, p. 43.
26. *Time* magazine website: http://www.time.com/time/covers/0,16641,19610 825,00.html.
27. "Reise nach Angeland," *Bild am Sonntag*, September 14, 2009: http://www.bild.de/politik/2009/see/mit-der-kanzlerin-in-die-uckermark-9413702.bild.html.
28. *Aufstieg zur Macht*, p. 53 (referenced in Note 14).
29. Merkel interview, Evelyn Roll, "Und es war Sommer," *Süddeutsche Zeitung Magazin*, No. 9, 2008: http://sz-magazin.sueddeutsche.de/texte/anzeigen/4578/1/1.
30. Ulrich Merkel quoted in "Eines Tages zog sie aus," *Focus*, July 5, 2004: http://www.focus.de/politik/deutschland/deutschland-eines-tages-zog-sie-aus_aid_200326.html.
31. *Aufstieg zur Macht*, p. 65 ff.
32. Ibid., p. 70.
33. Ibid., p. 112.

34. Speech by Merkel on 20th anniversary of the fall of the Berlin Wall, Berlin, November 9, 2009: http://www.bundeskanzlerin.de/Content/DE/Rede/2009/11/ 2009-11-09-rede-merkel-falling-walls.html.
35. "Reise nach Angeland" (referenced in Note 27).
36. Interview with Pöhl in *Welt am Sonntag*, August 29, 2004: http://www.welt .de/print-wams/article115077/Karl-Otto-Poehl-ist-ueberzeugt-Der-Kurs-beim-Umtausch-war-verhaengnisvoll.html.
37. Press conference with Merkel, Berlin, September 17, 2012.
38. Authors' interview, December 19, 2012.
39. Quoted in *Ouest France*, October 1, 2010: http://www.ouest-france.fr/actu/ international_detail_-Il-y-a-vingt-ans-l-Allemagne-retrouvait-son-unite-_ 3637-1531499_actu.Htm.
40. Press conference with Merkel, Berlin, September 17, 2012.
41. *Mein Weg*, pp. 16, 20.
42. Quoted in article "Fotograf damals wie heute," *Bild*, October 19, 2009: http://www.bild.de/politik/2009/fotograf/damals-wie-heute-9773250.bild .html.
43. *Aufstieg zur Macht*, p. 156.
44. Angela Merkel, "Der Marsch zur Macht," *Emma*, May–June 1993: http:// www.emma.de/hefte/ausgaben-1993/maijuni-1993/der-marsch-zur-macht.
45. Interview in *SUPERillu* magazine, June 22, 2011. Quoted on Chancellor's official website: http://www.bundeskanzlerin.de/Content/DE/Interview/2011/06/ 2011-06-22-merkel-super-illu.html.
46. Interview with Zahradník cited on Radio Prague website, April 3, 2012: http:// www.radio.cz/en/section/curraffrs/merkels-former-academic-boss-angela-is-what-we-call-a-constant-of-motion.

Chapter 4

Numbers (Germany's Subprime Scandal)

Merkel was attending the Salzburg Festival in Austria at the start of her traditional three-week summer vacation when the financial meltdown an ocean away intruded. Seated in the Felsenreitschule, a theatrical arena carved out of a former quarry, she received a text message on her mobile phone as the premiere of Haydn's opera *Armida* was about to begin. The text was from Jens Weidmann, her chief economic adviser in the chancellery and later president of Germany's central bank, the Bundesbank.[1] It marked the opening salvo of a financial and economic crisis that would dictate her policy choices for the rest of her time in office, challenges for which she was unprepared at the outset.

Merkel was less than 18 months into office when the financial crisis spawned in Wall Street seeped over to Europe, making landfall in Germany via the River Rhine. Dusseldorf, the city of Germany's biggest power company, E.ON SE, and steelmaker ThyssenKrupp AG, as well as electronic music pioneers Kraftwerk and artists like Joseph Beuys and Gerhard Richter, gained the additional distinction of being the scene of Germany's first victim of the financial crisis. IKB Deutsche Industriebank AG, founded in 1924 to process Germany's World War I reparation payments,[2] was the tip of a toxic iceberg that holed German state-owned lenders and national giants alike, prompting resignations, court cases, and monstrous losses that had to be covered by the government to avoid a collapse of the entire banking system. At its peak, in October 2010, the taxpayer was on the hook for 197.4 billion euros in loans and guarantees (29.4 billion euros in loans plus 168 billion euros in guarantees) provided to financial institutions via the government's bank-rescue fund.[3] Overnight, no-one talked in terms of millions of euros any more as bailout after bailout required sums in the multiple billions.

"The IKB is in trouble," Weidmann wrote in his text message. "What's the IKB?" Merkel tapped back. She later explained that the bank had simply not done anything until that point to mark itself out. Neither did the opera in Salzburg: the lead was no diva and there was a distinct lack of "stage magic," the *Hamburger Abendblatt* newspaper concluded.

Merkel and her advisers at that point regarded IKB as an isolated case and not an indication of a broad spillover into the German economy; the realization of wider contagion to Germany would only come later. For IKB, as with other German lenders with humble regional roots, the lure of the money to be made during the U.S. housing market boom was irresistible, and for a while it paid off. But as homeowners already reeling with debt saw the monthly payments rise on their variable rate mortgages, growing numbers defaulted, and spectacular profits turned into stellar losses for IKB. The bank's Rhineland Funding investment vehicle, based in Delaware, had gorged on securities tied to U.S. mortgage prices and found that they were rapidly turning sour. IKB's shares started to drop in April 2007 amid rumors of its subprime risks. In early July, the credit rating agency Moody's Investors Service said it needed to revise its assessment of some mortgage-related investment products known as asset-backed securities. That prompted write-downs of 117 million euros at Rhineland Funding alone, with the prospect of more to come.[4] Deutsche Bank, which provided credit to IKB that allowed it to invest in the subprime mortgage market, sought clarification as to what was going on. It received none, and Germany's biggest bank pulled its credit line that day. The chain reaction was rapid: Deutsche Bank CEO Josef Ackermann called Jochen Sanio, the head of the financial regulator BaFin, to let him know the situation. Sanio set up an emergency meeting over the weekend to negotiate a bailout. It was then that Weidmann at the chancellery in Berlin texted Merkel in Austria.

The first public hint of the subprime impact on Germany arrived on faxes and in email inboxes that day. IKB issued a press release on July 30 saying that it was in difficulty as a result of its exposure to the subprime crisis, 10 days after releasing a statement that said all was well. Even then, few realized the full import of the announcement. IKB received a bailout package the same day from the government-owned KfW development bank, the first public rescue of the crisis in Germany. The IKB secured as much as 12 billion euros in guarantees from a government rescue fund set up the following year.

Merkel's government, unsure of how to react at first, was persuaded that it had to step in. Without a financial injection, IKB faced imminent collapse that would have wreaked "incalculable effects" on the markets, Deutsche Bank's Ackermann told a court hearing in Dusseldorf into the events two years later. It was an argument that was to prevail for the rest of Merkel's first and second terms as she was confronted with crisis after crisis: that an individual institution – or, later, country – was too important to the financial system at large to be allowed to go under, and it would be cheaper in the long run to save it with public money. It was a stark illustration of the impact of globalization and lack of transparency on financial markets, and a realization that angered Merkel.

Merkel recalls the moment as a turning point in her chancellorship. "That was my introduction to a completely new type of role that none of us apart from the specialists had paid much attention to before then," she later said.[5]

Casting about for solutions and lacking any template, Merkel confronted the fallout of the financial crisis that began with the subprime implosion, fed through the entire banking sector, led to the deepest recession since the Great Depression and the implementation of government stimulus spending to turn it around, culminating in the sovereign debt crisis that wrought havoc in the 17-country euro region. Now, Europe has bailout funds and institutions in place to deal with such emergencies, but early on no such infrastructure existed. To get there, she deployed her scientist's approach to problem solving, allied to a dogged persistence and an ability to rapidly grasp complex technical matters, traits that she displayed repeatedly throughout the times of crisis ahead. "She can very well understand chains of cause and effect," said Anton Boerner, the president of the BGA German exporters' federation, who has met regularly with the chancellor since she entered office. "She's very intelligent, which I value greatly and which is not always the case with politicians." Merkel can think in the middle- and in the long-term and is very matter of fact, without being emotional in her deliberation, Boerner said. "When you argue with her based on the facts, you always have an open ear," he said. "She is always looking to see if there are contradictions in logic in her interlocutor's argument. When there aren't any, then she'll accept it."[6]

One of her first impulses was holding to account those in the financial industry whom she saw as responsible, a policy course that would lead to her later efforts during the euro-area crisis to forcibly impose losses on private investors to help pay for the mess. Merkel's initial response to the banking crisis on her watch was to see the problem as one limited to the financial world and isolated from the "real economy." She publicly blamed the bankers who had promulgated the problem and threatened to legislate to clamp down on bankers' pay and bonuses. That stance was popular with voters: polls indicated support for her party began to pick up after languishing for much of 2006 and into 2007. Deploying banker-bashing that came more naturally to Social Democrats than her conservative base, she managed to steal the SPD's thunder, carve out a profile, and bolster her popularity.

The coalition in Berlin set up a working group on manager pay, as the chancellor warned that growing wage disparities posed a threat to social cohesion. "Take this debate seriously," Merkel told business owners in a speech in December 2007. "Don't simply shrug it off."[7] As the crisis developed, the chancellor was accused by commentators of abandoning her political ideals and shifting to territory more usually occupied by the Social Democrats. She only intensified her calls. At her CDU party convention that month, she criticized "fantasy compensation" for executives. While she didn't mention him by name, Merkel was speaking two days after the *Wall Street Journal* reported that Porsche SE Chief Executive Officer Wendelin Wiedeking had been paid about $100 million in 2006. Party delegates, reveling in their party's rise to 40 percent in polls under Merkel — the highest score of the year, opening up a 16-point lead over the Social Democrats – applauded her loudly. Merkel, who governed at the head of a grand coalition of the two biggest parties in what was supposed to be alliance of equals, had found her feet and began to break free.

Vehicles making for the Baltic Sea coast the evening before Germany's G-8 summit were met by a sea of blue and green police vans parked at an autobahn rest stop two hours north of Berlin, a warning of the lock-down ahead. The traffic slowed to a crawl at the junction for Rostock-Laage airport, where a police cordon blocked the road and signaled all vehicles traveling in the direction of Rostock to the exit ramp. With the police expecting as many as 100,000 demonstrators to protest the summit, the only way through to the press center at Kühlungsborn was to take to the back roads with the help of a navigation system and the network of old East German farming tracks.

It was June 2007, almost eight weeks before Merkel learned of IKB's troubles, and the first signals of a looming financial crisis were only just being picked up, without yet resonating widely. Merkel, elected barely 18 months earlier, was facing her first sustained moment in the international limelight as both host of the annual summit of leaders from the Group of Eight leading economies and holder of the six-month rotating presidency of the European Union. The question was what she would do with the platform.

She had already pulled off a coup by hosting the G-8 in Heiligendamm, a spa resort developed in the final years of the 18th century by the Grand Duke of Mecklenburg, Friedrich Franz I, and restored to its for-mer glory 200 years later. Heiligendamm won renown as Germany's earliest resort to be built by the sea rather than the mountains, as the health advantages of the invigorating brine-filled Baltic air became fashionable for those able to afford it. The five-star complex of build-ings arranged around the former spa building that now occupy the site is in the east of Germany along the coast from Merkel's electoral dis-trict of Stralsund. It was a showcase for the benefits of reunification and a statement of intent by Germany's first eastern chancellor.

The German focus for the June 6–8 summit was on "Growth and Responsibility," intended to address the "economic, social and envi-ronmental aspects of the political shaping of globalization," themes that occupy Merkel to this day. A preparatory paper distributed by the German government noted that the U.S. housing market had "cooled off somewhat" after reaching its peak the previous year, while national budget-cutting efforts were making "good progress," both factors that helped to keep the world's economic advance on track. "The world economy as a whole is in good shape."[8]

As well as pledges to address climate change and to work more cooperatively with Africa, the centerpiece of the German G-8 presidency included moves to tighten regulation of financial markets. In pushing global efforts in particular to shine a light on the $1.4 trillion, largely unregulated hedge fund industry, Merkel knew that she was picking a fight that she was unlikely to win. Bringing greater transparency to financial markets, a policy goal shared by Merkel and her Social Democratic finance minister, Peer Steinbrück, was an issue that barely broke over the seawall of public consciousness at the time. It now seems prescient.

In reality, officials in Merkel's government were less visionary than grappling to understand some of the economic developments they were witnessing. They opted to push legislation as a means to gain a better grasp of what they saw going on in financial markets and which made them uncomfortable. They concentrated their efforts on hedge funds as the highest profile symbol of what would later be called the shadow banking system, a policy the Germans are still pursuing. At the time, European Commission officials viewed the German drive on hedge funds skeptically, as a sign of Germany's lack of understanding for the markets and their needs. It was seen as just another one of those crazy German ideas, according to one Berlin official, who conceded that the proposed regulatory efforts were not as focused as they could have been, and certainly not as focused as they would later become. Where Brussels was wary, the U.S. and the U.K. were downright hostile, seeing the German move as an unnecessary and wrongheaded intervention in the markets. In fact, the move was symptomatic of tensions that would flare up throughout the years of crisis between the German idea of a "social market economy" that could be better administrated though more regulation and the "Anglo-Saxon" ideal of the free market economy – a disconnect that exists to this day.

Merkel left the region's prime minister to greet the world leaders including U.S. President George W. Bush, U.K. Prime Minister Tony

Blair and France's newly installed president, Nicolas Sarkozy, as they arrived at Rostock airport. She met them later at Heiligendamm. The heavy thudding of helicopter rotors reverberated from the pine forests to the coastline as the G-8 chiefs were ferried from the airport to the summit venue, which had been sealed off behind a 12 kilometer-long security fence specially erected for the meeting in anticipation of protests. Before the advent of the more representative G-20 summits including the major developing nations, China, India and Brazil, meetings of the seven leading industrial nations – the U.S., Japan, Germany, France, Italy, the U.K., and Canada – plus from 1997 Russia, were at that time still the premier forum for international decision making. As such they were the focus of protests broadly grouped under the banner of the anti-globalization movement, which included environmentalists campaigning for more aggressive action against climate change, activists who demanded more money and energy be spent fighting global poverty, and demonstrators who rejected the G-8's right to dictate policy to the world. There were also anti-capitalist protestors, peace activists, black-hooded anarchists, and squads of sinister-looking circus clowns in paramilitary gear. After high-profile protests at international meetings in Seattle in 1999, Genoa in 2001 and at Gleneagles in Scotland in 2005, Heiligendamm was the next stop. Even as the demonstrations threatened to spin out of control, the chancellor appeared relaxed as she chatted with Russian President Vladimir Putin, shared a joke with Bush, and grinned for the cameras with Sarkozy. She met with Bob Geldof and U2 frontman Bono, who called for a greater G-8 commitment to aid Africa and later issued angry press releases questioning her figures.[9] Merkel, hosting a dinner on the first evening of the summit at the nearby Hohen Luckow estate, shook hands and greeted the locals like a member of royalty. The following day as talks began, protesters dodged tear gas and water cannon to block a narrow-gauge railway line running through the forest, preventing a steam engine known as the *Molli* from carrying journalists from the press center to briefings 10 kilometers (6 miles) away at Heiligendamm. A high-speed boat chase between a German naval vessel and Greenpeace activists in rigid inflatables played out in the Baltic directly offshore. Merkel again appeared unfazed and completely in control as she directed proceedings, usually seated between Putin and Bush. She was pictured drinking a glass of white wine in the evening sun with Bush, Blair, and Romano

Prodi, the Italian prime minister, on the hotel terrace. German broad-casters treated to pictures of world leaders at the German coast in glorious weather concluded the summit was a success. In terms of con-crete achievements, however, she had little to celebrate as her goals on climate change and financial-market regulation fell by the wayside.

One of Merkel's early policy achievements, as minister for the envi-ronment and nuclear reactor security in Chancellor Helmut Kohl's fifth and final Cabinet, was to broker a deal to tackle global warming in 1995 at a United Nations-sponsored climate conference in Berlin. After two weeks, the international talks ran into a morass of collid-ing interests and the conference, like climate negotiations since, ground to a standstill. Merkel, fearful of an embarrassing failure on her home turf, sought to break the deadlock. She toured each room in private, persuading and coaxing the delegations individually, carrying messages between them and cajoling them into a compromise deal. The Berlin Mandate, as the final declaration became known, contributed to the Kyoto Protocol that guided efforts to cut the greenhouse gases blamed for global warming. Merkel pulled off a "quite astonishing display of negotiating prowess" that got her noticed on the international stage, as Erhard Jauck, a career civil servant who was her deputy at the time, recalled in a 2009 interview.[10]

Merkel failed to secure a repeat at Heiligendamm. With no firm commitment to tackle global warming, the leaders' final communique referred only to a non-binding aim to halve global CO_2 emissions by 2050. She fared no better on regulation of hedge funds; her aim to mitigate the risks to global markets came to nothing. Bush and Blair united to thwart Merkel's push for an industry code of conduct, and she came away only with an acknowledgment that assessing risks "has become more complex and challenging." Given the industry's rise "and the increasing complexity of the instruments they trade, we reaffirm the need to be vigilant," G-8 leaders concluded.

It was an empty statement given the subprime mortgage crisis already eating away at the foundations of the financial markets, and one that Merkel was quick to hold against the U.S. and the U.K. In fact, world leaders didn't have to exercise vigilance for long. As soaring lev-els of U.S. household debt collided with a fall in real estate prices, the bottom fell out of the market for complex financial products backed by high-risk subprime mortgages. U.S. foreclosures multiplied and investor losses escalated, but the repercussions weren't confined to the U.S.; within less than two months of the Heiligendamm commitment to remain vigilant, the ripples of looming financial crisis had spread across the Atlantic, and banks in Germany that had been every bit as eager to indulge in the subprime bonanza were about to share in the bust.

By the end of February 2008, the U.K.'s decade-long housing boom was not only at an end, but Newcastle-based mortgage lender Northern Rock had witnessed the first run on a bank in the country in more than a century, prompting the Blair government to take the bank into public ownership. In the U.S., President Bush enacted an economic stimulus package comprising tax rebates and incentives to spur business worth $168 billion[11] as confidence among U.S. consumers sank to the lowest level since 1992. In Germany, meanwhile, the Bundesbank warned there was no need for a similar stimulus program because the economy was still in good shape. Under Merkel, Germany had briefly returned to a balanced budget in 2007 for the first time since reunification in 1990[12] and the central bank saw no good reason to divert from the virtuous path of consolidation by running up debt. While conceding there were "increased uncertainties" over the economic outlook, the Bundesbank judged that "embarking on an expansionary fiscal policy could prove to be an unnecessary and costly venture." Merkel stubbornly held to the coalition's goal of balancing the budget by 2011, describing the path of fiscal prudence as "indispensable if we want to be fit for the future."[13]

By July 2008, the world's biggest financial companies had posted almost $400 billion in writedowns and credit losses,[14] yet a survey of 5,000 German non-financial companies concluded that they were barely affected by the crisis. A majority of those surveyed by the KfW Group, the BDI federation of German industry, the BDA employers' association, the HDE retailers' lobby, and the ZDH association of skilled trades said that access to credit was unchanged; 12 percent even found that credit availability had improved. "Concerns that the financial market crisis has significantly worsened the financing conditions in Germany, and is spilling over into the real economy, so far haven't materialized," KfW Chief Economist Norbert Irsch said. Against that backdrop, Merkel refused to act.[15]

Then came September. Investor fear set in as the U.S. government, alarmed by the plunging market value of mortgage giants Fannie Mae and Freddie Mac, deployed an unlimited financial "bazooka" to take control of them, still failing to calm markets. Fear turned to panic within 10 days, as New York-based Lehman Brothers Holdings Inc., the fourth biggest investment bank on Wall Street, declared bankruptcy and the government stood by without stepping in. Some $1.3 trillion was wiped off the Dow Jones Industrial Average in one day, September 30, as the U.S. Treasury's request to Congress for the authority to invest up to $700 billion in toxic mortgage and other assets to clean up the balance sheets of the financial sector was rejected. Congress later passed the Troubled Asset Relief Program, known as TARP, but it was too late to halt the global meltdown.[16] Merkel's initial response as the events of September unfolded was to berate the U.S. for not listening to her earlier. The economic actors "must accept" rules on strengthening the independence of ratings companies, on greater transparency in financial markets, and take on board that high-risk products entail big gambles, she said in a September 22 speech in Berlin. "These measures aren't new, they were spelled out at the G-8 meeting in Heiligendamm," she said. "We must adopt them. Germany has always pointed out how necessary they are." In an interview with the *Münchner Merkur* newspaper the same week, she took aim at the financial markets, criticizing their "assumption that they're in the right" and taking a pop at the Bush administration and the U.K. government now led by Gordon Brown, who served as chancellor of the exchequer throughout the Blair years, for taking their side. "Sadly, backed by the governments in Great Britain and the U.S., they've resisted voluntary regulation," she said of the markets. "I strongly advocate that we use the latest crisis to draw the necessary conclusions."[17]

Steinbrück, her finance minister, insisted that the U.S. situation was not comparable to that in Germany, where the banking system is based on three distinct tiers: private banks such as Deutsche Bank and Commerzbank; cooperative banks known as Volksbanken; and public banks including the "Sparkassen," or savings banks, and the regional lenders, or "Landesbanken," owned by some of Germany's 16 states. He wasn't about to bring in a similar rescue program to that of the U.S.

because Germany's three-pillar banking system was stable, he said. He'd be proven wrong within seven days.

If the U.S. subprime crisis left few visible cracks in Germany beyond IKB in 2007, the full extent of the damage was exposed in September 2008 with Lehman's collapse. The lightning rod was Hypo Real Estate Holding AG of Munich, then Germany's second-biggest property lender. As with IKB, its rescue was deemed to be without alternative. Up until that point, there had been "no sign of life-threatening problems at German private banks," Merkel's adviser, Jens Weidmann, later told a parliamentary committee of inquiry set up to determine whether the government could have avoided the need to rescue the blighted bank.[18] The ensuing "dramatic developments were unforeseeable," he said.

While the Germans had little clue of what was to come even after the signals telegraphed by IKB's woes, Merkel had taken stock all the same. Two weeks after Lehman, Germany's financial system was seizing up as the flow of credit halted, and Hypo was in trouble. This time, Merkel dangled the bank over the edge, just as she would do with Greece three years later. She risked the biggest bank failure in Germany since the 1930s as she engaged in last-minute brinkmanship with the then head of Deutsche Bank, Josef Ackermann. Faced with a 35 billion-euro bill, she determined to wring as much as she could from the banks to mitigate the cost to the taxpayer. It was 12.45 a.m. in Berlin – 15 minutes before the markets opened at 9 a.m. in Tokyo – when she called Ackermann to accept his offer. The banks would provide 8.5 billion euros of the total.

"If she hadn't reached me at a quarter to one that morning, it would have been over," Ackermann told the inquiry the following year. "I ran back to our room and shouted: 'stop, stop, there is a solution'." If Merkel was playing politics, "it went pretty far," he said. "It was dangerous." Martin Blessing, the CEO of Germany's second-biggest bank, Commerzbank AG, which received more than 18 billion euros of aid under a bailout that included the government taking a 25 percent stake in the bank,[19] told the parliamentary inquiry that Merkel's government had managed to win last-minute concessions from the banks. Perhaps mindful of his audience, he said it was a "courageous" move, albeit "a strategy that caused high blood pressure for many of us."

The negotiating prowess that Merkel had honed all those years earlier during the climate talks in Berlin had again paid off, this time for
the German taxpayer. It was a warning for fellow euro-area crisis leaders such as Papandreou, who ignored it at their peril.

Within a week of the Hypo bailout, the package had to be increased
to 50 billion euros, and Merkel and Steinbrück stood side by side in
the Chancellery at a hastily called press conference on the evening of
October 5, a Sunday, to announce that the government would guarantee
bank deposits to avoid panic or a bank run. They were following in the
footsteps of Nicolas Sarkozy of France and Italy's Silvio Berlusconi, both
of whom promised to prevent losses for depositors. Merkel's pledge was
"political" and not enshrined in law, unlike that of Irish Prime Minister
Brian Cowen, whose government enacted legislation guaranteeing 100
percent of the deposits and debts of six banks that bore the brunt of
the implosion of Ireland's housing bubble – a boom so exaggerated that
property developers became billionaires and flew around the country by
helicopter. The bank guarantee became a millstone that crushed Cowen's
government and which his successor as Taoiseach, Enda Kenny, would
later have to carry to Merkel's door in a plea for relief.

Merkel's government, having stepped in to save the banks, called an
emergency session of the Bundestag that week, which she used to vent
her anger at the "greed, speculation and mismanagement" of those who
caused the crisis. "Irresponsible" loans in the U.S. had helped destroy
faith in the global financial system that must be rapidly restored.
"There'll be no blank checks or protection for managers who've made
mistakes," Merkel said, welcoming Hypo CEO Georg Funke's decision
to quit that day. The government went on to set up a 480 billion-euro
bank-rescue fund that month to stabilize the country's lenders, followed three weeks later by an economic stimulus package of 50 billion
euros. It was topped up to 85 billion euros in 2009 amid criticism from
economists including Paul Krugman that it was too little too late. A
further 115 billion euros of credit for companies was also made available. Merkel would recall that "after 2008, in certain areas the minimum
unit became the billion, and that was something we just hadn't experienced before."[20] The government slashed its economic growth targets
and finally abandoned the goal of balancing the budget by 2011.

In tandem, she was formulating a policy that went farther than anything imposed in either the U.K. or the U.S. in terms of demanding something in return for the money. Bonuses were barred at German banks in receipt of aid and a cap on executive pay set at 500,000 euros; business deemed by the state to be risky was banned, and the government took a stake in the banks that enabled it to impose management changes. In the U.S., executive pay above $500,000 at banks applying for a government aid program was allowed, merely subject to higher tax rates.[21] Polls showed the public were with her. Merkel's Christian Democratic bloc, which had fallen to 28 percent in a weekly Forsa poll on November 1 – the lowest level of support since her election and behind the Social Democrats – recovered and gained five points in five weeks as the SPD faded. Seventy-two percent of respondents to an Infratest dimap poll on November 7, 2008, said they considered Merkel to have done "good work" in dealing with the financial crisis. Bank-bashing was going down well again.

The banking crisis forced Merkel to shift gears and learn about complex new subjects, but she dealt with it without showing any sense of frustration at the direction in which it took her, according to an official who worked closely with her. Frustration only came later when the depth of the problem became apparent and tension arose between the banking sector and policy makers. She assumed a growing lack of trust toward the banking industry as she felt the information she received to be inadequate and the industry's ability to diagnose its own problems limited, if not distorted, by its own interests. As a scientist used to weighing the evidence before making her call, she needed to have the full picture. Instead, Merkel was dismayed by the difficulty in obtaining reliable facts from the industry on its status, and that shaped her perceptions of the banking sector and influenced her policy making.

Even when drawing up bank-rescue packages, she learned to view what she was being told with a grain of salt. Frustration turned to anger as Ackermann gave an interview to Der Spiegel magazine in which he said that he wouldn't be applying for state aid for Deutsche Bank because of the stigma attached. Faced with dismissive comments by the industry's main interlocutor that threatened to water down the effectiveness of the package days after it was negotiated, the government response was swift and to the point. Ackermann's comments were "extremely alarming, incomprehensible and unacceptable," said government spokesman Thomas Steg, employing unusually blunt language. Ackermann released a statement that night saying that of course he backed the government's actions. He declined to be interviewed for this book.

By March 2009, six months out from national elections, Merkel's coalition had agreed curbs on managers' pay and was preparing to put a vote to the lower house, the Bundestag, enabling the government to seize control of Hypo Real Estate if needed. In an interview with *Bild* newspaper, Merkel acknowledged that the crisis sweeping Europe's biggest economy was forcing her government to "overstep boundaries and do things that we wouldn't otherwise do."[22]

Merkel, who came to power after Germany broke EU budget limits for three years running, was never going to easily concede the need to raise Germany's debt and deficit as a result of fighting the financial crisis. She broke the budget to help dig Germany out of the economic malaise that followed on the heels of the financial crisis, the deepest recession since the 1930s, but returned to the path of consolidation as soon as she was able. In 2009, her government introduced an amendment to the constitution that locked in a "debt brake" obliging the federal government and the 16 states to balance their budgets. From 2011 onward, the two layers of governments that together control policy in Germany were legally bound to progressively lower their budget deficits. In the case of the federal government, its deficit must not exceed 0.35 percent of gross domestic product by 2016, though at the time of writing the government was on course to meet the target in 2013. The states must not run any deficit at all. Merkel went on to make the debt brake a cornerstone of her policy in the fighting the crisis to come, exporting it the rest of the EU.

Merkel's economic philosophy took shape during the financial crisis of her first term. At the core of her credo was a commitment to lowering debt, coupled with a distrust of the financial markets that she saw as having created the mess in the first place and which found expression in a push for transparency to avoid being sprung with a repeat. The principle of no aid without a commitment in return to reform was for now focused on banks, but would later be adapted to countries, together with a willingness to intervene in the financial sphere when the state deemed it necessary to protect German taxpayers. Her set of policy responses worked for the German public but diverged from those of the U.S. and others. During her first term, she consolidated her place as a world leader in times of crisis, holding her top spot on *Forbes* magazine's list of the most influential women in 2009 for the fourth consecutive year. Domestically, she asserted herself as the clear leader of her government, having relegated Steinbrück and Frank-Walter Steinmeier, respectively her finance minister and foreign minster from the rival Social Democrats, to the margins. That was by no means a foregone conclusion when they entered into the grand coalition together in late 2005. Heading into the election in September of 2009, Germany was undergoing its worst economic downturn in living memory as exports to its partners were hit by the global recession: The economy contracted 3.7 percent in the first three months of 2009 alone. Yet Merkel led her election challenger Steinmeier by 36 points in personal popularity polls. The SPD, unable to win any voter credit for its share of crisis-fighting after Merkel adopted its traditionally skeptical positions toward banks and financial markets, ended up with 23 percent support on election day, unchanged from its poll score at the beginning of the year. The main beneficiaries were the Free Democrats of Guido Westerwelle, who led his party to its best-ever result after campaigning for tax cuts and a return to a more economically liberal agenda. Merkel, whose Christian Democratic bloc won the election with its lowest share of the vote since the war, was still able to ditch the SPD and form a coalition with Westerwelle's party. Merkel was now unbound, with a mandate from German voters to set out on a fresh path with a coalition partner that backed her agenda. That's how it appeared at least. The following month, October 2009, as the coalition parties met in Berlin to tie up their joint program for the coming four years, in Greece, George Papandreou swept to power at the head of a Socialist PASOK government. One of his first acts upon examining the books was to announce that Greece's budget deficit was more than four times EU limits, a revelation that would again upend Europe's economic fortunes and determine the course of Merkel's second term.

Notes

1. Speech by Merkel to Christian Democratic Union/Christian Social Union event on financial market regulation, June 29, 2011: http://veranstaltungen .cducsu.de/rede-von-bundeskanzlerin-angela-merkel-auf-dem-kongress-zur-finanzmarktregulierung-nach-der-krise.
2. IKB Deutsche Industriebank Aktiengesellschaft, Registration Document, August 10, 2012: http://www.ikb.de/fileadmin/content/30_Investor_Relations /20_Fixed_Income/01_DIP/120810_Registrierungsformular.pdf.
3. Federal Agency for Financial Market Stabilisation, Press release dated April 27, 2012: http://www.fmsa.de/de/presse/pressemitteilungen/2012/ 20120427_pressemitteilung_fmsa.html.
4. Karin Matussek, "Ex-IKB CEO Convicted of Misleading Investors About Bank's Subprime Risks," *Bloomberg News*, July 14, 2010: http://www .bloomberg.com/news/2010-07-14/ex-ikb-chief-ortseifen-convicted-of-market-manipulation-over-subprime.html.
5. Speech by Merkel to Christian Democratic Union/Christian Social Union parliamentary group, Berlin, June 29, 2011: http://www.bundeskanzlerin. de/nn_683608/Content/DE/Rede/2011/06/2011-06-29-merkel-Kongress .html.
6. Interview in Berlin on January 9, 2013.
7. Andreas Cremer, "Merkel Says German Wage Disparities Threaten Social Cohesion," *Bloomberg News*, December 11, 2007: http://www.bloomberg .com/apps/news?pid=newsarchive&sid=aZd59B..otdA.
8. Andreas Cremer "G-8 Communique to Stress Improved Economy Outlook, Germany Says," *Bloomberg News*, June 5, 2007 (not on web).
9. Andreas Cremer, "Merkel Quarrels With Bono, Geldof Over African Aid," *Bloomberg News*, June 7, 2007: http://www.bloomberg.com/apps/news?pid= newsarchive&sid=akxhjbivrcEk&refer=Germany.
10. As cited in Leon Mangasarian and Tony Czuczka, "Merkel's Bargain with Ackermann Signaled Re-Election," *Bloomberg News*, August 24, 2009: http:// www.bloomberg.com/apps/news?pid=newsarchive&sid=ai2lW4fyMeas.
11. Alison Fitzgerald and Brian Faler, "Congress Sends $168 Billion Economic Stimulus to Bush," *Bloomberg News*, February 8, 2008: http://www.bloomberg .com/apps/news?pid=newsarchive&sid=aMljy8GxkKoc.
12. Deutsche Bundesbank Monthly Report, Frankfurt am Main, February, 2008, p. 10: http://www.bundesbank.de/Redaktion/EN/Downloads/Publications /Monthly_Report/2008/2008_02_monthly_report.pdf?__blob=publi cationFile.
13. Speech in Berlin to mark 60-year anniversary of the social market economy, June 12, 2008: http://archiv.bundesregierung.de/Content/DE/Archiv16/Rede/ 2008/06/2008-06-12-rede-merkel-60-jahre-soziale-marktwirtschaft .html?nn=273438.

14. Bloomberg terminal function detailing writedowns and capital infusions: {WDCI <GO>}.
15. KfW Bankengruppe, "Unternehmensbefragung 2008," Frankfurt am Main, July, 2008: http://www.kfw.de/kfw/de/I/II/Download_Center/Fachthemen/ Research/Studien_und_Materialien/PDF-Dokumente_Unternehmensbef ragung/Ubef2008_ZiVPKR_Endfassung_Internet.pdf.
16. Randall D. Guynn, "The Financial Panic of 2008 and Financial Regulatory Reform," Harvard Law School Forum on Corporate Governance and Financial Regulation, November 20, 2010: http://blogs.law.harvard.edu/corp gov/2010/11/20/the-financial-panic-of-2008-and-financial-regulatory-reform/#2b.
17. Interview with Merkel in *Münchner Merkur* newspaper, "Die CSU fasziniert mich immer wieder," September 22, 2008: http://www.merkur-online.de/ nachrichten/politik/interview-csu-merkel-10305.html.
18. Rainer Buergin, "Hypo Rescue Was Needed as World Faced 'Abyss'," *Bloomberg News*, August 20, 2009: http://www.bloomberg.com/apps/news?p id=conewsstory&tkr=DBK:PZ&sid=aw_9Uvh.N9qo.
19. Aaron Kirchfeld, Sonia Sirletti, "Commerzbank Plans to Repay $20 Billion in State Aid Using Capital Increase," Bloomberg News, April 4, 2011: http:// www.bloomberg.com/news/2011-04-06/commerzbank-to-redeem-20-billion-in-soffin-participations-in-capital-move.html.
Federal Agency for Financial Market Stabilization, "Stabilisierungsmassnahmen des SoFFin" (data as of December 31, 2012): http://www.fmsa.de/de/fmsa/ soffin/instrumente/massnahmen-aktuell.
20. Speech by Merkel to Christian Democratic Union CDU, June 29, 2011: http://veranstaltungen.cducsu.de/rede-von-bundeskanzlerin-angela-merkel-auf-dem-kongress-zur-finanzmarktregulierung-nach-der-krise.
21. Rainer Buergin, "Merkel Converts to Bank-Bashing," *Bloomberg News*, November 7, 2008: http://www.bloomberg.com/apps/news?pid=newsarchiv e&sid=aJGfmTuCaoPY.
22. Interview with Merkel in *Bild*, March 11, 2009.

Chapter 5

Job (Greece as Euro's Nemesis)

With the euro area in the midst of the seven most critical days since its creation, Merkel had an appointment in Moscow, the city she knew from her student days. Europe's wartime past, the fiscal contradictions set aside at the euro's birth and German domestic politics culminated in one of those weekends that European leaders seem to need to keep the continent from backsliding. It was May 9, 2010, a Sunday that marked the 65th anniversary of the Allied victory over Nazi Germany. Russian President Dmitry Medvedev put on the largest Victory Day parade since the dissolution of the Soviet Union in 1991 to mark the occasion. A flyover of 127 aircraft roared overhead, including Tupolevs, Antonovs, and the Mi-26 heavy transport helicopter, the largest in the world. SS-27 intercontinental ballistic missiles rumbled across Red Square in front of the visiting dignitaries standing on the spot where Soviet leaders and communist functionaries once stood before them. Whatever conflicting emotions Angela Merkel may have been feeling as she looked on from the viewing stand were set aside as she concentrated on the business at hand: halting the market meltdown that was rapidly putting Europe's economic future in doubt.

Merkel kept in touch with her key aides, who were back in their Moscow hotel ringing around their European counterparts to get a feel for the kind of size of rescue package that was needed to wow the markets that had been singularly unimpressed by the 110 billion-euro bailout for Greece announced seven days previously. The Germans were looking for a number that would underline Europe's collective commitment to stay together and give what Merkel termed the "speculators" cause to back off. At stake were soaring borrowing costs in Portugal, Ireland and Spain that were undermining the ability of the respective governments to service their debt and threatened to render each country effectively bankrupt, a prospect that until then had been unimaginable for Western Europe. These were seven days that shook not just Merkel's world, but also the foundations of Europe's postwar make-up. Greece was the keystone that became dislodged through financial mismanagement and a belief that nothing could reverse the gains brought since the advent of the euro. Its bloated budget deficit and inability to meet its payments had spiraled into a crisis that threatened to drag the rest of Europe down with it. If Greece went, then the eurozone was at risk of collapse causing untold economic and financial damage, an event that might even unwind the European Union.

Merkel flew to Moscow from Brussels, where European leaders held a crisis summit to discuss measures to stem the gathering panic on international financial markets. The previous Sunday, May 2, European Central Bank President Jean-Claude Trichet and EU Commissioner Olli Rehn had made a joint statement committing to help Greece in exchange for 30 billion euros in austerity cuts to be carried out over the next three years.

It didn't work. Markets, rather than being reassured by the help offered, took fright at the implications for the whole of the eurozone. The euro tumbled more than 4 percent during that week, the most since the aftermath of the Lehman collapse 20 months earlier, and borrowing costs for Ireland, Portugal and Spain measured in the interest rate, or yield, on government bonds soared. Greece's woes were infecting all of Europe as global market confidence in the euro region's ability to hold together collapsed. In the U.S., the Dow Jones Industrial Average fell 1,000 points briefly on May 6, prompting President Barack Obama to call Merkel and French President Nicolas Sarkozy to urge "resolute steps" to prevent the crisis from spreading in Europe and around the world. Merkel, her financial regulation agenda checked by the U.S. and the U.K., lashed out and declared war on the "perfidious" investors who were speculating against state debts and using Greece to try and expose the wider flaws of the euro. "I believe that we are experiencing a conflict the likes of which the world hasn't witnessed before," she said on German television that day. "Speculators are our opponents, so we must weigh our words more carefully than ever and show unity." Countries needed to get a grip on their debt and deficits, but markets also had to be subject to greater regulation, she said. Saying it was a "scandal" that hedge funds weren't regulated, she blamed the U.K., which had blocked her attempts at regulation three years earlier during Germany's presidency of the G-8. "It's almost like a battle of politics against the markets and politics must gain primacy," she said. "I am determined to win this battle." Within the month, Germany introduced a unilateral ban on naked short-selling of government bonds in the euro region, a practice blamed for driving up interest rates.

The next day, Friday May 7, the Bundestag held a special session to vote on Germany's 22.4 billion euro share of the Greek bailout. "There is no better alternative," Finance Minister Wolfgang Schäuble told the lower house. It passed by 390 votes to 72 against; the main opposition Social Democrats abstained.[1] The upper house met and passed the bill the same day and President Horst Köhler signed it into law at 7 p.m. that evening. German lawmakers would be called upon to aid ailing euro countries for the sake of the single currency for the rest of the legislative term.

The Bundestag was already behind the curve as European leaders met in Brussels that same day to deliberate efforts to stop the contagion that was spreading from Greece by providing a financial shield for those other countries with budget difficulties now in the eye of the financial storm. Trichet circulated graphics to the leaders to illustrate the gravity of the situation. On the table was a European Commission proposal to recycle 60 billion euros from the EU budget and channel it toward a Europe-wide rescue fund. As the talks dragged on past midnight into Saturday May 8, Merkel, who had already been accused of worsening Greece's predicament by delaying a deal on aid, blocked the Commission's plan, arguing that 60 billion euros would be a ludicrous sum to announce if the problems were as drastic as described.

Why expose ourselves to ridicule in the markets on Monday morning with something that is ill thought-through and clearly insufficient just for the sake of appearing to do something, she told the meeting.

Merkel demonstrated again that she wouldn't be rushed – and that she held the key. Risking further opprobrium to get a deal that would tackle the problem at hand, she called for the euro group of finance ministers to work on something more appropriate before the markets opened 48 hours later. She held sway. Merkel emerged at the street entrance of the Brussels EU summit building with a perfunctory statement to the media, who had been expecting concrete measures to be announced. Noting the "high level of speculation" against the single European currency, she said leaders had agreed "to take joint measures to defend ourselves against speculators." While they must be thoroughly prepared, there should be no doubt "it will be a very clear signal against those who want to speculate against the euro." She headed off into the night back to Berlin en route to Moscow.

Merkel was in Russia as finance ministers prepared to gather for what would be a 14-hour overnight session to hammer out Europe's collective response. The German chancellor, standing between Chinese President Hu Jintao and Russian Prime Minister Vladimir Putin, nipped on and off the podium to consult with her aides as a troop contingent 10,000 strong marched past on Red Square. Nicolas Sarkozy had cancelled his attendance at the victory parade the previous day to focus on what his office at the Elysée termed "euro-area issues," leaving Merkel as the only major European leader in Moscow. Even if she had wanted to, Merkel couldn't escape the crisis, as Hu Jintao delivered what one aide described as a very candid view of the euro area. Two years later, Merkel thanked Chinese Premier Wen Jiabao during a visit to Germany for maintaining confidence in the euro.

The military convoy rolled past, starting with a fleet of World War II Soviet T-34 tanks through to the SS-27 missiles that are designed to carry a nuclear payload. Members of the German contingent were negotiating firepower of a different sort with their colleagues across Europe. They settled on a sum of 500 billion euros – more than eight times the original amount proposed and about four times the entire revenue of the 27-member EU that year[2] – as both achievable and of a sufficient volume to impress markets, or at least buy enough time for more action to be taken. With the crisis diplomacy spanning nine time zones, Merkel called Obama to inform him. She and Sarkozy agreed on the plan in a call at 6 p.m. Berlin time.

That was the same time polls closed across the German industrial and coal-mining state of North Rhine-Westphalia, Germany's most populous region. With almost 18 million inhabitants, the state accounts for more than 20 percent of Germany's entire population, providing the first electoral test of Merkel's second-term coalition and her crisis policy.

In Brussels, meanwhile, the finance ministers were already deliberating when Schäuble, then 68, suffered an adverse reaction to a new medicine and had to be rushed to the hospital. Schäuble has used a wheelchair since he was shot by a deranged assailant after an election campaign event in 1990. His place was filled temporarily by a deputy, Jörg Asmussen, who had been a German government crisis troubleshooter since the collapse of Lehman Brothers in 2008. Merkel later nominated him to join the ECB's governing council. Faced with sudden uncertainty, Merkel called on Thomas de Maizière, her former Chancellery chief of staff and confidant from the days after the fall of the Berlin Wall, to sit in for Schäuble. It was a rare signal of her possible succession plans. De Maizière, who was interior minister at the time and later became defense minister, held positions in post-communist eastern German state governments from the 1990s until Merkel brought him to the chancellery in 2005. Thomas' cousin is Lothar de Maizière, the first and only democratically elected East German premier. His father was General Ulrich de Maizière, who fought with the Wehrmacht in Russia during World War II and later helped build the Bundeswehr, Germany's post-Nazi armed forces. Merkel wanted a full minister at the table, and someone she trusted.

The negotiations resumed, though it would take 14 hours for them to forge a deal that at last showed Europe was serious about tackling the threat it was facing. The package comprised the 500 billion euros as agreed by Merkel, Sarkozy and other European leaders, plus 250 billion euros from the International Monetary Fund (IMF). Translated into a dollar sum, it yielded a crisis-fighting fund in excess of $1 trillion. Germany's share of the fund, which came to be known as the European Financial Stability Facility, or EFSF, was 123 billion euros, and later climbed to 211 billion euros. Meanwhile, the ECB started a program to buy the bonds of those nations worst affected. Hailed at the time as the ultimate "shock and awe" package, the deal was credible enough to buy some time, that was all. The available firepower would later contract after taking into account the cash buffer needed to protect the EFSF's credit rating. And it came too late to save Merkel's domestic troubles.

Exit polls in North Rhine-Westphalia showed the Social Democrats led by Hannelore Kraft, a native of the Ruhrgebiet who served under Peer Steinbrück before he joined Merkel's first-term Cabinet as finance minister, with a narrow victory over Merkel's Christian Democrats. Party strategists ascribed the result to public anger at having to bail out Greece. Nationwide, polls showed backing for Merkel's coalition slumping as the wrangling over Greece dragged on through the spring of 2010, culminating in Germany assuming the largest share of the rescue in a parliamentary vote less than 48 hours before the state election. In the final tally, the Christian Democratic Union (CDU) in the state edged ahead of Kraft's Social Democratic Party (SPD) by 0.1 percentage point while taking the same number of seats, but it was Kraft who succeeded in putting together a minority coalition with the Greens that allowed her to win election as prime minister. The result gave the opposition SPD and their Green allies a key state and also allowed them to seize control of the upper house of parliament, the Bundesrat, where state governments are awarded seats according to population. With Germany's most populous state falling to the opposition, Greece and its aftermath cost Merkel her Bundesrat majority, giving the SPD the opportunity to flex its political muscles and to block her government's legislation. Domestically and internationally, Greece was Merkel's nemesis during 2010 and for much of the following year, dragging down her popularity, losing her further regional elections, and undermining her reputation abroad as she analyzed her response to each aspect of the unfolding crisis that came her way. Yet it was also the battleground that would establish her as the cautious leader who took charge of Europe's reply to the challenges presented. For Merkel, the events of May 2010 were a turning point, the moment when she started to fight back after being dictated to by the markets since Greece first emerged on the horizon as a problem eight months earlier.

Angela Merkel's concerns about Greece first became public through a chancellery blunder. In a speech to a private event in Berlin in January 2010, three months into her second term, Merkel told the audience that Greece and other countries which had allowed their budget deficits to swell unchecked were stoking up problems for all Europe. Without greater spending discipline, she said, the single European currency would be in trouble. Greece's example "can put us under great, great pressures," Merkel said, unknowingly setting the agenda for her second term. The euro, then shared by 16 countries, will be "in a very difficult phase over the coming years." The event was hosted by *Die Welt* newspaper, yet in an illustration of how the German government can operate, a blanket ban had been imposed on reporting the content of her speech. No-one had told Merkel's media aides, and a transcript was posted on the government website the following day. Her remarks were immediately reported – though not by *Die Welt* – and financial markets reacted to the news of her concern, ratcheting up Greek government borrowing costs. Such was the concern after Bloomberg reported the speech, the chancellery called and asked for the story to be removed from the wire, as if it had never happened. It was a slip that betrayed Merkel's concerns at what was to come. The German chancellor had until then studiously avoided any specific reference to Greece in public, almost as if she was hoping it would go away. If she was specifically asked about the country's problems, she said they were a matter for the Greek government to address. Savings and economic reforms would see the country through, she said. It was a stance she kept up in public even in the face of mounting evidence that Greece could no longer be considered a little local problem.

As Merkel spoke in Berlin, George Papaconstantinou was preparing drastic revenue-raising measures and budget cuts in Athens under a three-year plan aimed at bringing Greece back into the European fold. Greece, a relative backwater in economic terms accounting for only about 2 percent of the euro area's output, had committed the error of not only living beyond its means for years but also of covering up the extent of its binge. Athens Venizelos airport, built as part of the city's successful bid to host the 2004 Olympics, is gleaming, new and empty for whole periods of the year, as are the excellent motorways that connect it to the city and all points of the country. Papaconstantinou, an economist married to a Dutch travel writer, was finance minister in Prime Minister George Papandreou's PASOK government which had swept to power in October 2009. He served in the post for 20 turbulent months, during which he had to impose wage cuts and job losses on the Greek people in return for the financial help needed to keep Greece in the euro. By May of 2012, Papaconstantinou was out of office, he had lost his parliamentary seat and was wary of going out on the street for his own safety, such was the stigma of the job and the rage at what his government had enacted. During that time, Greece turned into a virtual pariah state as it became the detonator of a crisis that consumed Ireland and Portugal and marauded Spain and Italy, polarizing Europe into a rich north and a poor south and threatening to tear the euro region apart.

The day after Merkel's Berlin address, Papandreou presented the first of three austerity packages that were to be inflicted on his country in an attempt to wrestle down its deficit. The parlous state of Greece's finances was not a priority during the campaign for the October 2009 election, as neither side was willing to advocate the deep cuts that were later deemed necessary. With the economy in its third year of recession, PASOK trounced the government of Kostas Karamanlis, whose New Democracy party fell to its worst election result since its founding in 1974. Papandreou took office in Athens days before Merkel wrapped up negotiations with the Free Democrats in Berlin that sealed her second-term coalition. Their respective fates were bound together.

The Karamanlis government had notified Eurostat, the European statistics agency, that Greece was staring at a deficit of 6 percent of output for the year, already double the 3 percent limit laid down in EU statutes. On gaining office, Papaconstantinou opened up the books and saw the true extent of the damage. "It was horrible," he recalled. The figures for the first nine months of that year showed a deficit of 10 percent, meaning the full-year figures would certainly be higher. Though new in his post, Papaconstantinou wasn't expecting congratulations when he traveled to Brussels that month to his first meeting of euro-area finance ministers. Instead, he was burdened with an ominous message that would have ramifications for the whole group: Greece's budget deficit for 2009 was slated to be 12.7 percent of GDP. Taking into account the expenditure that was being hidden or massaged, the deficit ended up at about 15 percent, five times European limits. "I could see this was going to be a very short-lived honeymoon," Papaconstantinou said. "Whoever's fault it was, it was up to us to clean it up." He said that his fellow finance ministers already knew that Greece was a problem waiting to happen. He cited an internal report by the European Commission presented to the group in July 2009, which used data from the first quarter to show that Greece was looking at a deficit of 10 percent unless it took action to narrow the gap. As a result, the group of finance ministers knew the figures were worse than they were being told at the time, even if they didn't know the order of magnitude by which the government's finances were out.[3]

France had raised concern about Greece as far back as 2008 during the banking crisis, when the European Economic and Financial Committee, the group of senior treasury officials that prepares the ground for meetings of finance ministers, warned that Greece might have problems issuing debt in the wake of the Lehman meltdown. That was a scenario which it was judged would immediately trigger a problem for the rest of Europe. In the end, the problem didn't materialize then. Who knew what about Greece's debt and when they knew it wasn't important anymore as the crisis gathered force. Yet even with the Greek numbers out in the open, European governments were slow to react. Up until that moment, there had been a complacency bordering on arrogance at large, a feeling that this was Europe and the euro system was pinned together by trust, transparency and self-policing. When it failed, there was no immediate response.

"There was shock, there was embarrassment and there was also a lot of confusion about what to do," said Ángel Gurría, secretary-general of the Paris-based Organization for Economic Cooperation and Development (OECD), a think tank on economic and policy matters for its 34 member countries. "The theory that prevailed was that if you use the euro nothing wrong or nothing too bad could happen." Gurría too had clashed with the previous Greek government over its budget figures, and been told to butt out. A former finance minister in his native Mexico, he negotiated the country's debt restructuring in 1989, earning him a reputation as one of the world's experts on sovereign debt issues. "Our position – my position, maybe because I was familiar with the fact that countries go bankrupt and here in Europe no one has gone bankrupt for a long, long time – was you have to stop, pause and take a deep breath and face the music," he said. In Europe, however, "every time we proposed that we needed to go for some kind of debt management process, we were told that that was 'irresponsible'."[4]

Once the crisis began, alarm bells soon rang in Washington. The Obama administration recognized early on that Greece could blow up and lead to a row of very complicated problems, according to a senior U.S. official. More broadly, the U.S. understood the degree of contagion that was possible. In late 2009, the U.S. Treasury sent a delegation to Athens to hold talks with the Finance Ministry and the central bank. In early February 2010, Treasury Secretary Timothy Geithner and Federal Reserve Chairman Ben Bernanke confronted the Europeans at a G-7 meeting hosted in Iqaluit in the Canadian Arctic, asking them to come up with a game plan on Greece. The MSCI World Index of stocks had just fallen to its lowest since the previous October amid investor concerns that Greece and perhaps other European countries might default. German Finance Minister Wolfgang Schäuble told reporters in Iqaluit that Europe "isn't the only one with budget problems."[5] At that stage, the Europeans didn't understand at all what they were facing, nor what was around the corner, according to the U.S. official. They saw Greece as a run-of-the-mill fiscal crisis in a single country and failed to grasp the potential for interlinkages within the euro area with its highly interconnected banking system. By March, an official had been appointed at the Treasury dedicated to Greece, even though all they could do was monitor developments, offer support and advice. Treasury officials were calling Papaconstantinou's ministry twice a week to express their concern and ask if Greece was any closer to moving toward requesting outside help. "It was clear that as the markets were closing in, or as markets were closing out in the sense they were shutting us out, the worry on behalf of the U.S. was growing," said Papaconstantinou. "We were saying, you know it's not up to us, talk to the rest of Europe."

The question was famously attributed to Henry Kissinger: whom to call in "Europe" to get things done? Ultimately, that now meant

Merkel. Though she showed an understanding of the potential for spillover contagion from the outset, Merkel at first chose to play down Greece's troubles. Back in December 2009, as the leaders of the 27 EU states prepared to discuss the financial situation in Greece for the first time, Merkel intimated that she sensed what might be around the corner. She had returned to Bonn for a pre-summit meeting of the European People's Party, the European umbrella group that includes her Christian Democrats among some 74 political parties from 40 countries. It was being held in the World Conference Center, a complex by the Rhine that incorporates the former Bundestag building in which Merkel first took her place as a lawmaker 19 years earlier. On the agenda were climate change and the upcoming United Nations climate conference in Copenhagen; the economic and financial crisis that began with the 2007 subprime collapse and which was only then receding; plus a discussion of the "social market economy" as a model to defeat the crisis, a German-inspired addition to the program. Heads of state or government from 13 EU countries and a further six non-EU states attended as EU President Herman Van Rompuy exhorted nations to become "climate friendly" and his cohort, José Barroso, then freshly installed for a second term as EU Commission president, urged efforts be stepped up to reach a deal in Copenhagen. His calls went unheeded as, unlike in Berlin under Merkel's direction in 1995, no deal was forthcoming and a non-binding text backed by the U.S. was simply "taken note of" by the other country delegates.

Speaking to reporters, Merkel acknowledged that EU leaders traveling to Brussels for the summit later that day would be discussing Greece. It would be the first of what became a succession of crisis summits over the next three years as Greece and its aftermath went on to dominate European policy making. Merkel gave a first intimation of what might be to come, raising the need to help if a fellow euro member gets into difficulty. "If something happens in one country then all other countries are affected as well," she said. The common currency shared by euro nations means "we also have a common responsibility." Yet she also made clear that euro-area countries weren't alone in falling from the path of fiscal temperance, aiming an apparent jab at the U.S. "One shouldn't over-value" the matter, Merkel concluded. "There are deficits in other parts of the world as well."

At the meeting's close, Merkel stood at the center for the family portrait. On her left was Yulia Tymoshenko, then Ukraine's prime minister. To Merkel's right, Italian Prime Minister Silvio Berlusconi cracked a joke; laughing, the chancellor touched his arm, as if to reproach him for going too far. Within two years, Tymoshenko would be imprisoned as a result of what the EU called a politically motivated conviction and Berlusconi had stepped down, harried by Merkel and Sarkozy to make way for a government of technocrats to steer Italy through the crisis.

If Merkel chose to publicly deny the seriousness of the challenge posed by Greece, she was not alone to shrug it off initially. Financial markets, which had in the main been digesting the news about Greece since its woes became public three months earlier, only took fright going into 2010. The yield on Greece's 10-year bond reached a euro-era high of 6.248 percent on January 21, rising to 7.4 percent on April 4. The euro, which nudged past $1.50 in December 2009, went into a tailspin that took it below $1.20 within less than six months.[6] What's more, the crisis was beginning to impact on Germany, with the benchmark DAX index losing more than 500 points in the first six weeks of 2010. And still Merkel waited to act. As the realization dawned in Greece that whatever they could do it would not be enough to convince markets, Merkel refused to be drawn into agreeing to a backstop at European level. Her response was for Greece to keep doing the job, that it didn't need any outside help, and that there was no plan B. By the spring of 2010, EU leaders said they were ready to help Greece in exchange for stricter oversight and implementation of austerity measures. Yet no concrete measures were announced. The leaders of the euro region, the world's biggest economy after the U.S., were paralyzed. It was an inauspicious time for Merkel to commit financial resources: debt was rising to a record as a result of tax cuts and other stimulus measures introduced to escape the recession, while support for the parties in her coalition was at its lowest since 2001, prompting dissenters on Greece to speak out against providing help. The state vote in North Rhine-Westphalia further complicated matters. Merkel stressed the tough conditions being imposed on Greece and said the Greek government "doesn't want money from us." In March, European officials still expressed confidence in public that Greece's budget cuts, coupled with a statement of political support, would be enough to convince financial markets without the need for a bailout. Papandreou, who pushed an austerity package through parliament on March 5 with an additional 4.8 billion euros of cuts, really "grabbed the bull by the horns," Merkel told reporters in Munich that day. She held out the prospect of the ultimate sanction: euro expulsion. As a measure of last resort, it must be possible for "a country to be excluded from the euro area if it continually fails to meet the conditions," she told the Bundestag on March 17, 2010.[7]

Time was running out for Greece. A government bond of 8.5 billion euros fell due on May 19, and the government was facing a probable default unless help was forthcoming.[8] Behind the scenes, France was trying to swing Merkel round to a bailout. But there was a hitch: Merkel insisted on the involvement of the IMF in the face of opposition from France and the European Commission. She openly disagreed with Schäuble, her finance minister, who was against IMF involvement. A native of the Baden region across the Rhine river from France, he sided with Paris in arguing that bringing in the IMF would signal Europe was incapable of finding a home-grown solution to deal with Greece. Publicly, Merkel said that the IMF had experience in sovereign defaults and so it was natural that its expertise should be enlisted in helping Greece. It also helped that the IMF would go on to take a 30 billion euro share in Greece's bailout. Her insistence on having the IMF on board was also a vote of no-confidence in the EU Commission's ability to handle the task alone.

She was touting an eastern European precedent to back up her case. Latvia, one of the Baltic states that joined the EU in the wave of expansion to the former communist East in 2004, had just applied for an IMF program after the global crisis exposed its economic flaws. The bubble burst in August 2008 with a run on Parex Bank, the largest domestically owned lender, underlining the country's rising debt levels and unsustainable growth rates since EU accession. The IMF agreed to fund Latvia's financing needs from 2009 through 2011 in conjunction with European countries, the ECB, and the Commission. In return, Latvia committed to narrow its budget deficit drastically, achieving a reduction of some 15 percent of GDP over the next three years.[9] As Ilmars Rimsevics, governor of the Bank of Latvia, later noted: "Markets will punish the countries which are living beyond their means and trying to spend the future generations' income."[10] Latvians didn't have the benefits of the euro and got by with per-capita GDP almost one-third lower than Greece's. In Merkel's eyes, they had shown willingness to sacrifice.[11] Merkel, now in "Latvian mode," as the French called it, saw the precedent as an appealing one. Not only did it make economic sense, it also sent out the message that Germany was making no distinction with the Greek problem: Greece would receive no special treatment just because it was a euro member. Merkel made it her red line for participating in a Greek bailout and got her way, tightening the screws on Greece and sending a clear signal to her European partners that Germany could not be relied upon to pick up the tab this time. Merkel was accused of exacerbating the situation by delaying her response, a charge taken up by Joachim Poss, a budget spokesman for the Social Democratic opposition. "From February to May, you had no idea where you wanted to go. You failed to act," Poss told the chancellor in the Bundestag that fall, interrupting her as she delivered a speech to lower-house members. "You've made the crisis worse. The whole world knows it!" Merkel responded with typical coolness. "Herr Poss, stop shouting," she said. "Yes, I needed two months to convince Europe that first countries themselves had to make savings and that only then will solidarity come from the community."[12] That was her retort to the critics, be they investors or fellow leaders.

On April 23, 2010, one day after the European statistics office revised Greece's budget deficit for 2009 to 13.6 percent of GDP, Prime Minister Papandreou made a televised address from the island of Kastelorizo. Wearing a white linen suit and standing against a backdrop of turquoise blue waters, he called for international aid from the European community and the IMF, calling it a new Odyssey for Greece. "But we know the road to Ithaca and have charted the waters," he said. Like many of Papandreou's moves during the crisis, the announcement was spectacularly inappropriate, and seemed destined only to turn German politicians against aiding Greece. In fact, Papandreou had been due to visit the island anyway that day and didn't want to cancel, so decided to use it as the setting for making the plea for aid. He may also have wanted to use the opportunity to showcase a more positive image of Greece. Nine days later, the euro region and IMF agreed on a 110 billion-euro rescue package for Greece, with the IMF's share of the bailout at 30 billion euros. In return, Greece committed to 30 billion euros in austerity cuts over three years. The initial rate on the loans was more than 5 percent, higher for funds beyond the three-year duration of the program, plus a 50-point service charge. These were punitive terms intended to hurt, so much so that they later had to be eased when Greece couldn't meet them. It set the tone for Greece for more than two years until Merkel saw that being excessively harsh was counterproductive.

As Merkel prepared to seek a third term at the 2013 election, Greece was still on life support. Prime Minister Antonis Samaras was struggling to hold together a governing coalition amid what was projected to be a sixth year of recession. Merkel's stated determination to keep Greece in the euro did not extend to a willingness to write off all its debt and give it a clean slate to start anew. After all, that would imply her whole stance to date had been a failure. Greece had meanwhile been joined by Ireland, Portugal, Spain and Cyprus on the frontline of Europe's debt crisis as bailout recipients. Some were fighting to reduce crushing debt levels, others were suffering record levels of youth unemployment; all had economies that were stagnating – and were looking to Germany and to Merkel for relief. While she was at school, Merkel said she "tried to find a seat in the middle or at the back" of the classroom, because "I liked to have the overview."[13] Whatever overview Merkel has of Europe today from the Chancellery in Berlin, it is colored by Greece and its repercussions. In her speech behind closed doors back in January 2010 in which she first intimated the problems that might flow from Greece, Merkel anticipated that relations between European countries could suffer as a result of their budgetary woes. In Greece, "I don't know that they'll be enthusiastic about Germany giving them instructions," she said. It's not just Greece: Merkel's handling of the crisis in the euro area raised concerns about German control of Europe and put her country's reputation at a crossroads.

Notes

1. Patrick Donahue and Brian Parkin, "German Lawmakers Back Greek Aid Package," *Bloomberg News*, May 7, 2010: http://www.bloomberg.com/news/2010–05–06/germany-votes-on-greek-aid-as-merkel-pushes-for-increased-eu-discipline.html.
2. EU budget 2010 press release, December 17, 2009: http://europa.eu/rapid/press-release_IP-09–1958_en.htm?locale=en.

3. Interview in Athens, November 20, 2012.

4. Interview in Paris, November 19, 2012.

5. Simon Kennedy and Simone Meier, "G-7 Pledges to Keep Stimulus Even Amid Budget Stress," *Bloomberg News*, February 6, 2010: http://www.bloomberg.com/apps/news?pid=newsarchive&sid=aTXyM554cImg.

6. "Greek Crisis Timeline from Maastricht Treat to ECB Bond-Buying," *Bloomberg News*, September 5, 2012: http://www.bloomberg.com/news/2012–09–05/greek-crisis-timeline-from-maastricht-treaty-to-ecb-bond-buying.html.

7. Speech to Bundestag during general budget debate, March 17, 2010: http://www.cducsu.de/Titel__rede_herkulesaufgabe_haushalt_konsolidieren_und_wachstum_schaffen/TabID__1/SubTabID__2/InhaltTypID__2/InhaltID__15170/Inhalte.aspx.

8. Jones Hayden and Natalie Weeks, "Greece Gets First Installment of Emergency Loans," *Bloomberg News*, May 18, 2010: http://www.bloomberg.com/news/2010–05–18/greece-receives-18-billion-in-first-bailout-payment-from-european-union.html.

9. IMF news release, December 23, 2008: http://www.imf.org/external/np/sec/pr/2008/pr08345.htm.

10. IMF video: http://www.imf.org/external/mmedia/view.aspx?vid=1880771689001.

11. Eurostat: http://epp.eurostat.ec.europa.eu/tgm/table.do?tab=table&plugin=1&language=en&pcode=tec05114.

12. Merkel address to Bundestag, September 15, 2010: http://www.cducsu.de/Titel__rede_herbst_der_entscheidungen/TabID__1/SubTabID__2/InhaltTypID__2/InhaltID__16532/Inhalte.aspx.

13. Bunte-TV in 2003, as cited in *Die Welt*, November 22, 2005.

Chapter 6

Lamentations
(Safe European Home?)

T he French town of Deauville, with its hippodrome, grand hotels and beachfront promenade, is a resort that trades on its illustrious past. Developed in the 1860s during France's Belle Epoque, the town found its true vocation after enlisting the help of Eugène Cornuché, who had just given his Paris restaurant Maxim's an Art Nouveau makeover, ensuring the decor was as fashionable as the food. Cornuché set about redeveloping the town's casino, opening it in 1912, the year after the race course was inaugurated, thus establishing Deauville as a playground for the Paris smart set. Coco Chanel was attracted to the town by her polo-playing lover, Captain Arthur Edward "Boy" Capel, and opened one of her first boutiques there in 1913. Isadora Duncan arrived in the summer of 1914 during World War I and stayed for several months, working as a nurse in the casino, which had been converted to a military hospital. In the 1920s, the seaside boardwalk was constructed and the town cemented its reputation as a spa resort famed for its extravagant parties. Even in the late 1940s after World War II had brought its golden years to a close, Rita Hayworth and her racehorse-owning third husband, Prince Aly Khan, were regular visitors; Yves Saint-Laurent took up residence in the town in 1976.[1] Just along the Atlantic coast, traveling west toward Cherbourg through fertile farmland, the fields ringed by mature hedges, the spirit of the roaring '20s gives way to the wartime reality of two decades later. On June 6, 1944, better known as D-Day, more than 160,000 Allied soldiers fought their way ashore against unsuspecting German forces: the British Army landing at Sword Beach, Juno and Gold beaches, and the US Army at Omaha and Utah Beach. Normandy, for all its renown for horse racing and summer bathing, its Camembert cheese and calvados, is also a region fraught with 20th-century European history.

In the annals of the sovereign debt crisis and its existential threat to the euro, October 2010 in Deauville will go down for many as the scene of Merkel's biggest error and the moment contagion took hold, widening Greece's debt problems into a market rout. Ireland, bludgeoned by borrowing rates that soared to unsustainable levels after Deauville, was forced to call for a bailout five weeks later. Portugal fell victim in April the following year. Deauville was also where Germany and France began to impose their joint response on the rest of the euro region, stoking resentment. The euro, designed to make Europe more like one country, was splitting the continent into unequal northern and southern tiers, with France as something of a swing state. Merkel needed allies to back Germany's fix and the "German–French axis," linking the euro region's two biggest economies, was the natural centerpiece. If the aim was to avoid the impression in some quarters of a German diktat on Europe, it didn't work. In Greece, which suffered four years of German occupation during World War II, Merkel was vilified by protesters as a Nazi reincarnation. German President Joachim Gauck felt the need to address the matter in February 2013, using his first major foray into the political sphere to reassure Europe that Germany was not set on domination.[2] While Germany's image also declined elsewhere in Europe, polls show overall non-Germans' respect for the perceived homeland of hard work, thriftiness, and prosperity was still high.[3]

Merkel's breakthrough at Deauville was persuading Nicolas Sarkozy to go along with her plan to make investors pay for their role in bringing Greece to its knees and forcing governments to respond with tens of billions of euros in rescue packages. From the European Central Bank to the U.S., from Greece's government to the highest officials at the European Union, all agree that this was a tipping point in the crisis. After Merkel and Sarkozy strolled along the boardwalk in harmony, Greece's troubles ignited a fire that spread uncontrolled across the euro area and threatened to engulf the entire global economy. The occasion was a two-day meeting of Merkel, Sarkozy, and Russian President Dmitry Medvedev. Sarkozy was set to hold the rotating presidency of the G-8 and G-20 in 2011, and Deauville had been chosen as the location for G-8 leaders to meet in May of that year. The French–German–Russian meeting was meant to be an advance show of common purpose on issues such as the Middle East, Iran, and EU–Russian relations. Yet as so often during the debt crisis, the euro area's problems steamrolled the business at hand.

Merkel and Sarkozy met on October 18 to take the air before having dinner at a Deauville restaurant with Medvedev. The two were pictured walking on the boardwalk behind the setting sun, deep in conversation. They returned to announce a three-point plan that took their European peers by surprise. Merkel won agreement from Sarkozy to push for changes to the EU's guiding treaty to reinforce budget discipline, while he gained a concession that sanctions for countries breaching debt and deficit rules wouldn't be automatic, as Merkel had proposed. Rather they would kick in progressively, becoming in diplomatic-speak "more automatic." While the meaning of the agreement was obscured by European Union jargon, it yielded significant victories for each side. Sarkozy won by blunting the prospect of unelected outside bodies from imposing sanctions on national governments, an idea far more contentious in France than in Germany. Merkel gained by laying the groundwork for a Europe-wide treaty on budget discipline, her national goal since she took office in 2005 and one she was convinced was needed across Europe to tackle the root cause of the debt crisis. Aiming to pre-empt opposition to the prospect of cumbersome EU treaty revision, the two leaders stressed the limited nature of the changes. That failed to avert U.K. unease, with the *Daily Telegraph* foreseeing "the outbreak of political warfare" in David Cameron's coalition of largely Euroskeptic Conservatives and more EU-friendly Liberal Democrats. Thirteen months later, Cameron aligned the U.K. with the Czech Republic as the only two of the EU's 27 members that refused to sign up to Merkel's deficit-reduction plan, known as the fiscal compact.

The most contentious aspect of the Deauville deal, forcing investors to share in the terms of future country bailouts to mitigate the burden for taxpayers, merited a single line in the joint statement. Merkel and Sarkozy outlined the need to establish a permanent way to help crisis-hit countries once the fund that had been set up that May ran its course, saying the new instrument should ensure "an adequate participation of private creditors." At a subsequent press conference, Sarkozy was equally economical, saying they had charged EU President Herman Van Rompuy with studying "how the private sector can be involved" in the permanent crisis-resolution mechanism. It was left to Merkel to explain why. "We need treaty changes in particular to ensure that creditors are enlisted in helping make good in the event of a crisis, to help overcome the crisis," she said. "It's especially important that we construct this mechanism so that all those involved are held more responsible. That's precisely the lesson that we need to take from this crisis."

Sprung on markets in an off-hand way, the message on making investors pay was communicated poorly: the threat of sovereign-debt haircuts was meant to apply to a bailout system that was still being worked out and was only due to start operating about three years down the road. It was a miscalculation that backfired spectacularly. In the almost six months since Greece was awarded a 110 billion-euro bailout, followed by creation of the 750 billion-euro European Financial Stability Facility (EFSF), the spread in interest rates between Greece and Germany had tumbled by more than 300 basis points, or a full 3 percentage points. That trend reversed as Greek borrowing costs picked up again after Deauville, undoing the advances made in resolving the crisis. The announcement is blamed by Greece's then-finance minister Papaconstantinou as one of the main reasons the Greek program lost its way: "It made what was until that point a possibly containable crisis in one country into a full-blown, systemic issue." The U.S. judged that making private-sector involvement a precondition for future European programs would pull the floor out from under the little calm that had been achieved through the EFSF. In the words of a senior U.S. official, Deauville was a complete disaster that led the Europeans into another death spiral – and the U.S. told them as much.

While Merkel and Sarkozy met regularly to coordinate their stance before international meetings and issued joint statements, this time was different. It was one week before an EU summit and the same day as

European finance ministers were meeting to hammer out the details of the proposed permanent rescue mechanism. Merkel and Sarkozy not only reached an agreement without informing the other governments, they also pre-empted the outcome of negotiations that were about to take place. With the weight of Europe's two biggest economies behind one set of proposals, it was next to impossible for the other 25 states to resist, let alone for the 14 euro nations. ECB chief Trichet railed against the plan at a private meeting of finance ministers from euro countries. He took the highly unusual step of going public to express his reservations, saying that requiring investors to take losses in a sovereign rescue would undermine market confidence. Spain's then Prime Minister José Luis Rodríguez Zapatero, who was feeling the heat of rising borrowing costs, said he opposed it. Luxembourg's Prime Minister Jean-Claude Juncker, who chaired the group of euro finance ministers, said that pressing on with Merkel's proposals "could potentially drive investors from the eurozone, especially from the peripheral countries."

In November, almost four weeks after Deauville, an impromptu statement attempting to clarify what the plan entailed was handed out to reporters during a G-20 summit in the South Korean capital Seoul. Drawn up on behalf of European finance ministers, it was the result of negotiations between Germany's Deputy Finance Minister Jörg Asmussen, French government officials, and Trichet. It stressed that any losses on creditors would only apply after 2013 and that standard IMF practice for debt restructuring would apply. According to the U.S. official, it was the Obama administration that told the Europeans they had to issue a statement to try and take back what had been said at Deauville. The U.S. view was that Merkel and Sarkozy were building an obvious flaw into the design of the permanent mechanism that would strangle its effectiveness long before its birth. The trans-Atlantic finger-pointing intensified in the run-up to Seoul, so much so that Merkel and Obama addressed the issue head on during their bilateral meeting. They agreed in private that such unpleasantness did not get them anywhere and should not be repeated. The statement released was calming but the issue dragged on for months. The message had gotten out that investors in the euro area were to take a hit, and Merkel did little to lessen the concern which persisted until the idea of forcing losses was finally dropped a year later.

Merkel's proposal had its genesis in her May declaration of war on the "perfidious" speculators she regarded as turning budgetary troubles into a systemic crisis. They were the target of Germany's ban on naked short-selling introduced without warning overnight in June. Through her determination that creditors contribute to the cost of bailouts, Merkel broke a financial taboo – not by pushing for investors to take losses, but by announcing it in advance. The deal that took everyone by surprise had in fact been hatched in Brussels on the sidelines of a separate meeting several days before Deauville, according to Xavier Musca, Sarkozy's chief economic adviser. Merkel and Sarkozy both attended a summit of European and Asian leaders in the Belgian capital on October 4–5. Merkel was being advised at the time by officials including Otmar Issing, a former ECB executive board member whom she appointed to head an advisory panel on "new financial order" in 2008. He argued that the debt crisis was an opportunity to realign market incentives to account for differences in economic strength between euro-area economies, which had been leveled by creating a central bank with a single set of interest rates for the bloc. After governments bailed out Greece, Merkel was being told that market signals needed to be restored to highlight to investors that Irish or Portuguese government debt was riskier than German bunds. By warning private bondholders they would be the first to take losses in future sovereign-debt crises, lending would more accurately reflect states' creditworthiness and put pressure on profligate governments to change their ways. "It could have been an excellent idea at the start of monetary union precisely to tell the markets, don't rush to buy Greek or Portuguese debt," said Musca. "But if at the heart of the crisis you tell the market not only will these countries have difficulties, but in fact this risk will materialize and you will be the first to pay, the first reaction is to withdraw your investment from the euro-zone, and you create precisely the problems you're trying to cope with. So it's a disaster." Private-sector involvement, or PSI, went on to become the buzzword in the 2011 episode of the crisis.

Sarkozy was against PSI as he was convinced it would fan the flames of the crisis and cause it to spread. The German side didn't see the contagion threat and was more concerned about applying pressure on countries to get a grip on their own finances before the markets forced them under and prompted an international rescue, borne in large part by German taxpayers. Merkel said that any further German solidarity for countries in trouble was dependent upon the private sector taking its share of the cost. It was the principle that mattered, and in any case, as far as the French were concerned, Merkel thought it surely possible for the permanent mechanism to be devised in such a way that it ensured private-sector involvement without causing excessive harm to the markets.

The result of the political horse trading was kept secret until Deauville. Sarkozy agreed to PSI since he regarded it as the lesser evil to open conflict between France and Germany on the means of tackling the crisis at hand – and necessary to secure agreement on setting up the future rescue fund, known as the European Stability Mechanism. France set about trying to water down the commitment to PSI, but the damage was done; markets already suffering a collapse in sentiment toward the eurozone saw only that the relation between creditors and states had changed for the worse. One senior German official admitted that Deauville, which had to be unwound, was not the most fortunate package to have been struck – even if elements of PSI could still be seen in the eventual debt relief granted to Greece 18 months later in what would be the biggest restructuring in history. PSI might be politically and financially justified, but the price that had to paid for the principle was high and for the Germans it was, and remains, a double-edged sword.

By late November 2010 when she addressed the annual party convention of her Christian Democratic Union in Karlsruhe, home to Germany's equivalent of the supreme court, Merkel had a symbolic scalp to flourish. Combining a drive for individual budget responsibility across the region with the need to clamp down on those speculators who had taken advantage of euro states' moment of fiscal weakness, Merkel wasn't just beginning to latch on to a justification for her approach to crisis fighting; she was formulating a stance that served as a pitch for de facto leadership of the new Europe.

It was market excesses that caused the crisis, and "markets have to bear the consequences of their actions," Merkel told delegates. Dismissing British concerns, Merkel said that changes to EU treaties to stem the crisis, though regarded by some as a "utopian" idea, can and must be made. The collapse of the euro area would mean the end of

Europe's "uniting idea" that gave the continent peace and prosperity after World War II, she said. "If the euro fails, then Europe fails," and Germany's duty is to stop that from happening. Its task is no less than to "anchor a new stability culture in Europe."

The fervor of fiscal righteousness burned brightly within her party too. Leo Dautzenberg, then the CDU's finance policy spokesman, said the coalition had agreed on a set of proposals for the future bailout mechanism that included private investors "as a core element, involving if necessary taking a haircut," an enforced loss on their original invest-ment. And he knew well where to lay the blame – the Anglo-Saxons. "Wall Street investors have also got to shoulder their liabilities," he said. "We can't push everything on to taxpayers."[4]

Merkel that year assumed the greatest share of the liability for Greece and for Europe's bailout fund, lost Germany's most populous state in an election that cost her control of the upper house, and sur-vived a drop in public support for the CDU to the lowest in four years – yet she was re-elected party leader with 90.4 percent of the vote. Given Sarkozy's support and the political backing of her party for her stance, Merkel wasn't about to back down now. Opinion polls were meanwhile suggesting that voters were returning to her side as she dictated the terms of Europe's anti-crisis fight.

Deauville was also the birth of "Merkozy," the duopoly that was to dominate European decision making for the next 19 months. But with Germany's economy purring and France's sputtering, it was an unequal partnership from the start. After credit rating agency Standard & Poor's warned France that it was considering stripping the country of its AAA rating in December 2011 – a threat it carried out the follow-ing month – Merkel was very much in the driving seat. Sarkozy even said that France should be more like Germany during his unsuccessful 2012 campaign for re-election. Merkozy reached its apogee at the end of 2011, when German public broadcaster ARD reworked "Dinner for One," a mainstay of its Christmas television programming, with Merkel and Sarkozy as the main characters attending a crisis summit rather than hosting a New Year's celebration. As in the 1963 black and white original featuring the lady of the house and her increasingly inebriated butler, the skit ended with the two going upstairs to bed together, with

Sarkozy saying he'll "give it AAA." Merkozy, along with credit ratings, eurobonds and yield spreads, had gone mainstream.

Sarkozy and Merkel were polar opposites who had learned to cooperate as they were thrown together during the crisis. He was President Bling Bling with a model wife and an impetuous urge to make policy on the hoof; she an East German scientist married to a physics professor who carefully weighed her responses and preferred to do her talking behind closed doors. Merkel and Sarkozy had divergent economic philosophies, though their financial interests both lay in holding the euro together and stopping Greece's problems from spreading. While French banks' exposure to Greece was the highest of any European country, with overall claims of $56.6 billion in 2010, German banks were the biggest foreign holders of Greek government bonds, with $22.7 billion.[5] The German and French leaders toiled hard to overcome their divisions and forge a working relationship, taking their cue as the heads of Europe's two biggest economies to lead the response to the challenges. Over time, as they were forced to confront the situation in Greece and its multiple ramifications, Merkel realized that for all his ostentation Sarkozy could be taken at his word. They had disagreements on crisis responses, they negotiated, struck a deal, and he would stick to the accord rather than seek to undermine it. Then they both had to go out and sell it to the European Commission, the European Central Bank, and the member states. Sarkozy would seek to persuade the southern European countries that the deal was workable, while Merkel convinced the northern states it was acceptable to them. "I think Merkel at the start considered Sarkozy a Mediterranean, not very positive toward Germany, very French," said Xavier Musca. "She realized that he was reliable and he was doing the job and he was defending in public the positions they had agreed on in the bilateral meeting. So to a certain extent for her it was a good alliance and the atmosphere between them improved." Not that either leader agreed crisis-prevention measures just to please the other – each had their respective domestic constraints. Yet "at some point you had the feeling of two leaders not trying to oppose other national interests but finding the best solution for Europe," Musca said.

François Hollande unseated Sarkozy in May 2012 with a campaign based in large part on his rejection of Sarkozy's closeness to Merkel and collusion with her crisis-fighting policies for Europe. It came too late to dispel the resentment that had been building at the German–French crisis axis, although his election did serve to focus the anger on Germany alone. Tomasz Bielecki, Brussels correspondent for the Polish daily *Gazeta Wyborcza*, caught the European dilemma posed by the German–French axis in an article published in October 2011 and translated by Presseurop. "When the Germans and the French are unable to reach consensus, lamentations can be heard about the lack of real leadership in Europe; when they near agreement, protests against diktat mount."[6]

If Deauville gave Merkel a boost, it might just have tipped Ireland over the edge. Within 10 days Irish 10-year bond yields breached the 7 percent level and by early November 2010, Ireland was being told by Germany and the ECB that it was in the interests of the wider euro area if the Irish government applied for aid to quell the market unrest. The pressure was ratcheted up on Irish Finance Minister Brian Lenihan at a meeting of his euro region counterparts on November 16. Jörg Asmussen, who was by now at the forefront of Germany's crisis response, recalled it was made clear to Lenihan this was not just about Ireland but about the economic wellbeing of the rest of the euro region. Lenihan, who died of pancreatic cancer in June 2011, saw the bulk of the pressure for a bailout coming from the ECB, which had pumped money into the Irish banking system then on the verge of collapse. Germany's Wolfgang Schäuble was adding his weight, pressing Lenihan to announce publicly that Ireland was requesting a bailout program at the meeting's conclusion.[7] He refused; however, five days later, on November 21, the Irish government made the request. In a letter the same day to Trichet at the ECB's headquarters in Kaiserstrasse, Frankfurt, Lenihan cited concerns about Greece and a slowing economic recovery along with credit-rating decisions compounded by negative market sentiment for contributing to "a sharp reversal in financial conditions." That led to a "crisis in confidence" in Ireland's banks and the government's ability to meet its funding obligations, he said. Lenihan highlighted a fourth factor in his letter, which was released by the ECB and the Irish Finance Ministry after Freedom of Information requests made by Irish news websites TheJournal.ie and TheStory.ie.[8] "Uncertainty about the status of bondholders in the event of access to external support added to instability," Lenihan wrote.

Put more simply, Ireland's government saw German-led moves to force investors holding Irish government bonds to pay for future bailouts as a kick in the teeth when the country's financial system was already on its knees. If investors were thinking of pulling out of Ireland, Merkel had given them another reason to do so.

EU ministers met on November 28 and agreed on a rescue of 85 billion euros, and Ireland became the second country after Greece to lose control of its economic destiny by joining what is euphemistically called a "program." Measures were imposed by the triumvirate of the EU, the IMF and the ECB in return for the aid. Tens of thousands protested on the streets across Ireland, with feelings running high against what was perceived as outside interference forcing the country to go begging to Germany. Lenihan told a BBC Radio 4 program six months later that European pressure risked triggering social unrest. "They could push people beyond the brink," he said.

■ ■ ■

A crane winched up a burned out newspaper kiosk from the charred stump of its base as the Athens cleansing department began to sweep up the debris of rioting for the second time that year. The streets streamed with water, discarded placards were scattered on the ground, and smoke hung in the gardens of Syntagma Square where birds had hopped from branch to branch that morning before the demonstration began. The city's mayor demanded compensation from the central government for the cost of cleaning up central Athens. He had done the same four months earlier, without response.

Athens in October 2011 was a city under siege, with the focus of the protests the parliament building at the top of Syntagma Square. Protected by a ring of riot police holding back the demonstrators, inside besieged lawmakers deliberated late into the night over the latest round of wage cuts, reductions to pensions, job losses, and enforced privatization of state assets that were a condition of a sixth tranche of outside aid. Without it, wages would go unpaid, hospitals couldn't order drugs, and the garbage already piled high in the streets threatening to become a health hazard might never be removed.

International monitors from the so-called troika of creditors that were supplying the funds – the IMF, the ECB, and the European

Commission – had found the country's adherence to its bailout program wanting, but nevertheless recommended paying the next installment of aid "as soon as possible" after the government had made good
on its pledges. Even then, the country's "debt dynamics" remained wor-
rying. Successive rounds of enforced austerity were taking their toll
on the population of Greece, then enduring a fourth straight year of
recession. With the country on life support and no signs of economic
recovery on the horizon, the regime of cuts without visible progress
was pushing the population to breaking point. And they weren't alone:
across much of Western Europe, from Dublin to Rome, Lisbon to
Madrid, people were taking to the streets over the imposition of policy
measures that they saw as unjustly weighted toward austerity. Merkel,
as the principle paymaster for bailout nations Greece, Ireland and
Portugal and the chief proponent of reining in government spending
across the EU, was becoming the target of their fury.

It was a sign of Germany's increasing dominance during the crisis.
Volker Kauder, the parliamentary head of Merkel's Christian Democratic
bloc, captured the mood with an ill-advised remark during a speech to
a party convention in Leipzig in November 2011. Trumpeting Merkel's
success in persuading leaders to curb deficits, he noted that European
leaders who had at first refused to consider Merkel's deficit-reduction
proposals were emulating the German model of a "debt brake" written into the constitution. "Now, all of a sudden, Europe is speaking
German," Kauder said. "Not as a language, but in its acceptance of the
instruments for which Angela Merkel has fought so hard, and with success in the end."

The mood was dark in Athens that fall, as police in full riot gear
responded to volleys of petrol bombs and rocks with baton charges and
stun grenades. Some protestors had come prepared for violence, wearing
motorcycle helmets and face masks. They lit small fires in overflow-
ing garbage bins around the square in the belief that the smoke acted
as an antidote to tear gas. A man suffered a heart attack and died after
he was struck on the head by a rock near the Grande Bretagne hotel
on a corner of the square where the worst of the clashes took place.
It was at the Grande Bretagne, the most opulent hotel in town, that
the first International Olympic Committee convened in 1896 under

Baron Pierre de Coubertin. The Nazis made their headquarters there in 1941 at the start of the wartime occupation; Hitler and Field Marshall Rommel were both guests. At the war's end, the British moved in and Winston Churchill held talks there with George Papandreou, a member of the government in exile who would go on to serve as prime minister three times and found the political dynasty. Archbishop Makarios, the Greek Cypriot president dubbed the "Castro of the Mediterranean," addressed crowds from a second floor balcony of the hotel after the Turkish invasion of Cyprus.[9]

The Grande Bretagne's history mirrors that of modern Greece and it too bore the scars of the anti-austerity riots: its marble steps looked like they had been gnawed by a giant rat after demonstrators chipped away at the stone to hurl at the police. Greta Garbo, Elizabeth Taylor, Brigitte Bardot and Maria Callas all lodged in the hotel's royal suite in earlier times. What few guests remained the day after the anti-austerity demonstrations were greeted by the hotel's ancient dog and the bitter reek of tear gas.

The economic hardship and failure to achieve bailout targets was meanwhile undermining what little political stability remained. The current George Papandreou, who had followed his father and grandfather to serve as Greece's prime minister, saw his majority whittled down to single digits as members of his coalition balked at plans to reform the labor laws and force through 30,000 job losses in the state sector. Polls showed public support collapsing for the mainstream parties, Papandreou's PASOK and New Democracy, and a rise in backing for parties such as the left-wing umbrella movement Syriza. The teachers, kindergarten nannies, nurses and dockworkers who focused their rage on Greece's political leaders were beginning to see their own politicians as agents of outside powers, chief among them Germany. Where Merkel regarded austerity as a means of tackling the deficit and as justification for German solidarity, some in Greece saw a bid to enforce free market shock therapy on their country to crush the state dependence of past decades. For a country that suffered starvation and depredation under Nazi occupation, it wasn't much of a leap for some in the media and politics to project austerity through the prism of wartime atrocity; Germans seeking to finish by peaceful means what they had failed to achieve in World War II.

A *Time* magazine article from February 1942 described Greece as the hungriest country in the world, blaming the Nazi army of occupation's systematic stripping of the country's food supplies to send to troops in Africa. Between 1,700 and 2,000 people were dying each day as starvation coupled with cholera, typhus, typhoid, and dysentery ravaged the populations of Athens and the port of Piraeus.[10] Oxfam, the international anti-poverty non-governmental organization, was founded in Britain in 1942 specifically to aid Greece. Originally the Oxford Committee for Famine Relief, it campaigned for food supplies to be sent through an Allied naval blockade to the starving women and children of occupied Greece.[11]

Up a narrow side street just off the southern corner of Syntagma Square, the Jewish Museum of Greece details in gaunt terms the impact of the Nazi occupation. The Jews of Greece, known as the Romaniote, date back to antiquity, with Jewish settlement beginning in the 3rd century B.C. In the year 48 A.D., the Apostle Paul found a thriving Jewish community, and preached in synagogues in Corinth, Salonika, and Veroia. The Hebrew word "Tik" for the container used to hold the Sepher Torah, the Jewish sacred book of the law of Moses, comes from the Greek "Thiki," meaning case. The Jewish community flourished through the Roman and Byzantine empires, so much so that Greece became a refuge for persecuted Jews elsewhere in Western and Central Europe from the 14th century. They were engaged in textiles and glassware, printing, law, medicine, and shipping insurance. The first Greek constitution from 1844 granted all Greek citizens, including Jews, equal rights. At the beginning of the 20th century there were 10,000 Jews in Greece. That number rose to 100,000 after the expansion of Greek territory following the Balkan wars of 1912–1913, two-thirds of that total in Salonika. By the end of World War II, 87 percent of the population had been murdered by Nazi Germany, one of the highest rates suffered by any Jewish community in Europe. At the war's start, Jews fought with the Greek army against Italian forces after Mussolini ordered the invasion of Greece in October 1940. The Greeks counterattacked and drove the Italians back, pinning them down in Albania and inflicting the first land victory of the war over Axis forces. The Germans came to Italy's assistance, invading Greece on April 6, 1941, and occupying Salonika three days later. They took Athens on April 27. The mass deportations began in March 1943. Jewish properties and business were seized by the Germans, art treasuries confiscated, synagogues and cemeteries plundered and destroyed. When the war ended, only about 10,000 Jews were still alive in Greece.[12]

Merkel is the postwar chancellor with the least connection to Germany's wartime legacy, yet with Greece's unemployment soaring and the economy in ruins, there was a ready scapegoat to blame for the turmoil caused by the euro crisis. German flags were burned in the street, the embassy picketed, and a mock-up of Merkel wearing an SS uniform printed in Greek media and shown on television. Amid unrelenting pressure for more cuts to fulfill internationally imposed targets that were nowhere near to being met, George Karatzaferis, head of the LAOS party, said that Greece "could do without the German boot."[13] In Thessaloniki, Greece's second city, a German government official attending a conference of Greek and German mayors was hustled by local municipal workers who chanted "Nazis Out" and played Greek radio recordings from the war over loudspeakers.[14]

For President Karolos Papoulias, an octogenarian former pole-vaulting champion who fought in the wartime resistance against the Nazis, Finance Minister Wolfgang Schäuble's suggestion in early 2012 that Greek elections might have to be postponed was a step too far. Papoulias said he wouldn't "accept insults to my country" from Schäuble nor from any of the other countries that were united in pressing for more austerity, highlighting the north-south divide emerging across Europe. "Who is Mr. Schäuble to ridicule Greece? Who are the Dutch? Who are the Finns?" Papoulias said. "We always had the pride to defend not just our own freedom, not just our own country, but the freedom of all of Europe."[15]

In Germany, politicians and media showed no more restraint. The biggest-selling *Bild* newspaper regularly scorned the Greeks, running a front-page splash in early 2010 proclaiming: "So the Greeks DO want our money!" It later called for Greece to be forcibly ejected from the euro. Members of Merkel's junior coalition partner, the Free Democrats, demanded that the Greek government sell some of its islands to make up for the shortfall in its budget. *Focus* magazine ran a cover issue in February of 2010 featuring a statue of Aphrodite,

the Greek goddess of love, with her middle finger outstretched showing what in German is called the "Stinkefinger," beside the title:
"Fraudster in the Euro Family." Merkel was thrown into the web of
historic animosity that bubbles beneath the surface of contemporary
Europe without a lifebelt. Whereas her political mentor Helmut Kohl
turned his wartime experiences into a catalyst for European unity and
her immediate predecessor Gerhard Schröder's father was killed in
action in Romania, Merkel was born in 1954, almost a decade after the
war ended. Kohl thought that he could vanquish such European rifts
forever with the introduction of the euro, the glue that would bind
Europe together. Now, with fellow Europeans chafing at austerity they
see as imposed by an overarching, overly dominant Germany, his efforts
were being turned on their head.

For all the historic antipathy, the Greek–German relationship is a complex one. German tourists started arriving en masse in Greece barely
20 years after the war's end, and were welcomed with open arms.
Greece's first purpose-built tourist hotel complex opened in 1968 in
Agios Nikolaos on Crete. By 2011, over 2 million Germans were visiting Greece each year, more than from any other nation. The love affair
was to some degree mutual, even if for Greeks it was about work and
for Germans about play. Greeks traveled to Germany to earn a better
living as early as the 1950s, retracing immigration routes that began
in the 18th century. Germany's postwar economic miracle generated
a demand for foreign labor that attracted Greeks as well as Turks and
Italians to the urban centers of Frankfurt, Stuttgart and Munich, reaching its peak in the early 1970s. Among those to head north was Karolos
Papoulias, the future president, who fled to Germany after Greece's
military dictatorship seized power in 1967. He was granted asylum,
learned the language and studied at the University of Cologne, where
he gained a doctorate in law. It was awarded under the name Karl.

Migration patterns are shifting as the crisis in the euro area has
taken hold. Government statistics for the first half of 2012 showed that
501,000 people came to settle in Germany, an increase of 15 percent on
2011, which itself was up some 20 percent on 2010. The sharpest rise
was recorded in those coming from Greece – an increase of 78 percent –
followed by increases of 53 percent each in those arriving from Spain

and Portugal, fellow southern countries whose labor markets and economies have suffered during the crisis.[16] Not only is Merkel now predominant in European policy making, but Germany is the beacon of hope for many in those countries worst affected by the crisis.

In private, Merkel says she's resigned to the role assigned to Germany during the debt crisis. She compares Germany's relationship with other euro countries to that of the U.S. and the rest of the world: the nation at the top can't expect to be loved, and neither can its leader. That's something Merkel says she's prepared to live with while she goes about tackling the causes of the crisis to re-equip Europe for the future.

George Soros, the billionaire Hungarian investor and philanthropist, sees inward migration to Germany as an inevitable consequence of its policy: an insistence on budget cuts in the countries worst affected by the crisis serves only to deepen the recession there, leading, if unchecked, to depression. Merkel has it in her hands to resolve the crisis, but faces a choice, he says: She must decide whether to deploy Germany's economic might to commit to a "genuine" form of debt sharing across the euro region, or risk the collapse of the euro, fatally undermining the European Union that was forged from the ashes of the war to ensure the circumstances could never arise for another conflict. As it is, "the member countries are divided into two classes – creditors and debtors – with the creditors in charge," he said in a September 2012 speech in Berlin. "As the strongest creditor country, Germany is emerging as the hegemon."[17]

Soros was a boy of 13 in March 1944 when the Nazis marched into his hometown, Budapest, at the start of the occupation of Hungary. He was ordered to work as a courier for the Jewish Council until his father realized the notices George was to deliver were intended for Jewish lawyers as a means of registering them for deportation to death camps. His father told him to warn them instead. Soros assumed a false identity procured by his father, and spent the rest of the war pretending to be a young Romanian Christian named Sandor Kiss, the godson of a Ministry of Agriculture employee whom his father paid. After the Soviet army took Budapest from the Nazis in early 1945, the Soros family was able to return to their apartment. A bomb had destroyed the kitchen, so they cooked and ate in the living room.[18]

Soros argues that Germany's policy during the crisis is not due to malice, but rather a result of the Bundesbank, the central bank, being committed to "an outmoded monetary doctrine" rooted in Germany's traumatic experiences with inflation after World War I. That means Germany tailors policy to clamp down on inflation, even in times of recession when prices are depressed, rather than addressing the crisis on its doorstep. With the periphery in trouble, investors migrate to the perceived safety of Germany, buying up government bonds and allowing Merkel's government to enjoy record low borrowing costs. The relative economic health along the Rhine, Main, Danube and Spree is augmented while the misery elsewhere is compounded, widening the gulf and stoking antagonism.

"As time passes, there will be increasing grounds for blaming Germany for the policies it is imposing on Europe, while the German public will feel unjustly blamed," Soros said in his Berlin speech. "This is truly a tragedy of historic significance. As in ancient Greek tragedies, misconceptions and the sheer lack of understanding have unintended but fateful consequences. In the long run a eurozone permanently divided between debtors and creditors is politically unacceptable. The debtors are bound to revolt sooner or later."

Notes

1. Deauville official town website: http://www.deauville.org/fr/page.php?id=93.
2. Tony Czuczka, "Germany is not bent on dominating Europe, President Gauck Says," *Bloomberg News*, February 22, 2013: http://www.bloomberg.com/news/2013-02-22/germany-is-not-bent-on-dominating-europe-president-gauck-says.html.
3. Pew Research Global Attitudes Project http://www.pewglobal.org/2012/05/29/chapter-4-views-of-eu-countries-and-leaders.
4. Tony Czuczka and Brian Parkin, "Merkel Tells Her Party Europe Can't Afford to Let the Euro Fail Over Debt," *Bloomberg News*, November 15: 2010: http://www.bloomberg.com/news/2010-11-15/merkel-defends-debt-crisis-mechanism-prepares-cdu-for-trials-to-come-.html.
5. Boris Groendahl, "German Banks Top French With $23 Billion in Greek Debt, BIS Report Shows," *Bloomberg News*, June 6, 2011: http://www.bloomberg.com/news/2011-06-05/german-banks-top-french-with-23-billion-in-greek-debt-bis-says.html.

6. http://www.presseurop.eu/en/content/article/1065421-how-euro-will-divide-europe.

7. BBC Radio 4 programme from April 2011. Note copyright permission refused, so paraphrased: http://www.bbc.co.uk/news/uk-northern-ireland-13181082.

8. Lenihan letter widely published after made available through Freedom of Information: http://www.thejournal.ie/brian-lenihan-letter-trichet-bailout-648040-Oct2012/.

9. Grande Bretagne website: http://www.grandebretagne.gr/history/.

10. "Greece: Hungriest Country," *Time*, February 9, 1942: http://www.time.com/time/magazine/article/0,9171,777595,00.html.

11. Oxfam website: http://www.oxfam.org/en/about/history.

12. Jewish Museum of Greece: http://www.jewishmuseum.gr/en/index.html.

13. Maria Petrakis and Simon Kennedy, "Papademos to Ministers: Back Bailout or Quit," *Bloomberg News*, February 10, 2012: http://www.bloomberg.com/news/2012-02-10/greek-bailout-at-risk-as-party-pushes-back-against-german-demand-for-cuts.html.

14. AP report cited in: http://www.ekathimerini.com/4dcgi/_w_articles_wsite1_1_15/11/2012_470144.

15. Eleni Chrepa, "Greek President Papoulias Slams German 'Insults' as Aid Discussions Stall," *Bloomberg News*, February 15, 2012: http://www.bloomberg.com/news/2012-02-15/greek-president-to-forfeit-his-salary-in-solidarity-move-1-.html.

16. German federal statistics office release, November 15, 2012: https://www.destatis.de/DE/PresseService/Presse/Pressemitteilungen/2012/11/PD12_397_12711.html.

17. "The Tragedy of the European Union," Speech on Soros website, September 10, 2012: http://www.georgesoros.com/interviews-speeches/entry/the_tragedy_of_the_european_union/.

18. George Soros homepage: http://www.georgesoros.com/faqs/entry/howgeorgesorossurvivednazis/.

Chapter 7

Joshua
(Merkel and the U.S.)

T he debt crisis didn't only cause a north–south split in Europe. It also led to a trans-Atlantic disconnect on economic policy, re-igniting conflict between the U.S. and Europe just as friction over the Iraq war subsided. In the 1990s, American military power and diplomacy were needed to end warfare and atrocities in the Balkans, the EU's back yard. Now the Obama administration was publicly goading Europe's biggest powers on how to run their joint currency. Hackles went up in Paris and Berlin. U.S. Treasury officials viewed Germany as hamstrung by the Bundesbank's inflation-fighting tradition and slow to recognize the threat to the global economy. German leaders saw a U.S. administration too close to the financial markets and unable to deal with its own fiscal crisis after failing to honor debt-reduction goals agreed by advanced economies in 2010.[1] Two years of sniping and finger-pointing came to a head when Group of 20 leaders met in June 2012 at Los Cabos, a town at the tip of Mexico's Baja California peninsula where luxury hotel compounds and lush irrigated gardens fringe a desert land-scape dotted with cacti. Away from the marlin-fishing boats for tourists and the tequila bars, motorcades guarded by Mexican police with auto-matic weapons shuttled the leaders between air-conditioned sites in 35-degree-Celsius heat. The euro area had the world economy on the brink once again. Greeks voted on the eve of the summit in an election framed as a referendum on austerity that raised questions about Greece's future in the euro. Spain was seeking to avoid asking for a sovereign bailout, pushing the yield on its 10-year debt to a euro-era record of 7.16 percent the day G-20 leaders gathered at the brand-new Los Cabos Convention Center. [2] Italy's 10-year yield was at an almost five-month high. Bond spreads, the premium investors demand to hold southern European debt over German bunds, were back to haunt Italy and Spain. As the summit opened on June 18, Indonesia and China pressed euro-area leaders to get a grip on the crisis and restore market confidence.

Joining Merkel at Los Cabos were François Hollande, who had won the French presidential election in May on an anti-austerity platform, Italian prime minister Mario Monti and Spanish premier Mariano Rajoy, two euro-area leaders caught to varying extents in the debt trap of austerity, recession and high borrowing costs. Obama huddled with his European peers on the summit's sidelines and urged them finally to devise a financial backstop big enough to show markets that the euro area stood behind its biggest economies, according to a senior U.S. official. Facing a presidential election in November, he also pressed Europe to break the debt link between the state and troubled banks in countries such as Spain. With Merkel dead-set against pooling the euro-area's debt, Monti and Rajoy saw their pleas for joint EU action to reduce borrowing costs stymied. [3] So-called euro bonds were the endgame, yet they were out of reach. At Los Cabos, some European leaders, backed by Obama, tried another tack and floated a paper suggesting a cap on bond yields in the euro area, according to an official present at the talks. The proposal, which Germany opposed just as much as joint euro-area debt, was quickly taken off the table again, the official said. Obama and Merkel kept their post-summit comments general. The U.S. president said he was confident the Europeans were moving "with a heightened sense of urgency" and would "send a strong signal to the market," though there was no "silver bullet that solves this thing entirely over the next week or two weeks or two months." [4] Merkel didn't concede much in public, saying that while the euro area is determined to beat the crisis, it needs "the right mix" of deficit cuts and growth. Speculation about yield caps resurfaced in a report in Germany's *Der Spiegel* magazine in August. The ECB denied it was considering such plans, which would have put the central bank on the hook to buy more sovereign debt. With Germany and the U.S. as central players, the competing economic visions made for a difficult period in trans-Atlantic relations. At times, the U.S. was pressing Merkel to agree to changes in the euro-area's ground rules and principles that would have put her government at risk, according to a senior German government official. That didn't prevent Merkel from giving her nod of approval to ECB President Mario Draghi, the U.S.-trained economist and former Goldman Sachs vice chairman. Speaking in London five weeks after the summit in Mexico, he called the euro "irreversible" and said the ECB "is ready to do whatever it takes" within its mandate to preserve it. Faced with pressure for action by her euro-area peers and Obama, Merkel didn't dissent in September 2012 when Draghi put money behind his words and unveiled the threat of unlimited ECB bond buying to aid countries that commit to fiscal austerity.

Merkel and Obama didn't get off to an ideal start in the summer of 2008. Even before the Democratic senator from Illinois won the U.S. presidency, Obama got an inkling of Merkel's toughness when he set up a campaign tour of Europe. Berlin, the symbol of the U.S. commitment to freedom when the city was divided between East and West, was on the seven-nation itinerary. Trendy, international, and a hub of united Europe, it beckoned as the stage for a presidential candidate to pledge a change in U.S. relations with the world after the trans-Atlantic rift over the Iraq war. Polls at the time suggested that voters trusted Republican candidate John McCain's knowledge of world affairs more than Obama's.[5] The Brandenburg Gate, the city's Prussian-era landmark, served as backdrop when the late President Ronald Reagan stood at the Berlin Wall in 1987 and challenged Soviet leader Mikhail Gorbachev to "tear down this wall." When the wall fell and Germans celebrated national reunification in 1990, the main event took place at the arch. Hundreds of thousands of soccer fans celebrated German victories there during the 2006 World Cup. Merkel's government faced down Chinese protests when the Dalai Lama, the exiled Tibetan spiritual leader, held a rally at the gate in 2008. As Obama planned his European trip, his team sounded out Berlin city officials about letting the candidate give a speech at the Brandenburg Gate, according to

German news reports. While the world was abuzz with "Obamamania," Merkel drew the line. The idea of using the Brandenburg Gate as a campaign stage struck her as strange, a government spokesman said. "No German candidate for high office would think of using the National Mall or Red Square in Moscow for rallies, because this is not considered appropriate," said the spokesman, Thomas Steg. Merkel later said that while Obama was welcome, not every place in Berlin was appropriate for a campaign rally. "This may strike some as old-fashioned," said Merkel, who is seven years older than the president.[6] Obama made the trip to Berlin, was received by Merkel and on July 24 addressed a cheering crowd of 200,000 at the Victory Column, a monument about one mile from the Brandenburg Gate and Merkel's Chancellery. Global cooperation is "the only way to protect our common security and advance our common humanity," he said. Seven weeks later, Lehman Brothers Holdings Inc., then the fourth-largest U.S. investment bank, filed for bankruptcy, worsening the global financial crisis that was already straining cooperation between the U.S., Germany, and the rest of Europe.

Merkel had felt a female leader's kinship with Hillary Clinton, Obama's defeated rival for Democratic Party nomination, who "put up a great fight."[7] Once Obama became president and the financial crisis hit Europe with full force, he and Merkel clashed over the full range of economic challenges, from stimulus spending and debt reduction to the ECB's role in keeping the euro area whole. As Germany's economy shrank by the most since World War II in 2009, Merkel viewed what Germans sometimes call the Anglo-Saxon capitalism of the U.S. and U.K. as part of the problem rather than the solution. Her post-Lehman grievance that financial markets had resisted voluntary regulation for too long, "backed by the governments in Great Britain and the U.S.," hadn't really been redressed.[8] She wanted debt reduction and "sustainable" economic growth for Germany, not U.S.-style boom-and-bust cycles. In the German government's view, America's Keynesian ways had led the U.S. into its own debt crisis. The Obama administration berated her publicly and in private for failing to act sooner, not doing enough when she did, and for withholding sufficient resources to stop the turmoil from spreading worldwide. In Washington's view, Merkel held the key to limiting the spread of the crisis beyond Europe and backing a more interventionist approach by the ECB, in effect emulating the Federal Reserve. As Europe struggled through the first 18 months of the debt crisis, the tone on both sides grew more strident. After the first Greek bailout and the creation of the interim rescue fund known as the European Financial Stability Facility in May 2010, U.S. Treasury Secretary Timothy Geithner praised euro-area leaders for "acting forcefully to put strong reforms in place."[9] Fifteen months later, after contagion spread to Spain and Italy, Geithner traveled to Poland to attend a meeting of EU finance ministers for the first time. His calls for action drew a public rebuff from the Europeans, who in effect told Geithner to butt out. They didn't relish advice from the country they felt had triggered the financial crisis and had its own debt problem.[10]

Obama pulled out the stops in the summer of 2011, inviting the chancellor to receive the Presidential Medal of Freedom, the U.S. government's top civilian award. It was the highest-profile visit by a German leader to the White House in 16 years. The message behind the pomp and circumstance was clear: the administration expected Merkel to lead the euro area out of the crisis. "We think that America's economic growth depends on a sensible resolution of this issue," Obama said at a joint news conference on June 7. Preventing an "uncontrolled spiral of default" in countries such as Greece was needed to avoid "disastrous" harm to the U.S. economy, he said. Merkel responded cautiously, "If the euro as a whole is in danger, it's in Germany's interest – and in every country's interest – to help." Later that day, Obama presented the presidential medal to Merkel in the White House Rose Garden during the elaborate state dinner. On the menu were salad from First Lady Michelle Obama's garden at the White House, beef filet with Maryland crab ravioli, and a German-tinged dessert of apple strudel and whipped cream. This was not the home-made potato soup or grilled sausages served at Merkel's getaway in the wilds of eastern Germany. Guests included Merkel's husband, Google Inc. Chairman Eric Schmidt, and, at Merkel's invitation, former German national soccer coach Jürgen Klinsmann, who lives in California and went on to coach the U.S. men's team. Articles in the German press questioned whether the event served much of a purpose. Barack and Michelle Obama "are much better at conveying elegance" than Merkel and her husband, the *Die Welt* newspaper reported. Back in Berlin, Merkel didn't let up. Alluding to the subprime crisis, she criticized the U.S. for turning the sale of homes – something "that has been going on for centuries" – into a "deficit-financed economic stimulus program." The lesson remained that "every financial center, every financial product and every actor" world-wide must be regulated.[11] Three months after feting Merkel at the White House, Obama branded the European crisis a "severe strain" on the global economy and "the biggest headwind" to the U.S. recovery.[12]

Merkel's refusal to deploy the financial "bazooka" demanded by investors and the Obama administration became the focal point in a conflict between the German prescription for Europe and U.S. eco-nomic values, between Wall Street capitalism and Germany's more reg-ulated, European-style "social market economy." On top of that came differences in style between Obama and Merkel, who has an aversion to grand gestures. Obama placed himself in the arc of history when he launched his presidential bid in February 2007 outside the Old State Capitol in Springfield, Illinois, where Abraham Lincoln, the 19th-century U.S. president and slavery opponent began his career. Europeans disillusioned with the Bush administration's policies in the "war on ter-ror" after the September 11, 2001, attacks on the U.S. saw Obama as a beacon of change. "Yes We Can," his campaign slogan, became a buzz-word in Germany. By contrast, Merkel took office in 2005 saying she would make policy in "small steps." She stuck to her mantra even as the debt crisis threatened to blow up the euro area and reverse Europe's integration for the first time since World War II. Her rhetorical method is a steady series of speeches that shift and hone her position as events evolve, rather than one dramatic, well-orchestrated statement that drives home her vision for Europe. "I learned from Helmut Kohl that it's bet-ter not to make decisions right at the start," she said one year into her chancellorship. Kohl's approach "was criticized as 'sitting it out.' But in the end, his way of decision-making led to better results."[13] This way of doing business also grated on Greek policy makers, several of whom had U.S. or U.K. backgrounds. Gikas Hardouvelis, a University of California at Berkeley alumnus who advised Lucas Papademos dur-ing the latter's six months as Greek prime minister in 2011–12, scorned the German approach as "Calvinist" and ignorant of the real world. "The Anglo-Saxon will think, 'OK, we'll think of human nature' – and human behavior is to think, 'How do I avoid a restriction, how do I try to get out the rule that somebody imposes on me'," said Hardouvelis, the chief economist at Eurobank in Athens. "Therefore the economist's problem is to provide an incentive structure so that the individual behavior will be conforming with the rule that you impose. The Germans think: 'OK there's going to be a rule, I'm going to have a police and make you do it, whether you want it or not'."[14]

Growing up behind the Iron Curtain, Merkel looked to the U.S. as a land of freedom, constructing her image partly from books and films. Perhaps even more important, an aunt in the West "regularly sent jeans of a particular brand" that teenagers couldn't buy in the communist part of Germany. Merkel told the anecdote during a speech in 2009 to a joint meeting of the U.S. Congress, where House Speaker Nancy Pelosi introduced her as "Her Excellency Dr. Angela Merkel" to cheers and a standing ovation that made Merkel choke up. It was a high honor: she was the first German leader in more than 50 years to speak to Congress. The chancellor grinned when she recalled her craving for American denim – and looked taken aback when lawmakers stood up again to clap at a reference to the fall of the Berlin Wall, an event that still touched Americans as iconic 20 years later. "It was beyond my imagination even to travel to the U.S., let alone stand here before you one day," Merkel said.[15] "The land of unlimited opportunity was for me for a long time impossible to reach. Therefore I had to rely on films and books, some of which were smuggled by relatives from the West, to gain an impression of the U.S. (. . .) I was passionate about the American dream, the possibility for each and every one to be successful, to actually make it in life through one's own personal effort. I was passionate about the vast American landscapes that seemed to breathe the very spirit of freedom and independence."

In 1990, shortly after East Germany opened up, Merkel and her husband went to California on their first trip to the U.S. Previously, she had dreamed about being allowed to visit the U.S. after turning 60, the retirement age for women in East Germany. "We shall never forget our first glimpse of the Pacific Ocean," she told the assembled lawmakers in Washington. "It was simply gorgeous." For all her fondness for the American Dream, Merkel also drove home the message that her notion of freedom doesn't include a free-for-all in the financial markets. Freedom "does not stand alone" and "the world needs an underlying order," she said, likening the effort for global market regulation to the struggle to bring down communism. "A globalized economy needs a global order. Without global rules on transparency and supervision, we will not gain more freedom but rather risk the abuse of freedom and thus risk instability. In a way, this is a second wall that needs to fall – the wall standing in the way of a truly global economic order." As she spoke, the market meltdown triggered by U.S. homeowners who defaulted on subprime mortgages was already morphing into the debt crisis in Greece and the U.S. was in its deepest recession since the Great Depression. Before she was chancellor, Merkel expressed admiration for the dynamic U.S. economy and called the invasion of Iraq inevitable. Now the ideals of freedom came up against the reality of saving the euro without making German voters revolt.

Merkel's first official visit to the U.S. was a weeklong trip to San Francisco, Los Angeles and Washington in September 1991, when Kohl took her in tow less than a year after naming her to his Cabinet. She was introduced at the White House to President George H.W. Bush, who had helped Kohl the year before by welcoming speedy German reunification over British and French reservations. Merkel, transplanted to Bonn from Berlin, was still learning the ropes in the German political establishment and stayed in the background. Merkel spent much of the rest of the decade consolidating her power base in Germany. She returned to Washington as opposition leader in 2003 for a risky undertaking – to meet top aides to President George W. Bush, the former president's son, less than one month before a U.S.-led coalition invaded Iraq on March 20. The German, French and Russian governments publicly opposed the drift to war, which led to acrimonious rifts with the U.S. and between European governments. Taking a stand against German Chancellor Gerhard Schröder, Merkel met Vice President Dick Cheney; Condoleezza Rice, Bush's national security adviser; and Defense Secretary Donald Rumsfeld, who had just dismissed Germany and France as "old Europe" for opposing the administration on Iraq. Schröder, the Social Democrat who ended Kohl's 16-year tenure in 1998, had narrowly won re-election in 2002 on an anti-war platform. Days before the election, his justice minister reportedly accused Bush of emulating Nazi leader Adolf Hitler by using war to distract from economic problems. Rice spoke of a "poisoned" atmosphere and said "it's not been a happy time with Germany."[16] Against this backdrop, Merkel sought to set herself apart. Military force should never be excluded as a last resort, she argued in an opinion article in the *Washington Post*, because ruling out war "weakens the pressure that needs to be maintained on dictators and consequently makes a war not less but more likely."[17] To be sure, she wasn't writing a blank check or backing a German combat role in Iraq. Ties with the U.S. are as important as European integration, but "both will be successful only if it is possible to build new trust and we are able to formulate our own interests," she said. After U.S.-led forces took control of Iraq and captured President Saddam Hussein, Merkel insisted in early 2004 that the U.S. failure to find weapons of mass destruction shouldn't distract from the broader battle "between free societies and 21st-century threats." Germany must ensure it isn't an obstacle to European unity and trans-Atlantic friendship, she said.[18] In her first policy speech as chancellor, Merkel spoke of the values that bind Germany and the U.S. together: "peace and freedom, democracy and the rule of law, justice and tolerance."[19] Bush welcomed Merkel to the White House for her first visit as Chancellor two months later, immediately establishing a bond by admiring her rise from obscurity in communist East Germany to world leader. "There's something uplifting to talk to somebody who knows the difference between just talking about tyranny and living in freedom and actually done it," he said at a joint news conference in the White House. Merkel called the U.S. prison camp at Guantanamo Bay "only one facet in our overall fight against terrorism" and agreed on the need for UN action against Iran over its nuclear program. "It's vital that Germany take the lead on a lot of issues," Bush said. "She's got kind of a spirit to her that is appealing. So we're going to have a very good relationship."[20]

As Merkel and Bush turned around German-U.S. relations, the two economies chugged along without any obvious source of conflict. Merkel was back in Washington in May 2006 to address the American Jewish Committee's annual gala, the first German leader to be invited. At the Oval Office, she and Bush spoke of their growing friendship; he called her a "very sophisticated leader." She reciprocated by inviting Bush to her electoral district on Germany's Baltic coast, a rare

gesture she hasn't repeated for her peers from Europe's biggest economies. Wild boar was on the menu when Merkel hosted Bush and his
wife, Laura, for a folksy summer barbecue that year at Trinwillershagen,
a village that the communist leaders of former East Germany once visited to see a collective farm. She was showing him her homeland, 17
years after the defeat of communism and the fall of the Berlin – events
that were shaped by his father's presidency and allowed Merkel to enter
politics. "I respect her judgment and I value her opinion," Bush told
a cheering crowd in nearby Stralsund, the medieval port city whose
historic center is a UNESCO World Heritage site. Before slicing the
meat at the evening roast, Bush said, "Laura and I are from Texas, and
to invite us to a barbecue is the highest compliment you can pay us."[21]
Within a week, Bush got even closer at a Group of Eight summit in
St. Petersburg, Russia, surprising Merkel with a quick back massage as
she sat at the conference table. She hunched her shoulders and threw
up her arms, then smiled as Bush walked on. Women's rights advo-
cates in the U.S. protested the incident as a transgression. In Germany,
Der Spiegel magazine headlined its article "Bush's Grope-gate." Bush,
eight years older than Merkel, returned to the topic at their next
White House meeting in January 2007: when she spoke of setting "red
lines" in Middle East talks, he quipped, "No back rubs." Merkel played
host again that June at the Group of Eight summit at Heiligendamm,
a luxury compound at the Baltic seaside that provided a global stage
for Merkel and Germany, which presided over the G-8 that year. With
the U.S. and the U.K. blocking a code of conduct for hedge funds and
Bush resisting binding cuts in greenhouse gas emissions, Merkel fell
short of her summit goals. Yet she and Bush had made it clear in public over the previous 18 months that they wouldn't let policy disputes
flare into confrontation. "I have the impression that the American president, just as everyone else here, was interested in having an agreement
of which everyone can say, 'I have made my contribution'," Merkel
said at the summit, referring to climate change. The summit imagery
was harmonious. Merkel, relaxed and laughing, shared drinks on the
hotel terrace with Bush and others. When the leaders posed in a giant
covered beach chair, Merkel sat between him and Russian President
Vladimir Putin. Bush cemented his appreciation of Merkel by inviting her and her husband to his ranch in Crawford, Texas, in November.

After a one-hour hike around the 1,600-acre expanse, Merkel enthused about the "great American spaces and diversity of the landscape." When Bush told reporters he would now "feed the chancellor a hamburger," she made a rare mention of the city of her birth: "For someone from Hamburg, that's naturally a wonderful thing."

Bush paid tribute to Merkel in his memoirs, calling her "trustworthy, engaging, and warm" and "one of my closest friends on the world stage." He and Laura Bush were "fascinated" by Merkel's description of growing up in East Germany when they met in her home district. "She told us her childhood was happy, but her mother constantly warned her not to mention their family discussions in public. The secret police, the Stasi, were everywhere. Laura and I thought of Angela at Camp David when we watched *The Lives of Others*, a movie depicting life under the Stasi. It was hard to believe that less than twenty years had passed since tens of millions of Europeans lived like that."[22] Merkel put loyalty before public opinion with Bush, given that 77 percent of Germans rated him a bad president.[23] Finding a measure of common ground on Iran's nuclear ambitions and the war in Afghanistan offered a way out of the trans-Atlantic impasse over the war in Iraq – which Bush said on his last visit to Germany he didn't regret "at all." Merkel brokered a deal in her coalition government of the country's two biggest parties in 2007 to increase German troop strength and send Tornado reconnaissance jets to Afghanistan, though not for combat. She championed the Transatlantic Council, an EU–U.S. forum set up in 2007 to lower trade barriers and work for common financial standards. Yet from May 2007, Merkel also had a budding ally in newly elected French President Nicolas Sarkozy. When Bush pushed for the North Atlantic Treaty Organization (NATO) to grant pre-membership status to Ukraine and Georgia, opposition by Merkel and Sarkozy scuttled the plan at a NATO summit in April 2008. Even with Bush, camaraderie didn't get in the way of policy making. Three years later, Merkel snubbed Sarkozy and all of NATO on the military intervention in Libya. Once again, she insisted on going Germany's own way, raising questions about the Berlin government's consistency in foreign policy. Unlike in the debt crisis, her allies didn't need Germany and went ahead without her. When the U.N. Security Council voted in March 2011 for a no-fly zone to prevent Libyan ruler Muammar Qaddafi from attacking rebels inspired by the Arab Spring democracy movement, Germany abstained. Explaining why Germany aligned with China, Russia, Brazil and India, its leaders said the outcome of the military intervention was too uncertain and Germany didn't want to act like a big power. Though allied with Sarkozy in the debt crisis, Merkel refused to join his push for the NATO air and naval campaign, which ended in Qaddafi's ouster and death at the hands of his enemies in October. *The Economist* called Germany "the unadventurous eagle" – a reference to the bird in the country's coat of arms – with a foreign policy that still didn't match its economic power. Avoiding military action also meant that Merkel, after setting a different tone on war and freedom for her visit to Bush's Washington in 2003, didn't have to lobby German voters and lawmakers to back it. Obama swung around to intervention in Libya after some hesitation. He visited Europe in May, stopping in Ireland, the U.K., France, and Poland. His decision to leave Germany off the list prompted Helmut Kohl to take a rare public swipe at Merkel. "After everything that we Germans and Americans went through together, which still deeply bonds us today, I would never have dreamed that I would once have to witness an incumbent American president coming to Europe and flying over the Federal Republic," he said in an interview with a German foreign policy journal. "You could also say he is snubbing us. We urgently need to return to our old reliability."[24] Merkel, when asked about Kohl's comment, said different times require different approaches.

Merkel made a campaign pledge in 2005 to balance Germany's budget by 2011. In her first policy speech as chancellor, she called for a "change of course in budget policy" to lower deficits and help "make Germany stronger." It was a matter of demonstrating "seriousness," she said, and the rewards wouldn't be immediate. That would come later, as future generations would be saddled with less debt.[25] She almost managed it in 2008, when the shortfall was 0.1 percent of gross domestic product. Fallout from the U.S. subprime mortgage crisis forced her to abandon her target. In November 2008, Merkel objected when other EU leaders wanted her to back a joint 200 billion euro rescue package for the 27-nation trade bloc. As the global economic recession hurt German exporters, she relented and her coalition passed two national stimulus bills. In the U.S., Obama authorized $787 billion in crisis spending in February 2009 and his administration pressed its global partners to do more to spend their way out of recession. "It's time now for us to move together and to begin to act," Geithner said in Washington on March 11. Merkel demurred. "If we want to actually strengthen the effect of such packages you simply have to implement them and not talk about the next one before the first has actually taken effect," she said.[26] Germany's stimulus measures were worth about 1.6 percent of gross domestic product in 2009 compared to 2 percent in the U.S., according to the IMF. The clash played out at a global economic summit of Group of 20 leaders held in April at a convention center in London's Docklands, across a bend in the Thames from the financial-industry high-rises at Canary Wharf. Merkel, teamed up with Sarkozy for a pre-summit news briefing in a crowded hotel conference room, said she was concerned that leaders wouldn't "grasp the evil at the root." While anti-recession spending was needed, "the important thing is that we build a new architecture, a new constitution for the financial markets." This meant that "no place, no institution and no product" should escape oversight. From that G-20 summit, Obama headed to NATO talks in France and Germany, his first visit to the euro area since taking office. At a joint appearance in the city hall in the German spa town of Baden-Baden, he spoke Merkel's language. U.S. growth "can't be based on overheated financial markets or overheated housing markets or U.S. consumers maxing out on their credit cards or us sustaining nonstop deficit spending as far as the eye can see," he told reporters. Merkel was settling into a working relationship with the man she had snubbed over the Brandenburg Gate rally the previous year and who was as popular among Germans as she.[27] After Bush's effusive style, she said she enjoyed working with Obama because their "very serious, very thorough, ana-lytical discussions very often lead us to draw the same conclusions."[28] Obama repaid the compliment when Merkel visited the White House in June 2009, saying she is "smart, practical, and I trust her when she says something." Yet when Merkel mentioned deficit spending 10 days before the German election in a speech in Frankfurt, she indicated that she also had U.S. deficit and debt levels in mind. "I believe we have to start talking about how we can wind down those exorbitant stimulus measures," she said.[29] Der Spiegel, Germany's most-read weekly news magazine, said the Federal Reserve was creating "money out of thin air" and called Obama the "debt president."

Other sources of conflict emerged in 2009. German opposition parties put Merkel on the spot by taking up Obama's vista of a world free of nuclear weapons and calling for the removal of the remaining U.S. stockpile in Germany. Merkel reversed her stand and backed the demand under pressure from the Free Democrats, her second-term coalition partner, while saying any removal would have to be negotiated with the U.S. Another irritant was Merkel's failed effort to find a buyer for Adam Opel GmbH, General Motors Co.'s unprofitable German division. With 25,000 German jobs at stake in an election year, Merkel looked for ways to insulate the automaker from the turmoil at its U.S. parent, which filed for bankruptcy on June 8. She backed a joint bid for Opel by Magna International Inc., the Canadian car-parts maker, and Russia's OAO Sberbank for a 55 percent stake in Opel. As talks dragged on for more than six months, Merkel won re-election on September 27. GM's board scuttled the deal on November 3, citing the brand's importance for its non-U.S. market – just as Merkel was departing Washington after her speech to Congress and a White House chat with Obama. The German government was furious and Merkel, who had gone out on a limb, criticized GM's negotiating approach in parliament.[30] It was another trans-Atlantic disconnect.

As Merkel and other European leaders turned inward in 2010 to battle the debt crisis, Obama presided over the recovery from an 18-month recession, the U.S. economy's longest and deepest since the Great Depression. The U.S. jobless rate never fell below 9.4 percent during the year, even as the economy grew by 3 percent.[31] In Germany, unemployment declined from 8.2 percent in February to as low as 6.4 percent in November. In the six eastern German states, the jobless rate sank below that of California.[32] The divide on economic policy was becoming increasingly stark. Obama warned other major economies at the G-20 summit in Canada that "we can't all rush to the exits at the same time" and, in a hint aimed in part at Germany, urged countries with trade surpluses to "think about how can they spur growth and how can they spur demand." Merkel's government passed a deficit-reduction package, called for belt-tightening in weaker euro countries, talked about an exit strategy from stimulus spending and pressed for a global financial transaction tax. Sarkozy was the only euro-area leader to get a full-scale reception at the White House in 2010 and

Obama's major foreign trip of the year was a tour of Southeast Asia and Japan. "Merkel's demotion to the second tier," read the headline in the *Financial Times Deutschland*.[33] As the crisis moved into its second year, U.S. pressure for the euro area to use overwhelming financial force to stamp out the crisis grew. Paul Krugman, the Nobel Prize-winning *New York Times* columnist, steadily criticized Merkel's austerity-first policy. "German economic orthodoxy is misguided and a big problem," he wrote.[34] Nouriel Roubini, the economist who predicted the 2008 financial crisis, urged Germany to think of "Europe as a whole" and "postpone its austerity strategy."[35]

For all their differences, Merkel and Obama are bound together by shared responsibility for the global economy. Officials in both capitals said both leaders act in that spirit. Obama trusts Merkel and keeps the lines of communication open, a U.S. official reported. The two leaders share a cerebral approach to politics and speak candidly in person and on the phone, at one point discussing how to end public finger-pointing over policy differences, according to a German official. *Forbes* magazine ranked them the world's two most powerful people of the year in December 2012 – Obama first and Merkel second: "Merkel is the backbone of the 27-member European Union and carries the fate of the euro on her shoulders," Forbes said.

In his first inaugural address, Obama said the U.S. economy was "badly weakened, a consequence of greed and irresponsibility on the part of some, but also our collective failure to make hard choices and prepare the nation for a new age." The U.S. will meet its challenges, he said, rejecting the notion that "America's decline is inevitable, that the next generation must lower its sights." Merkel, addressing Germany's BDI industrialist association about the financial crisis a day earlier, took the practical view. "We will have to wrestle with our American partners, with the newly elected American president Barack Obama and his administration, to learn lessons from the crisis," she said. "This isn't a run-of-the-mill change in the economy, but rather a pretty fundamental challenge for all of us." Financial markets had engaged in "excesses," and the world must recognize that "no one can constantly live beyond their means."[36] The antidote, she suggested, is to design a kind of global version of the German social market economy. Merkel, whose CDU party claims credit for this German mix of market economy and welfare state, invokes it often as a counterweight to U.S.-style capitalism and the perceived domination of economic opinion by "Anglo-Saxon newspapers."[37]

Ludwig Erhard, the economics minister under CDU co-founder Konrad Adenauer, West Germany's first chancellor after World War II, is credited with originating the system, which blends social programs and labor rights with free enterprise and anti-trust rules that helped small and medium-size companies flourish. Erhard, a cigar-smoking Bavarian, worked with U.S. and British occupation authorities to carry out the currency reform that created the deutsche mark in 1948 and came to be considered the father of West Germany's economic boom. His system fits with the German public's aversion to the riskier sides of capitalism. New York-based A.W. Jones Advisers LLC, which bills itself as the first hedge fund, was founded in 1949. Germany legalized hedge funds under government regulation only in 2004, aiming to compete with Wall Street and the City of London. The social market economy drew on ideas developed by economists and legal scholars at the University of Freiburg in the 1930s known as "ordoliberalism," a German-style capitalism that gives government a natural role of setting the rules of the game. Unlike in the free-market traditions of the U.S. or the U.K., the state is seen as a natural partner in economic success. "Ordnungspolitik," a German term that roughly translates as "ordering policy," was invented by the Freiburg scholars. A year into the debt crisis, Merkel paid homage to them with a speech in the southern German city that delved into the topic. "The state has witnessed a rebirth as the guardian of order," she said. The need for a global "framework of order" meant that "Ordnungspolitik's finest hour still lies ahead."[38]

Notes

1. The White House, "The G-20 Toronto Summit Declaration," June 27, 2010: http://www.whitehouse.gov/the-press-office/g-20-toronto-summit-declaration.
2. Bloomberg generic price for 10-year Spanish government bond on June 18, 2012.
3. See Monti interview in Thomas Schmid, "Warum Italien mehr wie Deutschland sein sollte," *Die Welt*, January 11, 2012.

4. Barack Obama, "The President's News Conference in Los Cabos, Mexico," Gerhard Peters and John T. Woolley, The American Presidency Project, June 19, 2012: http://www.presidency.ucsb.edu/ws/?pid=101036.

5. Jesse Westbrook, "Obama Picks Site of Berlin Speech After Brandenburg Gate Flap," *Bloomberg News*, July 20, 2008.

6. Press conference by Merkel in Berlin, July 23, 2008: http://archiv.bundesr egierung.de/Content/DE/Archiv16/Pressekonferenzen/2008/07/2008-07-23-eingangsstatement-pk-sommerpause.html?nn=486326.

7. Alexander Osang, "Die deutsche Queen," *Der Spiegel*, May 11, 2009: http://www.spiegel.de/spiegel/print/d-65330394.html.

8. Merkel interview with *Münchner Merkur*, September 22, 2008, as cited on Christian Democratic Union party website: http://www.cdu.de/archiv/2370_24357.htm.

9. Rebecca Christie, "Geithner Says Europeans 'Acting Forcefully,' Need to Revamp Fiscal Policy," *Bloomberg News*, May 25, 2010.

10. Rebecca Christie, "Geithner Warning of 'Catastrophic Risk' Highlights Gap With EU," *Bloomberg News*, September 17, 2011.

11. Speech by Merkel to conference on financial regulation by the CDU-CSU parliamentary group, Berlin, June 29, 2011.

12. Hans Nichols and Mike Dorning, "Obama Says Europe Crisis 'Severe Strain' on World Economy," *Bloomberg Businessweek*, October 6, 2011.

13. Merkel interview with *Bunte* magazine, October 10, 2006. Cited on German government press office's website: http://archiv.bundesregierung.de/Content/DE/Archiv16/Interview/2006/10/2006-10-12-interview-merkel-bunte.html.

14. Interview in Athens, November 21, 2012.

15. Based on the recording of official English interpreter's translation of her remarks.

16. *Financial Times* interview quoted in Steven Erlanger, "Germans Vote in a Tight Election in Which Bush, Hitler and Israel Became Key Issues," *New York Times*, September 22, 2002: http://www.nytimes.com/2002/09/22/world/germans-vote-tight-election-which-bush-hitler-israel-became-key-issues.html.

17. Angela Merkel, "Schroeder Doesn't Speak for All Germans." Opinion piece in *Washington Post*, February 20, 2003. Reproduced on CDU-CSU parliamentary caucus website: http://www.cducsu.de/upload/merkel_wpost_200 30220.pdf.

18. Speech by Merkel to Munich Security Conference, February 7, 2004.

19. Speech by Merkel to German Bundestag in Berlin, November 30, 2005. Official minutes: http://dipbt.bundestag.de/dip21/btp/16/16004.pdf.

20. George W. Bush: "The President's News Conference With Chancellor Angela Merkel of Germany," Gerhard Peters and John T. Woolley, The American Presidency Project, January 13, 2006: http://www.presidency.ucsb.edu/ws/?pid=65176.

21. Claudia Rach, "Bush Walks in Communist Leaders' Footsteps in Germany," *Bloomberg News*, June 13, 2006.
22. George W. Bush, *Decision Points*, pp. 412–13 (Broadway Paperbacks, 2010).
23. EMNID poll for German broadcaster N24, June 11, 2008: http://www.presseportal.de/pm/13399/1208748/n24-emnid-umfrage-bushs-abschieds tour-deutsche-ziehen-negatives-fazit-der-amtszeit.
24. Interview in *Internationale Politik*, German Council on Foreign Relations, Berlin, September/October 2011 issue, pp. 10–17.
25. Speech to Bundestag, November 30, 2005.
26. Richard Tomlinson and Oliver Suess, "Merkel Makes Like Obama With German Stimulus Excluding Europe," *Bloomberg News*, March 25, 2009.
27. Poll for *Stern* magazine and broadcaster RTL cited in *Stern*, March 31, 2009: http://www.stern.de/politik/deutschland/forsa/stern-umfrage-deutsche-wuerden-obama-waehlen-659699.html.
28. Barack Obama: "The President's News Conference With Chancellor Angela Merkel of Germany in Dresden, Germany," Gerhard Peters and John T. Woolley, The American Presidency Project, June 5, 2009: http://www.presidency.ucsb.edu/ws/?pid=86248.
29. Speech by Merkel in Frankfurt am Main, September 17, 2009: http://archiv.bundesregierung.de/Content/DE/Rede/2009/09/2009-09-17-rede-merkel-iaa.html?nn=273438.
30. Speech by Merkel to German Bundestag, Berlin, November 10, 2009.
31. U.S. Department of Commerce, Bureau of Economic Analysis data.
32. Christian Vits and Alan Crawford, "Former East Germany Beats California on Jobs: Chart of the Day," *Bloomberg News*, October 6, 2010.
33. Claudia Kade, "Merkels Abstieg in die zweite Liga," *Financial Times Deutschland*, April 14, 2010.
34. Paul Krugman, "Ich Bin Ein Berliner, Or Something," *New York Times*, November 28, 2012: http://krugman.blogs.nytimes.com/2012/11/28/ich-bin-ein-berliner-or-something.
35. Interview in *Der Spiegel*, January 11, 2011: http://www.spiegel.de/international/business/spiegel-interview-with-economist-nouriel-roubini-europe-needs-growth-to-prevent-a-collapse-of-the-euro-a-738711.html.
36. Speech by Merkel at BDI New Year's reception, Berlin, January 19, 2009: http://archiv.bundesregierung.de/Content/DE/Rede/2009/01/2009-01-19-merkel-bdi.html?nn=273438.
37. Speech by Merkel to Alfred Herrhausen Society, Berlin, September 28, 2012: http://www.bundesregierung.de/Content/DE/Rede/2012/09/2012-09-28-merkel-herrhausen.html.
38. Speech by Merkel to Ordnungspolitik Foundation, Freiburg, Germany, February 23, 2011: http://www.bundesregierung.de/Content/DE/Rede/2011/02/2011-02-23-bkin-freiburg.html.

Chapter 8

Judges (German Model)

S tralsund, the biggest city in Merkel's electoral district, is enough
of a showcase that the chancellor invites foreign leaders such as
George W. Bush to the almost 800-year-old port, which began
as a Slavic fishing village. Restored after German reunification, the Baltic
city's gabled townhouses speak to the wealth of merchants who pros-
pered as part of the Hanseatic League trading bloc in the Middle Ages.
The Gothic-style brick town hall, begun in the 13th century, dominates
the town center, which won Stralsund its place on the World Heritage
list; St. Mary's church spire rises over the waterfront. Tourism has helped
replace lost industrial jobs, with tour buses flocking to the city's aquar-
ium and marine museum, opened in 2008. Stralsund's port now hosts
cruise ships on their way through the Baltic to St. Petersburg. A new
highway bridge to Rügen, a resort island that is part of Merkel's district,
symbolizes two decades of spending to modernize the formerly communist East, a testament to Germany's economic power. The city's jobless rate, once above 25 percent, fell to about 11 percent in 2012. Still,
that was almost double the national average. In the summer of 2012, the
Volkswerft shipyard filed for insolvency. Created as a communist "people's enterprise" in 1948, the yard built fishing trawlers for East Germany,
survived the threat of closure in the 1990s, and now has one of the
world's biggest ship assembly halls. While Stralsund Mayor Alexander
Badrow, a CDU member, pleaded for preserving the yard's more

than 1,200 jobs, a grim-faced Merkel visited the site to tell workers no more public aid would be forthcoming. Stralsund and the surrounding state of Mecklenburg-Western Pomerania, a rural region dependent on tourism and farming, were a stage for Merkel to make points about the economy. The state hit the brakes on spending and balanced its budget starting in 2006 to offset depopulation, a thin economic base, and declining post-unity federal subsidies. Local leaders of the two biggest parties, usually at least nominally at odds, felt they had no alternative: the state has Germany's lowest per-capita income and productivity.[1] When Merkel campaigned in the region before state elections in 2011, she praised voters' sacrifices as a model for other German regions, her federal government, and the whole euro area. Taken down to the market-square level, her implication was that if Germany's poorest state can balance its books, any euro-area government could. It was a variation of her theme, steeped in the experience of East Germany's collapse, that sacrifices must be made and politicians must avoid giving financial markets the upper hand over a country's future. "We know that if debt rises above, say, 80 or 90 percent of gross domestic product, it gets ever more difficult to maintain your independence," Merkel said more than a year later after talks with Irish Prime Minister Enda Kenny, whose country ran up the biggest budget deficit of the 17 euro-area countries. Ireland's shortfall reached 31 percent of GDP in 2010 and its debt jumped to 106 percent of GDP in 2011. That compares to the EU's deficit limit of 3 percent and debt to GDP of 60 percent. Before the Irish housing bubble collapsed and the government assumed the debts of the country's banks, debt stood at 25 percent in 2006.[2] Merkel said excess debt levels and the threat of loss of independent decision making "is a problem for Germany as well." Germany's debt-to-GDP ratio declined in her first two full years in office to 65.2 percent in 2007, before the recession and stimulus spending helped push it to 80.5 percent in 2011.[3] Of the four countries in the 17-nation euro area that had a AAA long-term sovereign debt rating at Standard & Poor's at the end of 2012, Germany had the highest debt ratio, followed in declining order by the Netherlands, Finland, and Luxembourg. Merkel was adapting an argument made by U.S. economists Carmen M. Reinhart and Kenneth S. Rogoff, whose 2009 book on the perils of debt, *This Time Is Different: Eight Centuries of Financial Folly*, became a best-seller. Published before Europe's debt crisis and loaded with tables and graphs, it offers a "quantitative history of financial crises," concluding, in effect, that policy makers tend to live in denial and the next debt-driven bust is always around the corner. In a related paper published in 2010, Reinhart and Rogoff argue that "above 90 percent, median growth rates fall by one percent, and average growth falls considerably more," with a similar threshold in advanced and developing countries.[4] Here was a U.S. view that fit with Merkel's take on the debt crisis, contrary to Nobel Prize winner Paul Krugman's calls for Germany to relent on austerity and boost deficit spending. Finance Minister Wolfgang Schäuble, Merkel's point man on the budget, publicly cited the Reinhart–Rogoff research as a reason for euro-area countries to reduce debt. As European leaders squabbled in late 2010 and early 2011 about the wisdom of writing off Greek sovereign debt, Rogoff praised Merkel as possibly "the only eurozone leader who is willing to face the likely prospect of future debt restructuring."[5] To be sure, Merkel, who met with Rogoff in Berlin in 2012, didn't take another piece of the Harvard economics professor's advice: to let Greece leave the monetary union temporarily to help it revive its economy.

Like the little rhymes about the virtue of saving painted on the former bank building in her home town of Templin, Merkel's political view of debt reflects German attitudes and history. When King Frederick the Great was short of funds to rebuild war-scarred Prussia in 1769, he let aristocrats, churches, and monasteries raise money by pledging their estates as security to investors. That started what today is Europe's market for covered bonds, known as "pfandbrief" in German, which are backed by assets such as mortgages as well as the seller's promise to pay. The German government says no bank has missed a payment on the securities in more than 100 years.[6] Debt – the kind that U.S. consumers run up with a wallet full of maxed-out credit cards – remains suspect, to the point that German polls in 2011 found 70 percent of respondents favored budget consolidation over tax cuts. More than half of all purchases in Germany, 53 percent, are paid in cash, followed by debit cards at 28 percent and credit cards with 7 percent, according to a Bundesbank report in 2012.[7] Most shops and restaurants and many retail chains in the capital of Europe's biggest economy don't even accept credit cards, leaving visitors from outside the euro area to load up on cash or take their chances. Aldi, the German supermarket chain that strips down grocery shopping to a generic-brand minimum, refuses credit cards to keep costs down. Karl Albrecht, who founded Aldi with his brother after World War II and saw the closely-held company expand to the U.S. and Australia, is Germany's richest man, with an estimated net worth of $23.6 billion on the Bloomberg Billionaires Index in January 2013. While German bank accounts come with a debit card (and overdraft for the reckless), no-fee credit cards are virtually unheard of except for introductory offers. The average German makes about 2,300 euros in card payments per year, compared with 6,000 euros in France and the equivalent of 9,200 euros in the U.K.[8] What the government encourages is saving, for instance by subsidizing accounts to build up money for buying a home. Though the Bundesbank expressed concern in 2012 about rising property prices in desirable urban areas such as Berlin, Munich and Frankfurt, Germany avoided a real-estate bubble after switching to the euro. Inflation-adjusted housing prices rose by 40 percent in France, 9 percent in the U.K. and 5 percent in Germany between 2004 and 2011, according to OECD data.[9] Almost 6 in 10 German residents are renters, one of the highest rates among rich countries, an indication of stringent loan requirements and the lack of tradition and incentives to buy real estate. The thrift industry urges Germans to start saving as early as in their teens by committing to a plan that requires monthly deposits. In the U.S., deregulation helped trigger a savings-and-loan crisis in the 1980s; Germany's savings and cooperative banks have political clout and the aura of safety. "Leave nothing to chance," LBS, the national umbrella group for the building-society system, says on its website.

To Germans, the global financial crisis and its spillover to the euro area only underscored the strength of their economic model, increasing their resistance to outside calls for change. Merkel laid down three markers: Germany must remain an export-led economy; a country that makes things; and a center of industrial excellence. She argues that "financialization" of the economy led the U.K. astray; consumer spending can't replace sales of power plants, BMW luxury cars, and precision machine tools as Germany's economic driver; and using joint bonds to paper over gaps in competitiveness between euro-area countries implies giving in to "mediocrity." That, she says, would hurt the EU in competing with China and other rising economic powers. Exports provide about every third job in Germany and accounted for half the country's GDP in 2011, compared with 22 percent in 1993.[10] France, Italy and Spain all rely on exports for less than one-third of GDP to fuel their economies.[11] In Germany, a 14.2 percent rise in exports powered the country out of recession in 2010. With at least eight euro-area nations in recession in early 2012, German companies tapped faster-growing Asian markets to boost sales. Demand in China and the U.S. buoyed Germany's three top carmakers – Bayerische Motoren Werke AG, Volkswagen AG and Daimler AG – and their suppliers. Total German exports rose at an annual pace of 4.3 percent in the first 11 months of 2012 as a 10 percent increase outside the EU offset declining shipments to euro-area nations.[12] The DAX, Germany's blue-chip stock index, rose 29 percent in 2012, its best annual performance since 2003.

Merkel's defense of the German reliance on exports is an unresolved conflict with Germany's partners, who view Europe's biggest economic power as selfish. Christine Lagarde, then in Paris as Sarkozy's finance minister, raised German hackles in 2010 by calling for a rebalancing of trade flows to reduce the surplus of countries such as Germany and China. Obama began that year by saying in his State of the Union speech he wanted the U.S. to double its exports over the next five years. The German view is that as Europe's engine, its economy pulls along the rest of the region. Besides, says the Confederation of German Employers, "no one is preventing countries from exporting their goods to Germany." They just "need to be better and/or cheaper" if they want to compete.[13] Business and labor share the unapologetic consensus that the global power of German products is well earned. "We have no alternative," says Anton Boerner, head of the Federation of German Wholesale, Foreign Trade and Services, a lobbying group that represents about 120,000 businesses. "Is Germany too dependent on global markets? Well, all of us depend on global markets." Germany's economic success "is based on thousands of individual success stories" by its world-beating companies. "So you'd have to wreck those thousands of success stories. And then? Europe collapses. It's absurd."

The Merkel economy benefited from the overhaul begun under her predecessor Gerhard Schröder, who cut jobless benefits and deregulated the labor market to spur part-time work and low-wage jobs. Unemployment declined from more than 5 million in 2005 to

2.7 million in 2011. Labor unions, faced with competition from lower-paid workers in Eastern Europe after 1990, agreed to wage restraint to stem job flight. It was one of those moments in which postwar Germany's comity between business, labor and government was seen as working wonders. Germany widened its competitive edge over euro-area peers, notably France, its key partner and Europe's second-largest economy, as cheap credit and rising wages fueled many other parts of Europe. Germany's vocational training also regularly gets high marks in international surveys of economic strengths. Obama cited it in his 2013 State of the Union address, saying "those German kids, they're ready for a job when they graduate high school."[14] Merkel, preaching the primacy of competitiveness, touted these accomplishments as Germany's jobless rate fell in December 2011 to the lowest since reunification while weaker euro nations flailed in the crisis. OECD economists wrote up a 36-page report for the chancellor that called for "policy actions to boost productivity in all euro-area countries," including wages that stay in line with productivity gains. On foreign trips, Merkel has taken to brandishing charts showing how unit labor costs in the rest of the euro area had surged ahead of Germany's.[15] Merkel is presiding over a newly confident Germany in the middle of the EU's biggest financial crisis. "We were considered the sick man of Europe at the start of the millennium, but right now we are in a very good position," she said in a November 8, 2012, speech in Berlin. "However, I know that the world isn't standing still and we have to look all the time at how we can improve our competitiveness." The German model of high-end manufacturing and export-led growth is reason for pride and envy. Halfway around the world in Vietnam, Merkel told local dignitaries in 2011 how Germany benefits from "a good mix of smaller companies, midsize companies and big corporations" that insulates Europe's largest economy from economic shocks and spurs innovation.[16] From soap bubbles and wooden pencils to bottling plants and industrial robots, Germany is full of regional or global champions whose manufacturing quality often allows them to sell at a premium. Sixty percent of Germans work in companies with fewer than 500 employees, the classic "Mittelstand" firms that make up the economy's backbone. Usually closely held, they avoid stock-market pressures as they tinker with new products and go global. Glasbau Hahn, run by the fifth generation of the Hahn family, constructs glass exhibition cases for collections around the world, from London's Natural History Museum to the Central Bank of Iraq in Baghdad, the Louvre and Pompidou Centre in Paris to New York's Metropolitan Museum of Art. Managing directors Isabel and Tobias Hahn "see themselves in the tradition of a global company that is committed to artisan perfection and rigorous quality."[17] William Prym Holding GmbH, which bills itself as Germany's oldest family-owned business, is a world leader in clothing fasteners, sewing supplies, and lingerie parts. Based in the Rhineland town of Stolberg near the Belgian and Dutch borders, the company was founded in 1530 and has been in the Prym family's hands for 14 generations. It expanded into precision connectors, including for the automotive industry, and now has offices or plants on five continents. Prym employs 3,600 people and had sales of 380 million euros in 2011. "Today Prym is known around the world," the company website says. "The Prym family shareholders are firmly committed to the business, providing the foundations for extensive, long-term development."[18]

Chinese demand for made-in-Germany equipment to fire China's exports to the world was key: German exports to China almost doubled between 2008 and 2011 to 65 billion euros – while China overtook Germany as the world's biggest exporting nation. Kuka AG, Europe's largest maker of industrial robots, planned to boost assembly capacity in China to 5,000 units in 2012 from less than 1,000 two years earlier. Robotics revenue at Augsburg-based Kuka rose 84 percent between 2009 and 2011 as customers including Volkswagen and Daimler bought equipment for new factories and China became the world's largest auto market.[19] The rise of the Mittelstand is not just an economic success, it's part of Germany's post-World War II order. Anti-trust rules designed by Ludwig Erhard, the economy minister in all five of Adenauer's Cabinets who succeeded him as chancellor in 1963, are credited with avoiding industrial concentration and ensuring competition, proving that "an orderly framework is absolutely necessary," according to Merkel. Germany's welfare-state safety net ensures "social cohesion that most others envy us for" and "our economic order has withstood the test of the financial and economic crisis as well."[20] Leaders in other advanced economies couldn't help but notice. Sarkozy said France should learn from Germany – then lost his bid for

a second term to François Hollande. Two months after becoming Italy's
prime minister, Mario Monti said he had "always worked for an Italy
that resembles Germany as much as possible." Germany "is the country that
has given Europe the most – a functioning, well-balanced model for
society," the economist and former European Union commissioner said
in an interview with *Die Welt*.[21] Ron Bloom, who worked as a White
House adviser on manufacturing between 2009 and 2011, recalled
Obama asking him why Germany is successful at running a high-wage
manufacturing sector. Bloom said Germany had a tradition of job training programs and its banks had made a top priority of financing man-
ufacturers, according to the *Washington Post*. "Why can't we do this?"
Obama asked.[22] Merkel's emergency measures in 2009 also drew attention. To help the auto industry, her government offered bonuses to
car owners who scrapped older, dirtier vehicles and bought new ones.
The U.S. emulated the idea in its "cash for clunkers" program. Merkel's
government also paid subsidies to help companies to shorten working
hours while avoiding layoffs, keeping skilled employees in the company and off the jobless rolls. The aid covered as much as two-thirds
of lost income for an average of 1.1 million employees in 2009, just as
U.S. unemployment peaked. "Kurzarbeit," the program's German name,
made it into Paul Krugman's column in the *New York Times*, where he
said Germany "avoided US-style mass layoffs even when it was slumping badly."[23] As she rebuffed critics of the German way, Merkel pointed
to consumer spending and rising wages as ways in which Germany was
helping the rest of Europe in the crisis; in other words, Germany wasn't
only exporting. As the euro area as a whole slipped back into recession in the third quarter of 2012, German retail sales rose year-on-year
in December for the eighth consecutive month, according to Markit
Economics in London. German employees' take-home pay rose the most
in at least a decade in 2010 and kept rising the next year. Consumer
spending, adjusted for inflation, rose in 2011 by the most since 2000.[24]
"Our wages and pensions have risen for the first time in years," Merkel
said in late 2012.[25] "We are making an effort for growth." As always,
the same data tell different stories. Consumption spending by indi-
viduals and the government contributed 1.1 percentage points to
Germany's 3 percent GDP growth in 2011, while exports accounted
for 0.8 percentage points. Yet exports were more dynamic, jumping

Angela Dorothea Kasner shortly before her fourth birthday in 1958. Her parents had moved to East Germany in 1954 when she was a few weeks old.

Credit: Ullstein Bild – P.S.I. Bonn

Für alle.

drshalb am 18 März

Wir schaffen soziale Sicherhe

DEMOKRAT AUFBR

Foto: Michael Ebner, Meldepress

Dr. Angela Merkel kam 1990 zur CDU und ging 2005 in die Geschichte ein: als erste Kanzlerin der Bundesrepublik Deutschland.

Merkel volunteered to help Democratic Awakening, an East German political group formed shortly after the Berlin Wall fell on November 9, 1989, before moving on to Helmut Kohl's Christian Democratic Union. The party used an image from those early days in a 2007 recruitment poster that referred to her mid-career jump into politics.

Credit: CDU – Michael Ebner/Meldepress – Creative Commons

As a spokeswoman for Lothar de Maizière (left), East Germany's first and only democrati-cally elected prime minister, Merkel joined him on a flight to Moscow in September 1990 for negotiations that led to German reunification on October 3 that year.

Credit: J.H. Darchinger/Friedrich-Ebert-Stiftung

A political novice, Merkel had to build an electoral base. Here she is campaigning in a fishermen's hut on the Baltic island of Rügen – a region she still represents in parliament – for the first postwar all-German election in 1990.

Credit: Ullstein Bild – Ebner

Merkel with Kohl in the Bundestag in Bonn, the former capital, in 1992. Kohl, her political mentor, had appointed her to his Cabinet as families minister the previous year.

Credit: German Government/Christian Stutterheim

Merkel's parents, Horst and Herlind Kasner, watching her swearing-in as chancellor from the Bundestag visitors' gallery on November 22, 2005.

Credit: picture alliance-dpa-dpaweb/Peter Kneffel

Merkel is a keen soccer fan and regularly attends the German team's games. She met the players after they won third place in the 2006 World Cup hosted by Germany, a feel-good event that dominated the summer after she took office.

Credit: Guido Krzikowski/Bloomberg

Merkel brought world leaders to the Baltic Sea coast in June 2007 when Germany held the presidency of the Group of Eight nations. Pictured in a beach chair (l-to-r) are Nicolas Sarkozy, Vladimir Putin, Merkel, George W. Bush, Tony Blair and Romano Prodi.

Credit: German Government/Jürgen Gebhardt

Merkel relaxes during the G-8 summit with Bush, Blair, Jose Barroso and Prodi on the terrace at the Heiligendamm resort, Germany's oldest seaside spa, inaugurated by Duke Friedrich Franz I of Mecklenburg in 1793.

Credit: German Government/Guido Bergmann

President George W. Bush serving roast wild boar to Merkel at a barbecue she hosted in the Mecklenburg–Western Pomerania region. He is one of very few leaders she has invited to visit her constituency in the nearby port of Stralsund.

Credit: German Government/Guido Bergmann

George Papaconstantinou, Greece's then finance minister, speaks to journalists after talks in Paris on December 15, 2009, telling them there was no discussion at that time of a bailout for his country. Less than five months later, Greece became the first euro-area country to request international financial help.

Credit: Antoine Antoniol/Bloomberg

Merkel and Nicolas Sarkozy walking along the Normandy coast at the French resort of Deauville in October 2010, a meeting that became one of the pivotal moments of the debt crisis. Merkel and Sarkozy built a close working relationship as the crisis forced them to unite in defense of the euro.

Credit: Philippe Wojazer/AFP/Getty Images

Public outrage at the job losses and spending cuts that Greek governments imposed as a condition for outside aid made violent demonstrations a feature of the debt crisis. Here police are under attack near Parliament in Athens on September 26, 2012, two weeks before Merkel's first visit to Greece during the crisis.

Credit: Kostas Tsironis/Bloomberg

President Barack Obama awards Merkel the U.S. Presidential Medal of Honor at a White House ceremony in June 2011. Behind the scenes, the U.S. was pressing her government to do more to stem the debt crisis as it spilled over to the global economy.

Credit: Andrew Harrer/Bloomberg

Street graffiti in Lisbon in March 2013 shows Merkel controlling Portugal's prime minister and foreign minister. As the crisis spread through southern Europe and forced governments to enact austerity measures, she was increasingly viewed as imposing her will throughout the euro area, raising uncomfortable echoes of World War II.

Credit: Mario Proenca/Bloomberg

At the Group of 20 summit in Los Cabos, Mexico, in June 2012, Merkel came under pressure from fellow leaders for Germany to take radical action to save the euro as the clash of views over how to stamp out the crisis intensified.

Credit: German Government/Jesco Denzel

Merkel's decision to shut Germany's nuclear plants and shift to renewable power poses a challenge to industry in Europe's biggest economy. Here she inspects a scale model of an offshore wind farm on the Baltic coast.

Credit: Hannelore Foerster/Bloomberg

Merkel hosting Dutch Prime Minister Mark Rutte at the Chancellery in Berlin with the refurbished Reichstag parliament building in the background.

Credit: German Government/Guido Bergmann

Merkel toasting fellow leaders of the Baltic Sea Council, which includes Scandinavian countries, Poland and Russia, in a Stralsund pub during a summit in May 2012. The chancellor has an affinity for the EU's northern and eastern countries and holds them up as economic examples for the south.

Credit: German Government/Guido Bergmann

8.2 percent from the previous year, while consumption rose 1.4 percent.[26] Demographics are helping reduce labor-market pressure: Germany's population shrank or stagnated for most of the decade through 2010. Numbers aside, Merkel's basic argument is simple: Germany doesn't have to choose between growth and debt reduction. She took the message to an international audience at the 2012 Hanover Trade Fair, the showcase of German manufacturing might. "We have to do a balancing act, because the international community expects Germany to contribute to growth and we are moving toward solid finances at the same time," she said. "These are the two pillars of the gateway to good performance with a future. I absolutely don't understand how some can see these as opposing pillars again and again."

While Germany's "social market economy" offers plenty of rules and traditions, organizing a sovereign default within a European currency union isn't one of them. When the first international bailout for Greece didn't stamp out the crisis, Merkel and other euro-area leaders had to find an exit route and she chose to make private bondholders pay. She had dropped early hints after the collapse of Lehman Brothers, criticizing market excesses and the financial industry's resistance to tighter regulation. When her government set up a 500 billion euro rescue fund for German banks in late 2008, Merkel warned bankers that the shoe was on the other foot and they now had to "accept our conditions."[27] In mid-2009, German lawmakers passed the "debt brake," a constitutional amendment backed by Merkel that obliges the federal and state governments to wind down budget deficits. After the debt crisis erupted, Merkel used that fiscal rule to press other euro-area countries to adopt similar commitments. She also set up an "Advisory Panel on the New Financial Order" to propose ways to tighten global financial regulation. Chaired by former ECB chief economist Otmar Issing, its members included Klaus Regling, who later became head of the euro area's temporary rescue fund, the European Financial Stability Facility, and Jens Weidmann, Merkel's chief economic adviser and negotiator at international summits, whom she chose to head the Bundesbank in 2011. To Greeks involved in crisis fighting such as Gikas Hardouvelis, the Eurobank economist in Athens, Merkel and "hardliners" who advised her had it backwards. "If you ask an economist from the most conservative to the most Keynesian, they will tell you that if you are in a crisis situation, you forget the issues of moral hazard and problems of incentives; you solve the crisis and get it out of the way and then you worry about fixing your problem, the architecture," Hardouvelis said. The Germans "believed that if you addressed the architecture issue, then the crisis will go away. I think that was a major mistake. Back then, in the end of 2009, early 2010, they could have simply bought the Greek debt and not allowed the crisis to get outside the Greek border, but they didn't."[28]

As with the Stralsund shipyard, Merkel wasn't in a mood to do banks any favors. Twenty years after the collapse of communism, "I couldn't imagine that an entire business sector would come to me and say: Only the state can still help us," she told a business association in Berlin in May 2009. Her government had rescued German banks not for their own sake, but to protect savers and to help avoid a credit squeeze for Mittelstand companies, she said. A year later, the sovereign-debt crisis was raging and Greece had its first bailout. On the eve of a May 2010 EU summit that sealed the rescue package, Merkel and Sarkozy issued a joint warning to the financial industry that they will "work nationally and internationally on a regime for fair contributions of the financial sector."[29] As the crisis deepened, Merkel won over Sarkozy for expanding that notion to private-sector involvement, or PSI, which was code for getting holders of Greek debt to accept losses to ease the burden on official aid creditors. Banks and governments agreed in October 2011 to work out the world's biggest debt write-off, an outcome Merkel had fought for. While Merkel was prepared to accept a 20 percent haircut at one point, Schäuble pressed for a bigger haircut as finance ministers and bank envoys haggled over the details through March 2012, according to Hardouvelis. "We would reach a point and then the hardliners would say, 'Well, this is not good enough, we want more.' Then it would start again," he said. In the end, the write-down was 52.5 percent, after governments extracted a last-minute concession to raise it from 50 percent. Hardouvelis recalls Lagarde, then IMF chief, ending the talks on a sober note, saying the target of Greece returning to capital markets in 2015 was illusory. "Everybody was congratulating themselves at 4 o'clock in the morning," he said. "Christine Lagarde turned around and told them, 'Look guys, don't celebrate, because you're going to babysit Greece all the way to 2020'." PSI helped Merkel fend off calls from within her coalition to get Greece out of the euro. Yet by declaring Greece's debt exchange a special case, euro-area leaders were attempting to signal that the option wasn't on the table for other debt-ridden countries.

By mid-November 2011, Spanish 10-year bond yields rose to the highest levels since the euro's debut. Flexibility was coming into play for Merkel. Sarkozy hosted her and Monti for a summit of the three biggest euro-area economies in Strasbourg, France, across the Rhine from Germany. The Christmas market, a tradition dating to 1570, had just opened, lending the Alsatian city a festive air as the three leaders met at the regional prefect's palace. The ECB, which had become an emblem of united Europe's disunity, was on the agenda. German politicians felt France was trying to soften up the ECB to become the euro area's lender of last resort, undermining budget discipline and the Bundesbank's anti-inflation tradition. Sarkozy saw the mirror image: Germans, while pointing to the ECB's statutory independence, were trying in fact to make the bank do things their way. Musca, who was at the Strasbourg meeting, said Sarkozy complained to Merkel that he "read every day in the newspapers" about what Germany said the ECB shouldn't do. "Don't you agree that the ECB is independent? It's up to the ECB to interpret its mandate," he quoted Sarkozy as telling her. "We should have only one message: we support the ECB and let them act."[30] Talking to journalists afterward, Merkel and Sarkozy said they agreed to refrain from trying to sway the ECB's anti-crisis policy. Mario Draghi ramped up the ECB's response two weeks later, cutting euro-area interest rates and offering banks unlimited cash for three years in an effort to spur lending. Merkel tacitly approved, letting Draghi do his job even as he insisted that ECB action can't substitute for economic reforms. Where Merkel insisted no silver bullet could replace step-by-step construction of a more stable euro, Draghi gave investors their long-awaited soundbite in July 2012: "Within our mandate, the ECB is ready to do whatever it takes to preserve the euro. And believe me, it will be enough."

Merkel has a domestic business constituency that wants to avoid turmoil in the euro area – people like Boerner, who runs a pump and sanitary-supply business in the Bavarian town of Ingolstadt and meets her regularly. "It's a big advantage that Draghi understands investment banking and the financial markets," says Boerner. "He knows what a trading room is." Had Merkel fallen in line with the Bundesbank and opposed the ECB's unprecedented offer on September 6, 2012 to buy sovereign debt, markets would have imploded. "Merkel understands this. This is why she had to say at that point: 'Yes, Draghi is right,'" Boerner says.[31]

Helmut Kohl's advocacy of European unification and the euro two decades ago was a matter of the heart, a historian's response to the worst moments of Germany's past. Merkel experimented with her tone for some time and looked forward, weighing the arguments before deciding that defending the joint currency would help Germany and the EU compete in the global marketplace. Six days before Ireland applied for a bailout in November 2010, her wording at a CDU convention speech suggested she was still honing her message: "All of us occasionally smiled when Helmut Kohl, at decisive moments in talks on Europe, never tired of saying 'It's a matter of war and peace.' That kind of language may sound a bit strange to us now. But his legacy should never be." In fact, ceding the deutsche mark for the untested euro, while backed by German industry, wasn't popular with ordinary Germans. Kohl had just returned from the December 1991 EU summit in Maastricht that put the euro on track when he told a CDU convention that the currency union will "quite necessarily" be followed by political union. At the end of the 20th century "it will be clear once and for all: this old continent will never see a fratricidal war again. Those are the tidings we can proclaim now," he said.[32] By the mid-1990s, people close to Kohl leaked comments to *Der Spiegel* magazine expressing doubt the project would work. Schröder, campaigning to unseat Kohl in 1998, called the euro a "sickly premature birth." He wound up presiding over its debut in people's wallets on January 1, 2002. Upon its introduction, there was anecdotal evidence that merchants simply substituted euros for marks even though the euro had been adopted at a rate of almost two-to-one, meaning that the cost of some items doubled overnight. That led to headlines that fed on the German fear of inflation and branded the new currency the "Teuro," from the German word "teuer," meaning expensive. That the myth of the euro's inflationary effect persisted is borne out by a December 2011 headline in the *Bild* newspaper: "It's official! The Euro is no Teuro!" The article cited figures from the Federal Statistics Office showing that in the almost 10 years from the euro's introduction in 2002 to the end of November 2011, inflation had averaged 1.6 percent per year, compared with an average 2.6 percent under the deutsche mark.

Merkel deployed the empirical evidence to justify her policy course, which had firmed up since the previous summer. "This currency has stood the test of time," she told members of the trade and industry chamber in Dusseldorf. "It gives more stability for prices than the deutsche mark did in the final 10 years of its existence." Yet with its failings "trotted out each day" during the international economic and financial crisis, Merkel pledged her "absolute political will" to strengthen the euro and reconstruct it as a more stable common currency fit for the future. "That will only be possible with more Europe and not less Europe," she said. The "visionary step" of a currency union must be supported by a political union, "the foundations of which have yet to be properly cast."[33] When the debt crisis exposed the joint currency's flaws and bailout commitments grew, polls showed Germans pining for a return to the deutsche mark. Merkel dismissed the idea, saying a revived national currency would appreciate against the currencies of Germany's trading partners, hurting exports and the economy. Germany, she said, is among the countries that has benefited the most from the euro. Martin Wolf argued as much in the *Financial Times*, saying the euro locked in "captive markets and a competitive exchange rate" for Germany. The debt crisis dragged down the euro's exchange rate, making German exports to the rest of the world cheaper. Meanwhile, many of Germany's partners in the euro region – the destination for 40 percent of German exports – were uncompetitive after a decade of relative rising costs. Germans, Wolf said, "have an overwhelming interest in the success of the eurozone."[34] Merkel's debt-crisis prescription for the euro area and championing of the social market economy didn't come out of nowhere. She laid the groundwork at the CDU's 2003 convention when she sought to rally her party out of the opposition doldrums. Germany was at a crossroads in the global economy and faced a choice: "Be submerged by change, or shape that change. That is the key question." Germany was "in a deep crisis" marked by a lack of jobs, high public debt, an inflexible labor market, and weak spending on research and development. "Returning to the good old days is out of the question," she said. Merkel expanded the vista when she first ran for chancellor in 2005, the year the number of jobless rose above 5 million for the first time since World War II and Schröder called early elections. Germany needed a "new social market economy," with a leaner state and a recognition that "Germany has no entitlement to open-ended prosperity."[35] Merkel says she was drawn to the social market economy's values while still in East Germany. Even so, life under communism shaped her first. Her take, long before the debt crisis, was that people learned to make do with less and still tried to improve their lot. East Germany "was a country where you practically couldn't buy wood – no piece of lumber, no board," she said. "Life in the GDR was tough and regimented and limited. But we tried to make the best of it."[36]

For all its strengths, the export-driven German model has drawbacks. Its success also tends to mask areas where Germany lags, from services and bank capitalization to broadband access and venture capitalists. Franz Müntefering, a Social Democrat who was vice chancellor in Merkel's first Cabinet until resigning for health reasons in 2007, once called private-equity firms "locusts." Between 2008 and mid-2010, German GDP declined more quickly and recovered more slowly than output in the U.S., which is less export-reliant. Thirteen percent of German exports went to the U.S. and China in 2011, yet the two countries accounted for 70 percent of German export growth in the first nine months of 2012, according to Deutsche Bank researchers. One-third of German exports come from two industries, automotive and mechanical engineering. "Such concentration harbors cyclical risks in the short term and structural risks in the long term," the Deutsche Bank researchers said. Another challenge is that companies such as carmakers are building up production – often with imported German equipment – in growth markets abroad, undercutting exports of the finished product from Germany. Services remain a relatively weak contributor to productivity, held back by regulations notably in the skilled trades, which still tend to operate under a guild-like system. Germany's license and permit system is more burdensome than in other countries, thus acting as a barrier to entrepreneurship in services, according to an OECD report, which reminded Merkel's government that reducing red tape boosts growth. German payroll taxes – which put the "social" in social market economy – are above the OECD average, increasing labor costs, while sales and property taxes are below average. German women work some of the lowest hours in the developed world, while the mix of tax and benefit policies "significantly favors single-earner over dual-earner couples," the OECD analysts said. Even as Merkel frets about Germany's aging, shrinking population, hurdles to immigration remain "significant" and the share of highly educated migrants is lower in Germany than in many other developed countries.[37] The digital economy came slowly to Germany as many large retailers, mindful of Germany's conservative consumer culture, wavered before embracing online sales. A survey commissioned by Google Inc. found that German professionals are less likely to use social technologies for business than counterparts in Spain, Italy, the U.K., Sweden, France, and the Netherlands. Seventy percent of fast-growing companies in Italy said they use social networks to improve work quality and generate ideas, compared with 28 percent in Germany.[38] Nationwide broadband internet coverage remains elusive in Germany, where travelers on the high-speed train corridor between Berlin and Hamburg – the nation's two biggest cities – struggle for a data connection. While other European cities roll out 4G networks, parts of downtown Berlin have patchy 3G coverage. Germany has Europe's second-highest number of rural households without broadband after Poland, the European Commission said in 2012. As Europeans load up on smartphones and tablets, mobile broadband's reach in Germany was below the EU average. Of the four biggest euro-area economies, only Italy had a lower score.[39] Merkel wasn't planning to use Twitter Inc.'s social networking service during her 2013 election campaign. She prefers text messaging by phone, an older and more private technology.[40]

Notes

1. As measured by GDP per capita.
2. Eurostat, "Public Balance and General Government Debt, 2008-2011": http:// epp.eurostat.ec.europa.eu/statistics_explained/index.php?title=File: Public_balance_and_general_government_debt,_2008-2011_(1)_(%25_of_ GDP).png&filetimestamp=20121023174050.
3. German Federal Statistics Office data.
4. Carmen M. Reinhart and Kenneth S. Rogoff, "Growth in a Time of Debt," Abstract, January 2010: http://www.economics.harvard.edu/faculty/rogoff/ files/Growth_in_Time_Debt_Abstract.pdf.

5. Kenneth Rogoff, "The Euro at Mid-Crisis," *Project Syndicate*, December 2, 2010.
6. Sebastian Boyd and Jody Shenn, "Hank the Great? Paulson Copies Frederick With Bonds," *Bloomberg News*, August 7, 2008.
7. Gabi Thesing, "Germans Still Favor Cash Over Cards for Payment, Bundesbank Says," *Bloomberg News*, October 17, 2012.
8. ECB data cited in Irish Payment Services Organisation, "Card Payments per Capita 2011": http://www.ipso.ie/?action=statistics&sectionName=EUStatistics&statisticCode=EU&statisticRef=EU07.
9. OECD (2012), "House prices," Economics: Key Tables from OECD: http://dx.doi.org/10.1787/hsprice-table-2012-2-en.
10. Confederation of German Employers, "Germany's Export Strength – Bad for Europe?" Berlin, September 2012: http://www.arbeitgeber.de/www/arbeitgeber.nsf/res/DtExportstaerke_eng.pdf/$file/DtExportstaerke_eng.pdf.
11. World Bank, "Exports of Goods and Services as Percentage of GDP," 2011 data: http://data.worldbank.org/indicator/NE.EXP.GNFS.ZS/countries.
12. Press release from German Federal Statistics Office, January 8, 2013: https://www.destatis.de/DE/PresseService/Presse/Pressemitteilungen/2013/01/PD13_005_51.html.
13. Confederation of German Employers, "Germany's Export Strength – Bad for Europe?" Berlin, September 2012: http://www.arbeitgeber.de/www/arbeitgeber.nsf/res/DtExportstaerke_eng.pdf/$file/DtExportstaerke_eng.pdf.
14. State of the Union address on White House website: http://www.whitehouse.gov/blog/2013/02/13/president-obamas-2013-state-union.
15. Speech by Merkel to German Bundestag, September 25, 2012.
16. Speech by Merkel in Ho Chi Minh City, Vietnam, October 12, 2011.
17. Company website: http://www.glasbau-hahn.com/en/the-company.
18. Company website: http://www.prym.com.
19. Richard Weiss, "Kuka Robots Invade China as Wage Gains Put Machines Over Workers," *Bloomberg News*, April 13, 2012.
20. Speech by Merkel to Ordnungspolitik Foundation, Freiburg, Germany, February 23, 2011: http://www.bundesregierung.de/Content/DE/Rede/2011/02/2011-02-23-bkin-freiburg.html.
21. Interview by Thomas Schmid, "Warum Italian mehr wie Deutschland sein sollte," *Die Welt*, January 11, 2012: http://www.welt.de/politik/ausland/article13808298/Warum-Italien-mehr-wie-Deutschland-sein-sollte.html.
22. Zachary A. Goldfarb, "Can Obama Save Manufacturing?" *Washington Post*, July 13, 2012: http://www.washingtonpost.com/business/can-obama-save-manufacturing/2012/07/13/gJQAe2zxhW_story.html.
23. Paul Krugman, "Kurzarbeit," *New York Times* website, September 2, 2010: http://krugman.blogs.nytimes.com/2010/09/02/kurzarbeit.
24. German Federal Statistical Office, "Volkswirtschaftliche Gesamtrechnungen, Private Konsumausgaben und Verfügbares Einkommen - 3. Vierteljahr 2012," Wiesbaden, 2012.

25. Press conference by Merkel and Hungarian Prime Minister Viktor Orbán, Berlin, October 11, 2012.
26. Statement by Roderich Egeler, President of the German Federal Statistical Office, at press conference in Wiesbaden, January 11, 2012.
27. Cited in *Focus* magazine, October 13, 2008: http://www.focus.de/finanzen/ boerse/finanzkrise/kanzlerin-merkel-es-gab-exzesse_aid_340448.html.
28. Interview by the authors in Athens, November 21, 2012.
29. German Government Press Office, "Joint letter of Chancellor Angela Merkel and President Nicolas Sarkozy to the Presidents of the European Council and the European Commission," May 6, 2010: http://www.bundeskanzlerin. de/Content/DE/Pressemitteilungen/BPA/2010/05/2010-05-06-brief-englisch.html?nn=74308.
30. Interview by the authors, Paris, November 30, 2012.
31. Interview with the authors, Berlin, January 9, 2013.
32. Speech to Christian Democratic Union national convention in Dresden, December 15, 1991: http://www.kas.de/upload/ACDP/CDU/Protokolle_ Parteitage/1991-12-15-17_Protokoll_02.Parteitag_Dresden.pdf.
33. Speech to Dusseldorf Chamber of Trade and Industry, January 9, 2012.
34. Martin Wolf, "Germans are Wrong: The Eurozone is Good for Them," *Financial Times*, September 7, 2010.
35. Angela Merkel, *Mein Weg: Ein Gespräch mit Hugo Müller-Vogg*, p. 68 (Hoffmann und Campe Verlag, Hamburg, 2005).
36. Quoted in interview in *Bild am Sonntag*, "So war mein Leben in der DDR," October 2, 2010.
37. OECD (2012), "Economic Survey – Germany," February 2012.
38. "How Social Technologies Drive Business Success," May 15, 2012: http:// services.google.com/fh/files/misc/google_emea_social_report_2012.pdf.
39. European Commission, "Digital Agenda Scoreboard 2012": http://ec.europa .eu/digital-agenda/sites/digital-agenda/files/scoreboard_broadband_markets .pdf.
40. German government chief spokesman Steffen Seibert quoted by *Spiegel Online*, January 6, 2013.

Chapter 9

Kings
(Merkel's Contemporaries)

A ngela Merkel smiled awkwardly as Gerhard Schröder insisted
he was staying on as chancellor. Merkel's Christian Democratic
bloc may have squeezed in ahead of his Social Democrats, but
in Schröder's eyes he hadn't lost the 2005 election. "There's only one
clear loser and that's Frau Merkel," Schröder said during a televised
debate between the main party leaders after the polls had closed. "The
result is clear: No one but me is in a position to form a stable government, no-one." Merkel, wearing dark eyeshadow that only seemed to
accentuate her discomfort, said she needed "a few more facts" before she
was able to fully analyze the results, but as the leader of the single biggest
bloc, she had the right to initiate talks with other parties to form a coalition.[1] Despite Schröder's chutzpah during a post-election performance
that entered German political folklore, within three weeks he had been
eased out and his party agreed to a coalition with the Christian Democrats with Merkel as chancellor. Schröder, who went on to take a post
with Russian gas giant OAO Gazprom, where he chaired the Nord
Stream project building a pipeline to Germany, was merely the latest in
a long line of people who underestimated Merkel.

A political outsider from the outset, Germany's first woman chancellor has made a career out of being misread and trivialized. Written off

because of her eastern origins and demeanor or her unemphatic speaking style, derided for her early bowl-cut hairstyle, Merkel nonetheless overcame all challengers from the earliest days of her political career.

She rose past her contemporaries at the Democratic Awakening political group set up in the weeks after the Berlin Wall's demise, and then, having opted to join Helmut Kohl's CDU, leapfrogged East Germany's only democratically elected prime minister, Lothar de Maizière, into Kohl's Cabinet from the relatively humble position of de Maizière's deputy press secretary. Once there, alongside the likes of Wolfgang Schäuble, Horst Seehofer, who would later become Bavarian prime minister and head of her CSU sister party, and Jürgen Rüttgers, the one-time prime minister of North Rhine-Westphalia, she bested them all. Even Kohl, who referred to her as "the girl," was deposed by Merkel when she publicly cut him loose over his role in a party funding scandal. Merkel's decision to break with Kohl was all the more effective because she had displayed such loyalty until that point. One illustration of her early dedication to Kohl came in the fall of 1991, as the first anniversary of reunification of East and West Germany approached. October 3 had been instated as a public holiday and Kohl's newly re-elected government – his fourth – let it be known that it would be a good idea if the churches that played such an important part in the peaceful removal of the East German regime rang their bells to mark the occasion. The Lutheran authorities refused, citing the historic separation between church and state in Germany, saying it's not the job of the church to celebrate state holidays. Merkel told her parents that Kohl was very upset, so much so that he had used a colloquial term of abuse to describe the church: "hinterfotzig," meaning devious and holier than thou. Merkel, whose father was a Protestant pastor, said she shared Kohl's view and the churches should stop being so obstinate, go along with the times, and recognize public sentiment. It was typical Merkel: not letting emotion get in the way of her rational opinion. "Of course she has a basic set of values, but her first step always is to look at the rational arguments on the issues and derive her actions from that," said Hans-Christian Maass, who has known Merkel since he helped organize the CDU's East German sister party for the first post-unity elections in December 1990. She is careful not to dwell "too much on differentiating between good and evil based on an ideological stand." It was still easy to dismiss Merkel in her early days in politics. She only took on significance when she was recommended by de Maizière for a Cabinet post after the election. Back then, "Angela was cautious. She absolutely didn't stand out. She was late to the game," said Maass. "But when she did something, she did it with her characteristic precision and reliability."

After Kohl was defeated by Schröder in 1998 and the Social Democrat-led coalition with Joschka Fischer's Green Party took office, the CDU was left to reflect on its failings and future direction after the longest reign of any chancellor of the postwar period. In the political wilderness of opposition, Merkel's star kept on rising. In January 2000, Kohl was forced to resign as his party's honorary chairman amid the party funding affair, then in February, Wolfgang Schäuble tendered his resignation as CDU parliamentary group leader after admitting accepting party donations from an arms lobbyist. Schäuble had been seen as Kohl's natural successor after having served as his interior minister and chief of staff, and his resignation left the CDU rudderless. Merkel, then general secretary, was blameless and a fresh face, a blank slate for the party tarnished by the descent into financial impropriety and disgrace. In April 2000, barely four months after saying it was time to look to life after Kohl, she was voted in as CDU chairwoman. With a sudden rush of interest in the new party leader about whom little was known, Merkel was forced to reveal details of who she was and where she came from. A sense of how anxious she was not to say the wrong thing can be seen in an interview from June 2001 in which she was asked about her childhood. "Before Christmas, I always used to go with my father into the forest to cut down a tree," she said, adding hurriedly: "legally, of course."[2]

Merkel's cautiousness and unwillingness to dissemble meant she continued to be underestimated. In January 2002, she heeded internal party pressure and made way for Edmund Stoiber, the head of the Christian Social Union, the CDU's Bavarian sister party, to challenge Schröder at that year's election. The CDU and CSU contest federal elections together, with the CDU not standing candidates in Bavaria and the CSU limiting itself to its home state, their votes counting together nationally. Schröder won the election after rushing to aid the victims of a 100-year flood along the River Elbe that struck the eastern states of Saxony and Saxony-Anhalt in August 2002, one month before the vote. His refusal to join the Iraq war, a popular decision even though it sent relations with the U.S. to their lowest level since the end of World War II, also helped give Schröder the edge over Stoiber. Defeated, Stoiber retreated to his Bavarian fastness and Merkel was the CDU/CSU bloc's undisputed leader. It was a tactical move that cemented her place as the head of her party, ensuring she would be the one to challenge Schröder at the next election when the economic situation had deteriorated further.

By then the signs of Germany's economic malaise were becoming unavoidable. Germany had been labelled the sick man of Europe by commentators as far back as 1997 under Kohl, not without a sense of Schadenfreude that the postwar economic miracle that had buoyed Germany was over. But it was during Schröder's time as chancellor that the rot set in. Schröder inherited an increasingly uncompetitive economy hobbled by high wages, an inflexible workforce grown accustomed to decades of boom, and a generous social welfare system. As globalization picked up pace, offering the prospect of relocating plants to cheaper locations further east, Germany faced the very real danger that its manufacturing-based economy would buckle.

Schröder's response was to initiate the Agenda 2010 package of reforms to make Germany fit once more. He faced down his own party and public protests modeled on the Monday demonstrations that contributed to the fall of the Berlin Wall as his government set about legislating to ease the restrictions on hiring and firing, cut pensions, and streamline unemployment welfare. Bernd Sickel, an unemployed real-estate clerk, helped organize demonstrations in the eastern city of Magdeburg against Agenda 2010 and the allied Hartz IV welfare reforms. In an interview in November 2004, he bemoaned the lack of progress, with unemployment rising inexorably and no end in sight to the reform path. "People want a vision for the future," he said. Merkel backed Schröder's policies while in opposition and was happy to benefit from them when she took over the chancellery in Berlin. Merkel feels no compunction about openly adopting opposition policies either piecemeal or wholesale if they suit, picking and choosing as the prevailing circumstances dictate and in accordance with the latest evidence. While she castigates Schröder's government for relaxing the constraints on the budget deficit as unemployment rose, causing Germany to breach EU limits for the first time, she praises his efforts to regain competitiveness. Albeit Germany acted "rather too late than too early," Merkel hailed the reform steps taken by Schröder's coalition in a speech to the BGA wholesaler and exporters' federation in October 2012, saying the measures helped unemployment to fall from over 5 million in 2005 to under 3 million, with the lowest rate of joblessness since reunification.[3] Youth unemployment halved in Germany over the same period, while in both Spain and Greece it rose to 50 percent. The OECD, in its 2012 report on Germany, attributed the drop in unemployment to "past reforms of the labor market" that were "arguably the most significant among OECD countries during that time." Those measures "contributed to the strong resilience of employment during the past recession by raising working hour flexibility and reducing structural unemployment."[4] Merkel is unfazed by the external praise for Schröder's reform course, saying that she supported the steps at the time and it doesn't much matter how progress was achieved. "It's no bad thing when someone else pushes something through," she said in her speech to the BGA in Berlin, "as long as it's the right thing."

As the 2005 election approached, Merkel was handed a campaign theme on a plate as unemployment peaked at a postwar high of 12.7 percent six months before the September vote. By the end of June, Merkel's CDU/CSU had opened up a 23 percentage point gap over Schröder's Social Democrats. With polls showing support for her bloc at 49 percent, Merkel was looking at an unprecedented result which would mean she could govern alone without the need of a coalition partner, the first single-party majority government in Germany's postwar history. By Election Day on September 22, even as most polls predicted she would win comfortably, her lead had collapsed and she squeezed home just 1 percentage point ahead of the SPD. While the result lay in part with Schröder's remarkable campaigning ability that allowed his party to catch up – helping to explain his election-night bravado – Merkel's own electoral missteps were also to blame. Key to the last-minute collapse of support was her platform's focus on tax policies that proved deeply unpopular with German voters. Faced with Schröder's take-no-prisoners campaigning style, she cast about for policies likely to appeal and in doing so her lack of economic nous was exposed.

The seeds of Merkel's platform were sown in October 2003 in a speech entitled "Quo Vadis Deutschland"[5] delivered at the German Historical Museum in Berlin to mark the 13th anniversary of reunification. In it, Merkel referenced an IMF assessment that found Germany's economy stagnating for three years and unable to maintain its standard of living without what then IMF Managing Director Horst Köhler, a German and a CDU member, called "a great deal of change." Citing "an excessive focus on preserving entitlements," he said that international respect for Germany's economic model was "crumbling quickly."[6]

Merkel set out an economic vision to reverse the decline and return Germany to the front line of global competitiveness. Germany had lived off the fat of the land for way too long and had to face up to the uncomfortable reality: too few jobs; a social security system on the rise; highly indebted public finances; a second-rate education system; and too few children. "Through bitter experience, those of us who lived in the former GDR have developed a keen sense of this painful truth," she said. "Our economic performance is trailing off. State institutions are partly atrophied or bound up in bureaucracy. Lots of small parts are moving but the whole is just treading water." Germany was at a crossroads, she said, its problems only able to be resolved by adopting a similar spirit of innovation to the founders of postwar Germany and by striking out on a second age of building the federal republic, with freedom, solidarity and justice as its guiding principles. "Freedom stands for the pleasure to be gained from performance, the development of the individual, joy in diversity, the rejection of egalitarianism, individual responsibility," and to attain it "a course of slashes, cuts and savings is indispensable," she said.

She went on to advocate high schools being allowed to select their pupils and performance-related pay for teachers. She urged a greater focus on financial services to add to Germany's manufacturing export industries, reform of social security and healthcare to place more emphasis on performance, a reduction of pensions and a "pensions age corridor" of 63 to 67. The income-tax system must be rebuilt to redress the "bad joke of a redistribution dogma." Wage tariffs must allow for longer hours or lower pay to attract inward investment, while protection from dismissal must be made "more flexible" and employers allowed to undercut wages to promote Germany as a leader in services. The state "must retreat to allow more space and individual responsibility for people."

Merkel's platform amounted to a radical break with Germany's past and it was backed at a party convention in Leipzig two months later, leading to what was termed the "Thatcherization" of the CDU. The problem was that the majority of Germans were not ready for it.

During the 2005 election campaign, Merkel floundered on economic policy. She confused gross and net income in more than one interview, prompting then SPD Finance Minister Hans Eichel to say that on questions of budgetary policy Merkel was "vastly out of her depth."[7] The SPD's general secretary, Klaus Uwe Benneter, added: "Life is more complicated than in a physics lab." Her biggest own-goal came in late August, when she appointed to her campaign team Paul Kirchhof, a professor of finance and tax law at Heidelberg University and a former federal court judge, who advocated overhauling the income-tax system to scrap all tax breaks and subsidies in favor of a 25 percent flat rate, down from a top rate of 42 percent. A flat tax had already been introduced in Eastern European countries including Georgia and Romania, as well as in the Baltic States. Germany's big industry lobby hailed the proposal as "magnificent," but the Mittelstand, the legion of small and medium-sized companies, many of them specialized and family-owned, were reluctant to see the subsidy system extinguished. And where big industry saw savings, the general public saw the rich paying less tax at their expense. Another Merkel adviser, Heinrich von Pierer, the former CEO of Siemens AG, Europe's biggest engineering company, criticized Kirchhof for confusing voters. Schröder referred dismissively to Kirchhof as "the professor from Heidelberg." Merkel, calling him a "visionary," distanced herself from the proposal.

She started August with a 19-point lead over the Social Democrats; going into September that lead had narrowed to 8 points. On the eve of the election, all six regular opinion polls put Merkel's Union bloc ahead by a margin of 41–43 percent to 32–34 percent for Schröder's SPD. In the event, voters had a last-minute change of heart and backed away from Merkel's vision. She took 35.2 percent to the SPD's 34.2 percent and was forced into a grand coalition with the Social Democrats, albeit without Schröder.[8]

What was left of her program amounted to a rise in the pension age to 67, spearheaded by SPD Labor Minister and Vice Chancellor, Franz Müntefering, and an increase in VAT sales tax to 19 percent from

16 percent from 2007 to help bring down non-wage labor costs by funding a reduction in contributions for unemployment insurance. Merkel, chastened by her ill-fated flirtation with a free-market ethos that was at odds with the majority of Germans, ditched most of the rest. She even agreed to raise the top rate of income tax to 45 percent.

Merkel saw that voters wanted change, above all an end to the economic malaise that had sent long-term unemployment to the highest level ever seen in Germany, but that they were exhausted by Schröder's Agenda 2010 reforms and were unwilling to swallow even more radical medicine. Not even when she won re-election in 2009 at the head of a coalition with her favored ally, the business-friendly Free Democratic Party, did she return to the "Quo Vadis" agenda. Germany by then was in the throes of the deepest recession in living memory and the public was financially challenged enough without burdening them further. Circumstances had changed, time had moved on, and so had Merkel.

When the CDU party convention returned to Leipzig in 2011 as the euro crisis raged, the *Rheinische Post* newspaper wrote in an article headed "The CDU's 180 degree about-turn," that of the free-market policies Merkel espoused in 2003, "not a trace remains."

Merkel's reversal left some in her party disgruntled with her policy course throughout her second term, but ensured that she was able to take the public with her as she faced the coming financial crisis. Nor would it be her last 180-degree turn. None of them harmed her political fortunes in the long run. As throughout her career, Merkel learned the lessons of Quo Vadis and the 2005 election that she so nearly lost. Having abandoned free-market thinking and appropriated opposition policies on pensions, jobs, and even wages, she denied her Social Democratic challenger Peer Steinbrück access to the center ground he needed to occupy if he was to have any hope of dislodging her. As she sought a third term in elections slated for the fall of 2013, Merkel wasn't allowing Steinbrück any purchase.

Dressed in a dark blue business suit with ivory colored buttons, Merkel stepped confidently down the few steps to the lectern in front of the packed Bundestag on October 30, 2005. Just eight days in office, it was her first speech to the chamber as chancellor. She used it to tear up her earlier program and to lay down a marker for her time in office, when pragmatism would take precedence over political ethos. "This has nothing to do with ideology," she said as she lay out her grand coalition's priorities for the four-year term ahead, "rather it's about practical, human expertise."[9] Like the internet, which links myriad small computers to create a machine greater than its parts, her government would not attempt great leaps forward, but focus instead on taking "many small steps." It was a stock Merkel phrase that she would repeat over and over during the euro-region debt crisis to explain her modus operandi. It is the nub of her policy making, her signature political style. "Let us not first ask what doesn't work or what has always been the case, but rather ask what is possible and look what hasn't been tried before," she said, speaking like the physicist she is. "Have the courage to then pursue it. Surprise ourselves with what is possible, surprise ourselves with what we can do."

Pulling off surprises became a leitmotif of her time in office. Back in May 2004 when she was still opposition leader, Merkel had succeeded in having Horst Köhler, the former IMF head, elected to the largely ceremonial post of president, outfoxing the Social Democrat–Greens coalition to put her man in the post in a demonstration of her political cunning. He quit in 2010, a year after being elected to a second term, over remarks he made about Germany's mission in Afghanistan in which he appeared to condone military intervention to bolster trade. Sensing a chance to turn the tables, the Social Democrats and Greens secured the candidacy for the post of Joachim Gauck, a Protestant pastor from the eastern German port of Rostock who for a decade ran the federal government's archives on the activities of the Stasi, the East German secret police. Polls showed he was the public's choice as head of state, but Merkel had other ideas. She maneuvered into place Christian Wulff, the CDU prime minister of Lower Saxony, bringing him and his young wife Bettina from the state capital Hanover to Berlin. He and Gauck went head to head at the Federal Assembly, a body comprising lawmakers, state representatives and a sprinkling of celebrities nominated by the regions that convenes specially to elect the German president. With a majority in both upper and lower houses, Merkel could expect to win the day, but it still took three attempts for Wulff to be elected president and gain the right to take up residence in Bellevue Palace on the edge of Berlin's Tiergarten, such was the backing for Gauck's candidacy.

While the German president is politically powerless and is mostly confined to representing Germany overseas, the post carries moral importance with the incumbent expected to give direction to public debates. Wulff's main contribution was to deliver a speech in which he said that Islam was a part of German society – until he resigned amid allegations of impropriety after a drawn-out scandal over property loans relating to his time as state premier. Having seen both her prior choices of president quit, Merkel backed Gauck's candidacy and he was elected president a little over 20 months after he first submitted to the vote. It was a farce unprecedented in Germany's postwar period and Merkel was its cause, but with the euro crisis never far off in the background attention was diverted and she suffered no visible damage: her party's poll ratings didn't waver. She had mastered the game of avoiding blame.

The supreme illustration of Merkel's ability to pull off a reversal without incurring lasting political damage was her overnight decision to ditch a planned extension of the lifespan of Germany's nuclear power stations. She won her second term in the fall of 2009 at the head of a coalition with the Free Democrats on a platform that included over-turning Schröder's policy of shutting nuclear plants by 2020. Merkel forced through a reprieve for the nuclear industry amid opposition from a populace that had been at the fore of the Green movement's rise: Germany was the first Western European country to have a Green Party foreign minister and vice chancellor, Joschka Fischer. Six months later, in March 2011, an earthquake and tsunami ripped through Japan, rupturing a reactor at Fukushima. Merkel performed a U-turn. Pledging to speed the transition to renewable energies and return to the original decision to shut down Germany's atomic-power capacity, Merkel the scientist said she had been convinced by the weight of evidence provided by the worst nuclear disaster since Chernobyl. She announced a moratorium on nuclear power to assess the facts, saying that Fukushima marked a turning point for the world.

The reversal came two weeks before a regional election in Baden-Württemberg, home to Porsche SE, SAP AG and Daimler AG, the maker of Mercedes cars, and a CDU heartland since the first post-war election in the reconstituted state in 1952. On March 26, the day before the ballot, about 250,000 people took part in demonstrations across the country calling for an end to atomic power, in what organizers said were some of the biggest anti-nuclear protests Germany had ever seen.[10] Baden-Württemberg, whose economy is bigger than Belgium and Luxembourg combined, was ruled by a coalition of the CDU and the Free Democrats, mirroring Merkel's federal government, but her atomic revelation came too late to save her regional allies. The CDU took 39 percent to win the election but slumped to its worst result of postwar times, while the Free Democrats only just managed to scrape back into the state parliament in Stuttgart with 5.3 percent, leaving the two parties three seats short of a majority.[11] The Greens reaped the advantage of their long campaigning against nuclear power and capitalized on their opposition to a contentious railway development known as Stuttgart 21 to take a record 24.2 percent, more than doubling their seats. The SPD placed third with 23.1 percent to depose the CDU regional administration and replace it with a Greens–SPD alliance. Winfried Kretschmann became the first Green Party prime minister ever to rule in one of Germany's 16 states.

It was a disaster for Merkel, who had made several campaign appearances in the state for her party. Seventy percent of respondents in one poll said her about-turn was a campaign ploy. The political landscape was shifting in Germany and it came on Merkel's watch. Nationally, polls showed the CDU dropping 6 points to 30 percent, its lowest level of support that year and just 2 points ahead of the Greens, which were enjoying record backing. The run of bad results continued through 2011 in regional elections that saw the Social Democrats enter into government or retain each state they contested. By year's end, Merkel's party had either lost control or lost vote share in five of the seven states contested, ceding ground to the SPD on each occasion. Her Free Democratic partner, riven by infighting and unable to win any profile in the coalition dominated by the CDU, had been eviscerated, dropping out of five state administrations. In domestic political terms, it was Merkel's *annus horribilis*.

Yet she recovered as the crisis in the euro area came to her aid. Trying to balance domestic concerns with international obligations, the crisis was her demon and her savior. In November 2011, Merkel's poll ratings crept back up as she threatened Greece with euro exit at the G-20 in Cannes, sparred with Berlusconi, and went on to push through

her plan for budgetary restraint at European level, winning agreement
from all but two of the 27 EU nations to lock in rules clamping down
on debt and deficits. By December she had regained a lead over the
SPD's Peer Steinbrück in a monthly Infratest survey for ARD television of voter preference on who should be chancellor. She ended the
year with her Union bloc on 35 percent support, 1 point more than at
the start of the year and 5 points above her low point reached in March
when she backtracked on nuclear power. Nothing stuck for long as she
demonstrated an ability to take the German public along on her cautious and deliberate route of "small steps" for Europe. "Even though I
can criticize certain decisions, what I admire is that she has managed to
keep the German public behind her, which is a huge feat," said George
Papaconstantinou, the former Greek finance minister. "She has shifted
positions without losing the core of her constituency."

Merkel's most propitious 180-degree turn was on Greece. Whereas she
had chided the Greek government for its ruinous ways and extracted
additional cuts in return for help, even raising the prospect in early 2010
of expelling wayward countries from the euro, by late 2011 and into
2012 she signaled a thaw. Greece had been in political limbo since Prime
Minister Papandreou scrapped his referendum and resigned in November
2011, making way for a caretaker government headed by a former vice
president of the ECB, Lucas Papademos. The Papademos administration was left to pick up the pieces, securing an aid tranche and guiding
through a 100 billion-euro writedown of its debt held by banks and other
private investors, before early elections were held in May 2012. With support collapsing for the two main parties, Papandreou's PASOK and the
main opposition New Democracy party led by Antonis Samaras, polls
suggested that Syriza and other parties opposed to the country's austerity
program might win the vote. The prospect of Greece defaulting and having to leave the euro, triggering a market meltdown, again reared its head.

As well as the risk of an uncontrolled euro exit, a number of other
factors influenced Merkel's change of heart on Greece, according to
Gikas Hardouvelis, Papademos's chief economic adviser. The IMF was
pushing very hard "to persuade the hardliners that they should give
Greece another chance," he said. The decisive issue, however, was the
potential political cost to Merkel of a Greek exit leading to the euro
area's dissolution. Such a horror scenario would inevitably be pinned on

her as the dominant figure in the fight against the crisis. What's more, after weighing the evidence and gathering expert opinions, Merkel had concluded the fallout from a Greek default was incalculable. She started signaling as much as early as October 2011, when she gave a speech rejecting the option of a Greek default, saying that the consequences were unquantifiable, would lead to speculative attacks on other highly indebted euro countries, and risk sending German economic growth into reverse. Letting Greece default would trigger "a gigantic loss of confidence" in euro-area sovereign bonds, she told CDU members in Magdeburg, eastern Germany. "No one can say with certainty" what would happen. Before embarking on "an adventure," she said, "I have to ask whether we can really handle this and can we oversee what we are doing?" It was a message she returned to and sharpened in the coming months. "I won't take part in any effort to push Greece out of the euro," Merkel said in February 2012. Ultimately caution worked in her favor.

In the Greek elections, New Democracy placed first, almost 15 percentage points below its 2009 result, while PASOK came third, more than 30 points adrift of its 2009 tally. The big winner of the night was Syriza, led by Alexis Tsipras, which picked up 39 seats to place second. First Samaras, then Tsipras, and finally PASOK leader Evangelos Venizelos tried and failed to forge a coalition. Fresh elections were called for the following month, June 17, a Sunday, leading to yet more instability and a prolongation of the agony. Tsipras, who was now leading in the polls, took his campaign to Paris and then to Berlin, where he briefed reporters in the federal press building on the opposite bank of the River Spree to the Chancellery. The chancellor didn't receive him. As the second election neared, opinion polls suggested an upsurge in support for anti-bailout parties and a slim lead for Samaras's New Democracy, which had campaigned on a renegotiation of Greece's international aid deals, but with the last surveys published more than two weeks before the election, no-one knew for sure. Merkel was notably silent, saying only that Greece had to stick to the terms of its agreements. The results were due to come in as Merkel was on her government Airbus A340 heading for a G-20 summit in Los Cabos in Mexico, at the southern tip of the Baja California peninsula between the Pacific Ocean and the Sea of Cortez, where Greece threatened to dominate the third G-20 summit in succession. Markets were on a knife-edge as Greece and the rest of the euro area looked into the abyss. In the end, voters pulled back from the edge, giving Samaras a 2 percentage point advantage over Syriza that enabled him to form a coalition with PASOK and a third party, Democratic Left. Greece had a government with which Merkel and other European leaders could negotiate.

From the start of Greece's budget difficulties until he became prime minister, Samaras had obstructed the Papandreou government's attempts to adhere to its international bailout terms, refusing to back policy measures, attempting to block his austerity plans, and rejecting Papandreou's offer of a national unity government to secure outside aid. In November 2011, Samaras held out on signing a document requested by Greece's international creditors giving his assurance that he would stick to the agreed terms in return for an aid tranche. Merkel shunned him for a year and a half during that time even though he is a member of the same European umbrella party, according to two Greek officials. Once he became Greek leader and recommitted to the path assigned by the troika of creditors, she relented and welcomed him back into the fold.

The reconciliation was rapid. Samaras announced his first overseas trip as prime minister would be to Berlin. On the day that Samaras was due to arrive, *Bild* reported that Merkel had called him a few weeks previously when he was admitted to hospital for treatment for detachment of the retina on his left eye. Merkel comforted him by telling him that her father, who died the previous year, had suffered the same condition. Samaras told *Bild* that he felt a "special bond" with Merkel.[12] Merkel couldn't have been clearer in the meeting the next day: she told Samaras she'd do all she could to keep Greece in the euro and said she was "deeply convinced" he'd make every effort to solve Greece's problems. Acknowledging that Greeks blamed Germany for painful austerity measures and that Greece's difficulty in meeting its pledges on overhauling the economy triggered "impatience" among Germans, Merkel said she wanted to helped overcome the division. "Now it's the task of those who have political responsibility in Europe to bridge that gap," she said. She committed to visit Athens, a trip she undertook a little more than six weeks later, following it with a trip to Lisbon.

The softening on Greece led to the December 2012 release of 49.1 billion euros in aid, the first tranche of rescue funds in six months. Greece reduced its debt burden by agreeing to pay 11.3 billion euros to buy back 32 billion euros of bonds, with European officials holding out the prospect of additional debt relief if necessary. Merkel, speaking to reporters in Brussels, hailed recent "very successful days" for Greece, saying that Samaras could at last begin to focus on spurring economic growth and the "final steps" still necessary to reform the Greek economy. Within four days of Merkel declaring the corner had been turned on Greece, Standard & Poor's upgraded the country's credit rating from selective default to B- with a stable outlook, the highest grade it had awarded Greece in 18 months. Standard & Poor's cited the Samaras government's commitment to get its budget under control and carry out structural reforms as well as European countries' "determination to support Greece's eurozone membership."

Merkel, hitting a wall on Greece as it struggled to meet its commitments and yet unable to take the logical next step of letting it go, was forced to think outside the box. While not a natural German trait, who better to do it than the most unconventional chancellor of the postwar period.

Returning to her annual party convention in December 2012, this time held in Hanover, the capital of Lower Saxony state, Merkel faced re-election as CDU chairwoman as she does every two years. She took 98 percent of the votes cast, the best result in her 12 years at the party's helm and almost East German in its absolute dominance. One of the words of the year for 2012 determined by a band of German philologists was "Kanzlerpräsidentin," a compound noun which translates as Chancellor-President, signifying both her presidential style that has elevated her in the public imagination above a mere head of government to become the de facto head of state as well. A monthly "Deutschland-trend" survey by Infratest-dimap for ARD showed that voters rated the CDU/CSU twice as competent on resolving the euro-area crisis than the opposition Social Democrats. And 44 percent of those questioned said voters would back the CDU because of Merkel, with only 7 percent citing the party's policies.[13] Going into an election year that would determine whether she overtook Gerhard Schröder's record and won a third term, what was seen by Germans as her mastery of the euro crisis was Merkel's biggest campaign asset, and she was the undisputed star in her party's firmament. The test for Merkel going forward was how she would adapt to the challenge of no longer being underestimated by domestic voters or the outside world.

Notes

1. German 2005 election "Elefantenrunde": http://www.youtube.com/watch?v=IG0okkBYBVA.
2. *Bild am Sonntag*, October 6, 2001, as cited in *Die Welt*: http://www.welt.de/print-welt/article179563/Die-Kanzlerin-ueber.html.
3. Merkel speech to BGA, October 24, 2012: http://www.bundeskanzlerin.de/Content/DE/Rede/2012/10/2012-10-24-merkel-bga-unternehmertag.html.
4. OECD Country Survey for Germany 2012: http://www.oecd.org/germany/economicsurveyofgermany2012.htm.
5. Merkel speech on October 1, 2003, "Quo Vadis Deutschland" via Konrad-Adenauer-Stiftung: http://www.kas.de/wf/de/33.2830/.
6. IMF Managing Director Horst Köhler interview with *Manager Magazin*, June 20, 2003, carried on IMF website: http://www.imf.org/external/np/vc/2003/062003.htm.
7. *Der Spiegel*, August 3, 2005: http://www.spiegel.de/politik/deutschland/cdu-panne-brutto-netto-merkel-a-368085.html.
8. Six regular polls carried on http://www.wahlrecht.de.
9. Bundestag record: http://dipbt.bundestag.de/dip21/btp/16/16004.pdf#P.76.
10. Tony Czuczka and Patrick Donahue, "Merkel's Nuclear Policy Under Fire as Greens Surge in Elections," *Bloomberg News*, March 28, 2011: http://www.bloomberg.com/news/2011-03-27/merkel-s-coalition-trails-greens-surge-in-state-elections-exit-polls-say.html.
11. German state assembly seats by party: http://www.election.de/cgi-bin/content.pl?url=/ltw_bw.html.
12. "How Angela Merkel Comforted Samaras With a Story of Her Father's Eye Complaint," *Bild*, August 24, 2012: http://www.bild.de/politik/inland/griechenland-krise/merkel-troestet-samaras-25837098.bild.html.
13. DeutschlandTrend by Infratest dimap ARD television: http://www.tagesschau.de/inland/deutschlandtrend1606.pdf.

Chapter 10

Apostles
(How She Works)

Merkel's chancellery stands at the heart of the rebuilt German capital, an island of glass and concrete eight times the size of the White House. Constructed on the banks of the River Spree, the vast postmodernist structure occupies a space in the center of Berlin left blank after the war and throughout the subsequent 40 years of division. It is part of a complex of government buildings – parliamentarians' offices, committee rooms, a canteen, a creche for lawmakers' children – envisaged as a "ribbon of the federal government" binding the two sides of the city that intersected at the river, forming the East–West border until 1989.

As a statement of intent, the chancellery is anything but subtle. Architects Axel Schultes and Charlotte Frank were influenced by the monumental structures of ancient Egypt;[1] one bend in the river opposite the Reichstag building, with a gleaming stone staircase leading down to the water, evokes Thebes or Luxor. Adolf Hitler's plan for Germania, the future capital of world domination, called for the massive Hall of the People with a 290-meter-high dome and space for 180,000 people to be erected at the site. With reunification and the decision to relocate the seat of government to Berlin, driven by Helmut Kohl and carried out in 1999 during Gerhard Schröder's chancellorship, came the historic opportunity to build anew the entire center of the city after the devastation of the war. The transfer of government from Bonn posed "an epic design challenge," at the root of which lay "the painful memories of past regimes," Michael Z. Wise wrote in *Capital Dilemma: Germany's Search for a New Architecture of Democracy.* "Berlin is haunted by its history as font of Prussian militarism, seat of a failed bid at democracy under the Weimar Republic, headquarters of genocidal Nazi rule and the cold-war fault line between East and West."[2] The transition's beginning wasn't grandiose. Schröder's interim office was an old East German government building, complete with stained-glass windows depicting scenes of socialism. One of his first official acts was to join Berlin's mayor in sampling a cake ringed with marzipan bears, representing the animal on the city's coat of arms. The chancellery building, opened in 2001, was controversial. "Is it too grandiose and formal?" asked the *Architectural Review*.[3] Merkel's office describes the building in which she works as representing "openness, democracy and an awareness of history."

The act of reinstating Berlin as Germany's capital, moving it 560 kilometers (350 miles) to the east from the River Rhine, was disputed at the time even in Germany. A campaign was mounted to retain Bonn as the capital. When that failed, civil servants were offered free removals, subsidized accommodation, and counseling to help them get over the shock of the shift east. For Merkel, however, the move was a return home. She lives in the former East, does her shopping in the east, her electoral district is the city of Stralsund and the island of Rügen in Germany's far northeast by the Baltic Sea. While others continue to scorn Berlin – six ministries are still based in Bonn – Merkel is completely at ease in the capital, which she knows from childhood. Even the government retreat at Schloss Meseberg north of Berlin, leased from the Messerschmitt Foundation established by the fighter plane maker, is just 40 kilometers (25 miles) from where she grew up. British Prime Minister Margaret Thatcher and French President François Mitterrand famously opposed reunification, fearing a return of a "bad" Germany once again intent on domination of Europe. The advent of the euro crisis has achieved German preeminence by other means: by dint of its economic size, Germany is the biggest contributor to international bailouts and thus holds the key to policies adopted in the 17-member euro region. Under Merkel, Berlin and the chancellery that lies at the city's core has come to reflect Germany's status as the fulcrum of European decision making.

Inside, the chancellery is a mixture of open airy spaces, attenuated corridors running off into the distance, and nondescript meeting rooms that could be in any modern office block. In a way, that's just what it is: the building houses 370 offices and some 450 staff. Yet it is flooded with light. The floors are of Italian granite, the metallic walls are painted a color architect Axel Schultes christened Porsche Green, olive and fig trees are planted in inner courtyards. Contemporary art is everywhere, most of it German: Georg Baselitz, Bernd Zimmer, Rainer Fetting. Painter Markus Lüpertz, born in Liberec (then Reichenberg) in the Sudetenland in what is the present-day Czech Republic, devised six "color rooms" located around a central staircase, with each curved wall painted a color representing a traditional virtue: blue is for wisdom; red for courage; umber for strength or fortitude; ochre for justice; and the combination of green and white for prudence.[4]

The Cabinet meets on the sixth floor of the chancellery each Wednesday morning at 9.30 a.m. A clock is placed on the oval table around which ministers sit, a gift from Konrad Adenauer, Germany's first chancellor of the postwar period, on his departure from office in 1963 after presiding over five Cabinets.

According to Merkel, the architects "very deliberately made sure of the views of parliament from many parts of the chancellery, that goes for the Cabinet room and for my office."[5] The result of the alignment is to constantly remind the Chancellor of the primacy of parliament in exercising its legislative power and the executive role of the government charged with implementing laws.

Merkel's office is on the seventh floor, with one aspect looking south over the Tiergarten and beyond to Potsdamer Platz, the crossroads of prewar Berlin, when the city during the Weimar years was home to the likes of Albert Einstein, Marlene Dietrich and Christopher Isherwood. The other wall of Merkel's office looks east to the Sir Norman Foster-designed glass cupola of the Reichstag building. The Reichstag's original cupola was destroyed in a fire in 1933, an act of arson blamed on the communists that the Nazis used to swiftly eliminate all political opposition and cement Hitler's hold on power. During the Cold War, the building marked the very extremity of Western territory, with the Berlin Wall wrapped around its northeastern flank by the River Spree.

Merkel's bureau offers a view of 20th-century history unlike any afforded her European counterparts: no other European capital so reflects the contemporary realities of the age than Berlin. In the 21st century, when economic might has replaced military firepower, Berlin is once more at the nexus of history. Germany is coming full circle under Merkel.

For all its global importance, the court of Merkel is unusually insular, even parochial, a characteristic accentuated during the euro crisis as policy making was brought closely within the chancellery. Mistrustful by nature, she learned quickly which media needed to be stroked and which could be ignored. Merkel can give a 90-minute press conference and say nothing of news value; she feels no need to deploy a soundbite that will make the front pages. She is an atypical politician in that she doesn't seem to care much if she imparts a message or not, at least not unless it is on her terms. Briefings with senior officials are typically on a non-attributable basis. Foreign media are regularly excluded. Interviews with German media are vetted by tradition, with quotes having to be resubmitted for approval prior to publication. Unlike in the U.S. or the U.K., Merkel's speeches are never distributed in advance, partly because she likes to fiddle with them, making adjustments until the last minute.

All the same, she can be remarkably candid. Merkel doesn't dissemble, rather she openly signals her intentions. "If I take my position in a political negotiation, then that's my position," she told an interviewer before she became chancellor. "If I'm not sure that I won't have to give it up, I won't take it."[6] She won't win prizes for public speaking: she is no Obama, whose soaring rhetoric can inspire with the poetry of his convictions; in fact she is the polar opposite. But she says what she plans, telegraphing her meaning in successive speeches that never amount to a grand vision but adhere to her guiding principle of "many small steps." The trick is to interpret them.

In public, Merkel can appear severe. She publicly upbraided her deputy spokesman, Georg Streiter, during a visit by the Croatian Prime Minister Zoran Milanović in September 2012, halting a joint press conference with Milanovic to berate Streiter for talking and telling him to pipe down. In April 2009 at a NATO summit held jointly in Strasbourg and at Kehl on French and German sides of the Rhine, Merkel was visibly displeased as Italian Prime Minister Silvio Berlusconi broke with protocol and kept her waiting on the red carpet while he took a call on his mobile phone.

Early on in her first term, in May 2007, *Der Spiegel* christened Merkel "the queen of the backrooms" because of her negotiating prowess behind closed doors. In Berlin, crisis policy is kept extremely tight within a close-knit circle in the chancellery, where loyalty to Merkel is a matter of obsessive importance. She has two gatekeepers, both women, who rarely appear in public. They control who shall be granted an interview with the chancellor and who can travel on her plane on her many foreign trips. Scenes like the public infighting between Obama's economic advisers early in his first term are anathema to Merkel. Those who witness her at close hand say she approaches problems in a calm and sober manner, analyzing without becoming emotional about the situation or the people involved. Her approach to crisis fighting has evolved with developments in Greece, Italy and Spain and as the economic situation has changed. But the constants of Merkel's analytical nature coupled with her sobriety are cited as the traits that have best served her during the crisis.

Ever the scientist, her background also ensures she is unafraid of challenging conventional wisdom. Having seen an entire system collapse, when the certainties conveyed by those in charge broke down almost overnight, Merkel is wary when told that things have to be the way they are. She is always ready to question the foundations of the system. Something she never understood about Kohl, she once said, was that he clung to some policies even after it was obvious that they weren't working. During the crisis, she canvasses outside opinion so that she can best assess the course of action to take. On more than one occasion she has sought the input of the Chinese government, of Indian Prime Minister Manmohan Singh, of Russia's Vladimir Putin. She is always keen to get outside views on the euro area and its problems, however candid. Her own administration sends her articles such as papers by economists Kenneth Rogoff and Carmen Reinhart with a non–technical summary to allow her to read the latest thinking that is shaping the political debate. After all, this is a woman who told the *Frankfurter Allgemeine Zeitung* she took along the libretto of the Richard Strauss opera *Die Frau ohne Schatten* by Hugo von Hofmannsthal for summer reading in 2011 before seeing the opera in Salzburg.

Merkel took some time to digest how the financial markets function. To help her, she read the work of Polish-born mathematician Benoit Mandelbrot, who held joint French and American citizenship. Famous primarily for his work in fractal geometry that brought order to apparently random phenomena like the wind, the leaves of a fern or Britain's ragged coastline, fractal theory found applications in everything from computer graphics to the paintings of Jackson Pollock. However, Mandelbrot also studied financial markets. In 1999, he wrote a piece for *Scientific American* entitled "A Multifractal Walk down Wall Street." It was followed in 2004 by a book co-authored with Richard L. Hudson, a former managing editor of the *Wall Street Journal's* European edition, called *The (Mis) Behavior of Markets: A Fractal View of Risk, Ruin, and Reward.*[7] Merkel began to read and digest it as the euro crisis spread from 2010 and into 2011.

Chapters have subtitles including "How the operations of mere chance can be used to study a financial market" and "Orthodox financial theory is riddled with false assumptions and wrong results." It begins with a description of how Mandelbrot's father escaped death during Germany's occupation of France during World War II. Taken prisoner by the Germans, he was sprung along with the rest of the inmates by Resistance fighters who told them to run before there was time for a retaliatory attack. While the other prisoners left together, Mandelbrot senior saw danger in sticking with the crowd and took off by himself into the forest. A German Stuka dive-bomber strafed the road along which the prisoners were traveling; Mandelbrot, by taking his own path home, was unhurt. Meant to illustrate the unorthodox thinking of the author, who was professor of mathematical sciences at Yale University until his death in 2010, it might also serve for Merkel's approach to tackling the financial crisis.

"From the start, Mandelbrot has approached the market as a scientist, both experimental and theoretical," Hudson writes in the book's prelude. Noting that the economics establishment "finds him intriguing,

and has grudgingly adopted many of his ideas," Hudson says "the establishment also finds him bewildering." Not Merkel: She became fascinated with the theory that financial actors and policy makers always
assume normal distribution and hence underestimate "tail risk," according to a person familiar with her economic reading. She would confront her guests with her new-found knowledge, asking them "What
do you think of the fat tail theory?"

Unlike some of her counterparts, Merkel consults widely to better
formulate her approach to policy making. She is not given to snap,
intuitive decisions, but is rather very deliberate in the way she reaches
her conclusions. Each year she invites the heads of the main international economic organizations to the chancellery for a discussion
on policy as it relates to Germany. Most recently, in October 2012,
she discussed competitiveness with IMF chief Christine Lagarde,
Ángel Gurría of the Organization for Economic Cooperation and
Development, the World Bank's Jim Yong Kim, Pascal Lamy of the
World Trade Organization and head of the International Labour
Organization, Guy Ryder.

"She's full of just downright common sense and she's very
approachable," says Gurría, the OECD's secretary general. "She listens,
she asks questions and she doesn't seem to have all the answers. She
may or may not like what you're saying or may or may not agree, but
she wants to listen. She wants the input, for the evidence."

In such meetings, she speaks German while the others use English
even though her English is fairly good. She sticks to the agenda, dealing thoroughly with each item in order, checking them off methodi-
cally before moving on to the next subject. Later, over dinner, she'll
speak English when the discussion is more relaxed and wide ranging.
French President François Hollande emulated Merkel's consultation
with the same group after his election.

Merkel's desire to take counsel can prompt her to change her
mind, a sign of humility and ultimately leadership, according to Gurría.
"If you have a scientific method, mind, and you find out that reality is
different than you thought, you change your mind, you change your
way," he says. "It takes some humility. It takes wisdom to have
your mind open to new facts, opinions and points of view. It also means

that you leave your thoughts, your convictions and also your ego at the entrance."

All the same, simply by exercising it she has become increasingly comfortable with Germany's leadership role in Europe, growing accustomed to the fact that little can be achieved without her giving the final word on policy issues during the crisis. Merkel's willingness to consult can help bring about a convergence of views, said Gurría.

"What is very important is that she is looking to put herself in the shoes of others. She may or may not share [their view], but she at least wants to know what's in the minds of others who think differently from her," he says. "It's not nice to go to Greece and have thousands of people with banners and burning your effigy – but in order to talk to the leader, this is a question of courtesy but it's also a signal.

"Let's not forget these are not people like us. They have been touched with the vote, which makes them different. They have also been touched by another element: they lead. They are the ones who set the roadmap and that makes the leaders different. And when you see one that is literally reaching out to the others to say: OK, tell me your story and I'll tell you mine. We may or may not agree, but at least we'll understand each other better. That has made her better today. She understands better what's going on because she reached out. She got out of the chancellery to find out. These are things that are in classic literature since the beginning of time, when the prince would disguise himself and find what people really wanted. Here you can't disguise yourself but certainly go out and talk to the interlocutors."

Merkel adopts a similar tone when negotiating with fellow leaders. She takes command in meetings, setting aside all chit-chat and getting straight to the point. She has an agenda and wants to go through it, checking off each item. She doesn't like to beat around the bush. In one meeting, she challenged then-Greek Prime Minister George Papandreou directly on his inability to stick to agreed targets in return for international aid. "Why are you not doing more on privatization?" she asked. In private, she likes to joke and is a congenial host. In the words of one southern European official, when business is over, however difficult it may have been, she is the model of hospitality: she comes across as a woman who has invited you into her house and takes care of you.

"High Politics, Housewife-Style," ran the headline in a regional newspaper, the *Märkische Allgemeine*, after Merkel's post-summer press conference in 2012. Indeed, the chancellor's nickname in Berlin political circles is "Mutti," or mom, because of her maternal ways, whether a concern for others or a scolding. Merkel is actually childless. German media have conjectured that the name may have originated with her former economy minister, Michael Glos, who resigned from the Cabinet in February 2009 feeling he had been poorly treated by Merkel. The term "manages to combine respect, subservience and insult in one," according to *Der Spiegel*. It dubbed Merkel's approach to governing, "Mutti politics," which it boiled down to trying to please everyone.[8] Certainly, after she won a second term, Merkel said that she aimed to be the "chancellor of all Germans." In the years since the euro crisis erupted, however, she has moved on from a mom to a matriarchal figure with absolute power over her household: her party, her coalition, and her regional adversaries – leaders with power bases in the states who might one day have challenged her. Her sway over Europe cements her position.

Merkel's role model is Catherine the Great, the Prussian princess who ruled Russia alone for 34 years. Merkel has a small portrait of Catherine alongside a globe on her office desk in the chancellery, a gift from before her time as chancellor, when she was leader of the CDU parliamentary group. Asked on a television show what she admired in Catherine, Merkel said she "was very courageous and accomplished many things under difficult circumstances." She also cited her ability as a "clever strategist."[9]

Catherine was born Sophia Augusta Fredericka in 1729 in the Pomeranian port city of Stettin – present day Szczecin in northwestern Poland – the daughter of the Prince of Anhalt-Zerbst, who was the city's governor, a Prussian general, and a devout Lutheran. Using her mother's royal connections, she determined early on to ascend to the Russian throne. She learned Russian, changed her name to the more acceptable Yekaterina, or Catherine, and abandoned her Protestant faith for Russian orthodoxy. After 17 years of marriage to the prospective czar, Peter III, she conspired to have him overthrown as soon as he succeeded to the throne. In 1762, just six months after he became czar, he was deposed and killed during a palace coup and Catherine became empress of Russia. She went on to rule until her death in 1796, expanding Russian territory to the south and the west during what came to be known as a golden age for Russia.

Merkel has read the journals of Catherine the Great and discussed her with Vladimir Putin. While the parallels are easy to make – both women came from similar geographical areas, had strongly Lutheran fathers and extraordinary levels of drive, and both prevailed over their male counterparts – Merkel never mentions Catherine other than on the rare occasion she is asked. If she genuinely sees Catherine the Great as a role model, it is another aspect of her life that she prefers to keep to herself.

Directly opposite Merkel's desk in the chancellery, several wooden chess figures stand knee-high by the south-facing window, gifts from the German forest-owners' association. The first chess piece she received upon becoming chancellor was a queen; she was subsequently given two pawns and a king.

Merkel is "an excellent chess player," according to Xavier Musca, Sarkozy's former chief economic adviser. "She never starts by putting all the cards on the table and saying, 'that's what I want to do'." That was a significant difference she had with the French president and which gave her the upper hand in the beginning. She would also canvass civil servants for their views of a specific problem, discussing the issue with the whole team.

Merkel was dismayed when Sarkozy brandished any concession he had won from her, as she kept quiet about whatever political bartering had taken place. It led to her being reproached domestically for sacrificing German interests and being too lenient toward the French. Merkel was transparent during negotiations on the constraints put on her by the need to satisfy her coalition and to retain a majority in parliamentary votes, by the Bundesrat, the Bundesbank and the high court. Musca recalls one caricature in a German newspaper depicting Sarkozy and Merkel as prehistoric cave dwellers, he beating her over the head with a club.

In 2011, Sarkozy realized he was making it more difficult for her to agree to crisis-fighting measures and revised his approach to dealing with Merkel: he no longer proclaimed the concessions he had wrung from her and stopped presenting his positions up front. After meetings, they would claim a united front on tackling the crisis, even when it was evidently not the case. "For the sake of Europe, he chose another way, which was politically, domestically extremely difficult – to be silent," Musca says. "The discrepancy between the German and the French line was destroying Europe and was also detrimental to France because it would put France in the camp of the southern countries" that were in trouble and demanding more help from Germany.

Merkel, while candid on her constraints, is not afraid of appearing at odds with her own Cabinet members in discussions. In one meeting with European counterparts on the debt crisis, she openly told those attending that she disagreed with her finance minister, Wolfgang Schäuble, on purchasing government bonds on the secondary market as a means of calming the bond markets. Those present were taken aback at her frankness.

She can be tough. Merkel is known to raise her voice at times to shout at her political adversaries, and it can be fearsome. One target of her temper was cited anonymously in *Die Welt* newspaper as relating the experience with a mixture of shock, perplexity and respect. It was clear that he never wanted to be confronted by a wrathful Merkel again.[10] Merkel admits she had temper outbursts as a child, boiling over when a series of grievances had built up.[11]

In May 2012, Environment Minister Norbert Röttgen witnessed her displeasure, becoming the first and only Cabinet minister to be dismissed from his post during Merkel's term. Röttgen was in charge of the transition to renewable sources of power from nuclear – the biggest energy overhaul in German history – after Merkel abandoned her support for atomic power in response to the 2011 tsunami and nuclear disaster at Fukushima. Among Merkel's closest confidantes, Röttgen had been touted as a possible chancellor one day, but to advance up the political ladder the more swiftly he needed a regional power base. So he took on the additional role of leading the Christian Democratic Union in North Rhine-Westphalia into regional elections. He made a name for himself for the wrong reasons, fighting a lackluster campaign that ended in Merkel's party falling to its worst-ever electoral result in the state.

North Rhine-Westphalia was more than just politically significant as the most populous of Germany's 16 states. It was symbolically important for Merkel. Two years earlier, in May 2010, the main opposition

Social Democratic Party had snatched the state from Merkel's CDU at an election overshadowed by voter anger at her last-minute decision to aid Greece. Her about-turn then cost her the state and her majority in the upper house, the Bundesrat. She wanted it back, and personally campaigned for Röttgen in North Rhine-Westphalia at least nine times.

He repaid her by leading the CDU to a postwar low score of 26 percent, a drop of more than 8 points on the last result. Not only did he fail to recapture the state, but the Social Democrats' vote share increased to 39.1 percent, allowing them to form a more stable government with the Greens. Hannelore Kraft was returned as North Rhine-Westphalia's state premier and went on to challenge Merkel's popularity in national opinion polls. If ever there was a regional election with national ramifications, this was it.

Yet the dismal result shouldn't have had any impact on Röttgen's ability to carry out his role as a Cabinet minister. *Bild* ran an unsourced story saying that before she dismissed him, Merkel had talked to industry officials who complained that Röttgen didn't listen to them over the energy transition. The reality was that he had lost Merkel's trust and that of his party and had to go: three days after the election, she fired him. Merkel never gave a reason for her decision. In a hastily convened statement to the press lasting just 1 minute and 40 seconds, she said simply that, in accordance with Article 64 of the constitution, she had asked the president to release Röttgen of his duties. "The energy overhaul is a central theme of this legislative period," she said. "The foundations have been laid, but we've got quite a bit of work ahead of us." She thanked Röttgen for his work and nominated in his stead Peter Altmaier, her party's chief whip and a close confidant. Merkel had come to her conclusion, and moved swiftly: Röttgen's Cabinet career lay in tatters.

Altmaier and Röttgen, who was CDU chief whip during her first term, were both members of Merkel's inner circle. In November 2005, they were among a select band of Merkel loyalists who attended a party in the chancellery held on the occasion of her election. *Focus* magazine reported that the others included Willi Hausmann, a close adviser from her time as families minister under Kohl; Volker Kauder, a lawmaker from Rottweil in Baden-Württemberg who followed Merkel as CDU/CSU floor leader; Ronald Pofalla, the CDU general secretary whom Merkel appointed her chief of staff in her second term; and Peter Hintze, a deputy minister in the Economy Ministry who as the official responsible for aerospace matters was instrumental in Germany's decision to block a proposed merger of EADS and BAE Systems in October 2012.[12] Hintze, who trained as a Protestant theologian, has since 2002 been a vice president of the European People's Party, the umbrella group of European center-right parties including Merkel's CDU, a position that puts him at the heart of EU strategizing.

Altmaier, the lawyer son of a miner and a nurse, worked at the EU Commission in his early career until his election to the Bundestag in 1994. In Merkel's first term he served at the Interior Ministry as deputy to Wolfgang Schäuble until 2009. He grew up in the Saarland on Germany's western flank, bordering Luxembourg and France. Now he is tasked with running the most politically charged ministry after that of finance, one that might yet trip up the chancellor over her decision to overhaul the power mix keeping Europe's biggest economy turning.

He sees the chancellor's greatest strengths as a cool head, an ability to laugh and a willingness to listen to other viewpoints. "Even in the most difficult situations, Mrs. Merkel doesn't lose her calm consideration," he said. "She has humor. And she allows herself to be convinced through argument."[13]

Those character traits are the secret ingredient that have helped her to master the complex, existential problems posed by the crisis in the euro area while retaining public support, according to Altmaier. "To govern successfully requires the ability not to be pressured by events and to stick to what you hold to be right even in the face of resistance," he says. "Mrs. Merkel has both qualities, and both have helped her during the euro crisis in successfully confronting countries like Greece or Italy as well as shoring up her profile domestically." While investors, political foes and media pundits accuse Merkel of lacking vision, opinion surveys suggest German voters trust her. A December 2012 poll for *Stern* magazine found 76 percent view Merkel as a strong leader and 56 percent say she is "trustworthy." Peer Steinbrück, her designated Social Democratic challenger in the 2013 general election, was rated a strong leader by 49 percent.[14]

It may not prove to be enough. Merkel may have to abandon her iron ways and learn to give ground on Europe if she is to succeed in pressing her agenda. With Sarkozy's defeat to François Hollande at France's presidential elections in May 2012, Merkel lost her foil during the crisis. The demise of Merkozy meant the dissolution of a partnership forged over five years of tackling financial and economic turmoil. Merkel was forced to start from scratch with a political leader she campaigned against and who makes clear his alignment with the southern arc of Spain and Italy in rejecting her antidote of austerity. In private, the chancellor concedes she is still very much finding her way with Hollande.

Horst Teltschik, who served as Helmut Kohl's deputy chief of staff, advising him during the diplomacy that led to German reunification, says Merkel will have to learn to be more sensitive to Hollande's concerns. Just as Kohl bent over backwards to take into account the sensitivities of his French counterpart, François Mitterrand, so she needs to grant Hollande the space he needs to rally domestic French support for the economic reforms necessary and to get him on board for her European agenda. That may mean allowing him to trumpet the concessions he gains from her, something she railed against with Sarkozy.

"It's hard for the French to take Germany as a role model. Kohl used to always say 'I salute the French tricolor three times before I turn to the German flag'," Teltschik said. "Kohl always tried to make it easier for the French to take joint decisions and make reforms. Merkel has to think about what she can do to make Hollande's domestic policy decision making easier."

Under her leadership, Berlin has moved from the eastern periphery of Europe to its core. She has unprecedented sway to take Europe in whichever direction she wants. The irony is that she may have to cede some of that power if she wants to get France back on board. She faces a choice: go it alone, breaking with Germany's entire postwar philosophy on Europe, or bend and do more to get others, notably France, back at her side. "Merkel is in the dominant role in Europe, though it's not something she has sought," Teltschik says. "Germany is now in its most dominant role in Europe since World War II. So the question is, does Merkel make it easier for Hollande to agree to a new agenda or not?"[15]

Nineteenth-century German author Theodor Fontane wrote a description of Berliners that could equally apply to Merkel and her time as chancellor. Fontane was born in Neuruppin, less than 65 kilometers

(40 miles) from Merkel's hometown of Templin, and was a pioneering German proponent of the novel through works such as *Effi Briest*. He also wrote about his wanderings in Scotland and through the Prussian state of Brandenburg which he and Merkel called home a little more than a century apart. Among his travels, in 1870 he went to the front to witness the Franco-Prussian war in eastern France, where he was captured and held prisoner for three months. The Berlin way, wrote Fontaine, is to be "frank and sincere." Yet "hidden behind is a whole lot of shrewdness." The following year, 1871, France was defeated and the German states unified under the Prussian leader Otto von Bismarck, the first Iron Chancellor, with Berlin his capital. Modern Germany was born and the face of Europe changed irrevocably.

Notes

1. Catherine Croft, *Concrete Architecture* (Gibbs Smith, October 2004).
2. Michael Z. Wise, *Capital Dilemma: Germany's Search for a New Architecture of Democracy* (Princeton Architectural Press, April 1998).
3. Catherine Croft, *Concrete Architecture* (Gibbs Smith, October 2004).
4. Tour of the chancellery: http://www.bundeskanzlerin.de/Webs/BKin/DE/Kanzleramt/Rundgang/rundgang_node.html.
5. Ibid.
6. Angela Merkel, *Mein Weg: Ein Gespräch mit Hugo Müller-Vogg*, p. 121 (Hoffmann und Campe Verlag, Hamburg, 2005).
7. Benoit B. Mandelbrot and Richard L. Hudson, *The (Mis) Behavior of Markets: A Fractal View of Risk, Ruin, and Reward* (Profile Books, November 2008).
8. "Angela the Great or Just Mom?" *Der Spiegel*, November 3, 2009: http://www.spiegel.de/international/germany/angela-the-great-or-just-mom-merkel-s-dream-of-a-place-in-the-history-books-a-659018.html.
9. Ibid.
10. "The EU Today is Angela Merkel's GDR," *Die Welt*, May 2, 2012: http://www.welt.de/politik/deutschland/article13850962/Die-EU-ist-heute-Angela-Merkels-DDR.html.
11. *Mein Weg*, op. cit.
12. *Focus Magazin*, November 28, 2005: http://www.focus.de/politik/deutschland/kanzlerin-aller-anfang-ist-leer_aid_209905.html.
13. Interview courtesy of Stefan Nicola.
14. *Stern*, December 5, 2012: http://mobil.stern.de/politik/deutschland/stern-umfrage-zu-peer-steinbrueck-guter-kandidat-mit-schlechten-chancen-1936800.html.
15. Interview courtesy of Leon Mangasarian.

Chapter 11

Proverbs (Where To?)

For a glimpse of Europe's future, go back to December 2011 and a meeting of EU leaders in Brussels. There, at the traditional post-summit briefing for journalists, Angela Merkel began by hailing a decision to grant Croatia entry to the EU club, saying it "once more shows that the idea of European unity hasn't lost its draw – in fact, perhaps the opposite." The accession of a new member "is a signal that every effort for Europe and the euro is worthwhile." She was speaking on the morning after an all-night meeting of the EU's 27 leaders which ended in success for Merkel and defeat for Prime Minister David Cameron, who managed only to sideline the U.K. Poland, the biggest of the eastern members, which is accorded equal voting rights to Spain, took Germany's side.

Merkel had gone into the talks intent on securing agreement for her plan to tighten the rules on limiting debt and deficits to tackle the root cause of the crisis in the euro region by ensuring that no country was able to flout with impunity the existing Stability and Growth Pact. It had been broken 60 times in all, most notably by Germany itself for three years running under her predecessor, Gerhard Schröder, and Merkel determined to shut off that avenue for good. She pushed for new budget constraints to be inserted into each country's constitution with the European Court of Justice patrolling the rules, but to do so she needed agreement to alter the EU's treaty.

Fellow European leaders remembered the EU's ponderous attempt in 2004 to enact a single constitution which was knocked down in referendums the following year in France and the Netherlands, and some had expressed reservations about the prospect of more treaty change becoming similarly bogged down. Cameron said he was prepared to veto any such move. Ana Palacio, the former Spanish foreign minister and Senior Vice President of the World Bank who served as a member of the European Parliament for eight years, said the entire EU was "paralyzed by the navel-gazing attitude of a Germany beset by 90-year-old memories of the doomed Weimar Republic."[1]

Merkel was unsure how much support she would receive at the summit. While she wanted all 27 member states to sign up to her fiscal treaty, she'd settle for however many she could get. "We are absolutely determined to say the euro is so important to us that we'll go with the 17 euro nations and be open to others who wish to come along," she said in Paris on December 5 at a press conference with France's Nicolas Sarkozy as they laid out their joint position three days before the summit.

During the talks in an unseasonably mild Brussels, Cameron bet all his cards on gaining assurances that London would remain immune to future EU finance measures. When Merkel and Sarkozy refused to grant the blanket guarantee he sought, Cameron rejected the notion of treaty change, safe in the knowledge that refusing to sign up to a European concept promoted by Germany would prove popular in his English heartlands. Cameron appeared ill-prepared for the summit, with no fallback position and little grasp of the detail, according to officials present. He relied too much on the support of other non-euro countries mainly in Scandinavia and Eastern Europe. What he failed to appreciate was Merkel's resolve, her prowess in European negotiations of this kind, and her long-standing connections with the EU's Eastern members.

Merkel emerged in the early hours of the next morning with what would turn out to be the backing of 25 of the 27 EU states, after the Czech Republic sided with the U.K. She singled out for praise Poland's Prime Minister Donald Tusk for rallying to her cause. Those with her would enact the necessary legislation through their own parliaments, resulting in what was called a "fiscal compact" rather than a new treaty.

The U.K. delegation briefed the British press that Cameron had exercised his veto to scupper the treaty, and said he would fight to stop the others from using the EU institutions to further their fiscal compact. However, as *The Economist*'s Bagehot columnist noted on his blog, Cameron did not stop the 17 euro countries from going ahead with their plan, nor did he win safeguards for the City in the face of French and German opposition, therefore he did not veto anything.[2] Thus, Cameron became the latest leader to underestimate Merkel.

At her press briefing later that morning, Merkel reveled in the support she had received from all corners of Europe. It was a moment that signaled her dominance of the EU, Cameron's abjuration notwithstanding. "There was only one country that clearly stayed more at a distance and that was Great Britain," Merkel said. "But I want to stress once more – and this was also made clear in talks with David Cameron – Great Britain is just as reliant on a stable euro as we all are because it affects the economic situation in all of Europe. That means we're all in the same boat."[3] Noting that it was exactly 20 years since European leaders agreed on the Maastricht treaty that created the EU and the euro, Merkel said those states that had chosen to go along with her fiscal compact were helping to chart the future political direction of the European Union. "This is the breakthrough to a union of stability," she said. "The stability union, fiscal union, will be developed step-by-step over the coming years, but the breakthrough to this union has now been achieved." Alongside, the political union that was omitted at the euro's birth will inevitably make progress, she said, reversing the order proclaimed by Helmut Kohl after German reunification.

The same summit brought forward the start date of the permanent rescue fund, the European Stability Mechanism (ESM), by one year to 2012 and finally buried Merkel's push, announced with Sarkozy at Deauville 14 months earlier, for private investors to take compulsory losses on their government bond holdings under the ESM. All future proceedings would adhere to standard IMF practice while Greece, which was about to undergo the biggest debt restructuring in history, was a "special case." At a stroke, one of the most divisive issues of the debt crisis was removed from the agenda, one that had been blamed for worsening the turmoil by further undermining trust in the euro area. For the German chancellor, what mattered was that the way to her chosen path for Europe had been cleared – despite the U.K., with the support of France and the help of Poland as a conduit to the east. "The message of this European Council meeting is clear," Merkel said. "We're using the crisis as an opportunity for a new beginning."

An indication of the fresh start Merkel was alluding to could be seen 11 days previously in a ground-breaking call for German leadership issued by Polish Foreign Minister Radek Sikorski, an Oxford-educated former journalist. Sikorski used a speech to the German Council on Foreign Relations in Berlin, a foreign-policy think tank, to open a critique of Europe's crisis-fighting strategy and to demand that Germany – read Merkel – step up and lead. If she did so, Poland would be at her side. The greatest threat to the security and prosperity of Poland today "is not terrorism, it's not the Taliban, and it's certainly not German tanks. It's not even Russian missiles," which the Russian president had just threatened to deploy along the EU's eastern border. The biggest threat we face is the collapse of the eurozone, Sikorski said.

"And I demand of Germany that, for your own sake and for ours, you help it survive and prosper. You know full well that nobody else can do it. I will probably be the first Polish foreign minister in history to say so, but here it is: I fear German power less than I am beginning to fear German inactivity. You have become Europe's indispensable nation. You may not fail to lead. Not dominate, but to lead in reform. Provided you include us in decision-making, Poland will support you."[4]

He listed a series of measures to make Europe more governable, from synchronizing labor, pensions and social policies through establishing the EU Commission as a genuine economic supervisor of states to making the ECB the lender of last resort. The aim must be to restore credibility by building "institutions, procedures, sanctions that will convince investors that countries will be capable of living within their means." Europe faces a stark choice, he said: deeper integration or collapse. It was a prescription at odds with the U.K.'s vision of a Europe primarily focused on the single market and clearly signaled Poland's alignment with Germany, so long as Merkel grasped the opportunity to save the euro as she repeatedly said was her goal.

Sikorski also had a message for Britain, which he said gave the EU its common language, developed the single market, and offered an indispensable link to the U.S. All the same, it's dangerously over-indebted and can't simply expect to walk away from the consequences of euro-zone collapse. "We would prefer you in, but if you can't join, please allow us to forge ahead," he said. "And please start explaining to your people that European decisions are not Brussels diktats but results of agreements in which you freely participate."

Norman Davies, the British historian who has written widely on Poland, Europe and Britain, singled out Sikorski's speech as a turning point, with Poland's relationship with Germany the pivot. Davies, whose works include *God's Playground* and *Europe: A History*, said that for historical reasons Germans were full of complexes and had traditionally left political leadership to France, but that in an EU of 27 countries that was no longer acceptable.

"Sikorski's call is for rapid political reorganization to provide common structures to deal with economic problems," Davies said in an interview for Polonia.nl, a website catering to Poles in the Netherlands. "This signals a shift in political patterns in Europe. New member states like Poland were naturally reluctant to take the lead. It could well be that Poland, whose economy is now in better shape than it ever was, could become one of the political leaders in Europe."[5]

Davies said that Poles, like all the peoples of Eastern Europe, understand the threat posed by the euro area's troubles better than those in the West since they are acutely aware that systems can collapse – from the breakup of the Soviet Union, the withdrawal of Soviet troops and equipment stationed on their territory, through rapid economic and monetary collapse with hyperinflation in 1989: the Polish state had to be rebuilt and the foundations for the market economy laid. "They have seen a systematic collapse in their lifetimes," he said. "People in the West have forgotten. You have to be 80 years old to remember World War II and since then everything here was getting better."

More than 65 years after the end of the war, Sikorski's speech demonstrated that there was greater convergence on Europe between Germany and Poland than Poland now shares with its wartime ally, the U.K. The Warsaw rising of 1944, the systematic German destruction of the Polish capital, and the abomination of Nazi concentration camps located on Polish territory serve to underline the importance of the founding ethos of the European Union: to make war on the continent impossible. It is not surprising if Poland opts for Merkel's view of a more closely integrated Europe over British euro-skepticism. For

Merkel, who witnessed collapse first-hand with the rapid degeneration of East Germany, Poland is every bit as natural an ally as France.

On November 15, 1989, less than a week after the Berlin Wall fell and the way to the West was opened, Angela Merkel took the train east to Poland. She traveled to the city of Toruń on the banks of the great River Vistula, where she was due to speak at a physics seminar at the Nicolaus Copernicus University, named in honor of the Renaissance mathematician and astronomer who is the city's most famous son. Merkel was to deliver a speech on an aspect of chemical physics known as electron paramagnetic resonance (EPR) spectroscopy, which facilitates the study of chemical reactions at molecular level. She was picked up from the railway station by some Polish friends, who expressed astonishment that she had shown up. "We were convinced you wouldn't come," they told her. "How could you come when just six days ago the wall fell – when world events were taking place in Berlin and Germany stands to be united next year? What are you doing here?" Whether typically Merkel, typically German or perhaps a bit of both, she saw it as her duty to fulfill her commitment to speak, Merkel related more than two decades later.[6] "The Polish hosts at Toruń university were pleased, and a speech on EPR spectroscopy has its exciting and lively sides, even in epochal times of change," she said. "Perhaps too I was keen to travel to Toruń because I already realized what we all now know: We Germans can never forget that it was the Poles, Solidarnosc and the power of Pope John Paul II that first set Germany and Europe on the path to freedom." Merkel's relationship with Poland goes back to childhood: her mother was born in Gdansk, Prime Minister Tusk's home city. In common with most Germans, Merkel refers to Polish cities by their German names – Danzig for Gdansk, Thorn for Toruń, Breslau for Wroclaw, Bromberg for Bydgoszcz – since many cities and regions of Poland were at one time part of Prussia or home to significant German-speaking communities before most of them were expelled after World War II. She has described Gdansk as a "melting pot of Polish, Kashubian and German tradition," a centuries-old Hanseatic port and trading metropolis which "serves as a symbol of the regional diversity of Europe."[7]

While Merkel doesn't flaunt her Central European connection, she has mentioned having "Polish parts of my family" on her grandfather's side and attributes aspects of her personality to the region. "Sometimes, for instance when I get that pensive or melancholy look, I think it's the Slavic element coming through."[8] Marek Prawda, who served as Polish ambassador to Germany for six years, recalls Merkel telling director Andrzej Wajda at a screening in Berlin that she went to Gdansk as a doctoral student and saw *Man of Iron*, his 1981 anti-communist film about Solidarity. Led by strike organizer Lech Walesa, the independent labor union had been born in the city's Lenin Shipyard the year before. Though she didn't understand the Polish soundtrack and had to travel all night by train, Merkel could "breathe a bit more freely" in Gdansk compared with Stalinist East Germany. Nostalgia aside, Merkel's background and Tusk's premiership are shifting a relationship framed for decades by recrimination rooted in World War II. In 2011, Prawda gave Merkel and her husband a private two-hour tour of an art exhibit in Berlin marking 1,000 years of Polish–German history, reminders of the Nazis' atrocities included. "We talked a lot about German–Polish relations, about this phase in which we are really looking forward," Prawda said. "European policy has given us the means to make them rational so we are not constantly standing in front of the old backdrop."[9]

Gdansk, where the first shots of World War II were fired on the Westerplatte peninsula as the Germans invaded, was the scene of Nobel Prize-winning novelist Günter Grass's *The Tin Drum*. It was also the birthplace of the Solidarity trade union movement, Solidarnosc in Polish, which Lech Walesa led out of the Lenin Shipyard and ultimately into power. East Germans were regular visitors to Poland until the authorities clamped down on travel with the official formation of Solidarity in 1980. As Merkel said: "The road to freedom and European unity began at the Gdansk shipyard gate and led from there to the Brandenburg Gate." In office, Merkel waited until her second term to develop Polish relations. Her foreign minister, Guido Westerwelle, was dispatched to Poland on his first trip upon assuming the post in late 2009. German President Joachim Gauck also chose Warsaw for his first official foreign trip, in March 2012. Merkel and her husband paid a private visit to Polish President Bronislaw Komorowski on the Baltic

Sea peninsula of Hel and nearby Gdansk in July 2011, a highly unusual event for the chancellor, who prefers to spend spare time at her home in rural Brandenburg. The German Foreign Ministry says there is a "new quality" to bilateral relations, especially since Tusk came to power in 2007.

After the big bang of EU enlargement to the east in 2004, only Ireland, the U.K. and Sweden opened up their labor markets to workers from Poland and the new member states; Germany did not. With German unemployment then on the rise, reaching a postwar record in early 2005, allowing unfettered access to Polish workers was a political risk that Chancellor Schröder was not prepared to take. Those restrictions were lifted on May 1, 2011, and Poles are now largely free to work in Germany, where the jobless rate has since halved. As of the end of 2011, there were 1.5 million ethnic Poles in Germany, constituting the second-largest immigrant population after Turks, who numbered 3 million.[10] With Poland's unemployment rate forecast by the EU Commission to rise to 10.8 percent in 2013, almost double the rate in Germany, the movement of workers looked likely to continue.[11]

All the same, the outlook for Poland's economy is for growth of 1.2 percent in 2013 and 2.2 percent in 2014, faster than Germany's 0.5 percent and 2 percent respectively and a blistering pace compared to the 0.3 percent contraction and 1.4 percent growth forecast for the 17-nation euro area.[12] While Germany has been Poland's most important trading partner for the two decades since the fall of communism, as prosperity has grown so Poland has gained in economic importance: from nowhere, it is now Germany's No. 10 biggest trading partner. Bilateral trade was worth 76 billion euros in 2011, and more than 25 percent of Polish exports now head west over the rivers Oder and Neisse (Odra and Nysa in Polish) to Germany.[13] That will help Poland's budget deficit to narrow to 3.3 percent of GDP in 2013 before reaching the EU's 3 percent limit in 2014, a trajectory of prudence that Merkel has praised.

Merkel and her Cabinet colleagues convene each year for joint government consultations with their Polish counterparts under Tusk, an honor otherwise reserved for France, Italy, Spain, and Russia in Europe. Merkel inaugurated similar joint Cabinet meetings with Israel in 2008, then China and India in 2011. At the most recent such meeting, in November 2012 in Berlin, Merkel and Tusk agreed to pursue joint marine and air surveillance missions in the Baltic region, upgrade rail links, and better tackle cross-border crime. They also discussed the upcoming EU summit and their differing positions on the EU's seven-year budget, with Merkel keener to clamp down on costs than Tusk. "European policy is increasingly a kind of domestic policy," she said. The joint meetings date from the German–Polish treaty on neighborly relations signed in 1991 by Helmut Kohl and then-Polish Prime Minister Jan Krzysztof Bielecki as the start of "practical reconciliation" of both peoples. It followed bickering over Kohl's timetable for Germany to recognize Poland's western border, a sore point that links back to the Nazi invasion at the start of World War II. The two countries finally signed the border treaty in 1990 in Warsaw, six weeks after German reunification.

Under Merkel, the debt crisis became the catalyst for upgrading the relationship from neighbors to partners. To her mind, Poland's transition from communism and economic collapse to prosperity by way of bold reforms and hard work exemplifies the mindset and policies needed to beat the crisis. It's precisely where she wants all of Europe to be so the continent can compete in an ever more globalized economy. She views Tusk as a reliable partner who has proven his worth, from his student days working with Solidarity in Gdansk to his determination in directing Poland toward Europe and away from the kind of euro-skepticism seen in the Czech Republic. Poland's proximity and potential clout as a nation of more 38 million people, the fifth most populous continental country after Germany, France, Italy and Spain, makes it an obvious partner if the political constellation is right. Marek Prawda, who was named Polish ambassador to the EU in 2012, noticed a "remarkable confluence" between Poland and Germany when the debt crisis and Merkel's response to it became Europe's dominant topic. "That was the first time I sensed that we in Poland understand instinctively what Merkel is trying to say," said Prawda. "You can date a sense of closeness about the diagnosis back to that time." Suddenly, German politicians who viewed Poland as a poor cousin were asking about the country's 1997 constitutional amendment that caps national debt at 60 percent of GDP, the same limit that applies to countries using the euro. Freedom for Poland also means low financing costs for its government, a "typically Eastern European view" that resonates with Merkel, according to Prawda. "We have gotten to the point where each country has something to offer the other."

When Tusk was awarded the Germany-based Charlemagne Prize in 2010 for his European engagement, Merkel – who was afforded the same honor two years earlier – delivered the keynote speech. She again spoke in his honor in May 2012 when Tusk was awarded the Walther Rathenau Prize for his work on European integration and in promoting German–Polish reconciliation. Merkel, addressing him as "dear Donald," said his call for more Europe "spoke to my heart" because "it's precisely during the current crisis in the euro area that teaches us we need more Europe and not less. Curing the symptoms alone isn't enough. We need structural reforms to tackle the root of the crisis and prevent it ever being repeated again – in the euro area as in the European Union as a whole. That requires a lot of perseverance and strength." Poland, she said, can serve as the template. Its deep reforms during the 1990s meant that "many lost their jobs, many more doubted the necessity of the drastic cuts and the majority questioned the point." Even in Gdansk, the well-spring of the freedom that swept across Europe, many former Solidarity members were embittered by the radically changing face of the labor market, she said. "That's why the people of Poland can understand especially well the difficult situation that people for example in Greece find themselves. But we also know that back then in the 1990s Poland laid the foundations of its economic upswing – as a result, it was the only EU country to come through the recent global economic crisis in the black. So however bitter the efforts were, they've paid off."[14]

West Germany's rapprochement with Eastern Europe, known as Ostpolitik, was begun by Social Democratic Chancellor Willy Brandt, who famously fell to his knees at the memorial to the Warsaw ghetto in 1970. Brandt was deliberately turning away from the course of confrontation adopted by his Christian Democratic predecessors, most notably Konrad Adenauer, in an attempt to normalize West Germany's relations with its eastern neighbors. Merkel has the option of bringing that policy to its logical conclusion as she channels the experiences of the eastern countries she knows so well into the service of Europe.

The "Weimar Triangle" of Germany, France and Poland is one possible vehicle. The three countries' leaders have met only twice since

Merkel took office in late 2005. Summits have been sporadic as first Poland suffered economic difficulty, then flirted with euro-skepticism under twin-brother leaders Lech and Jaroslaw Kaczyński, and as Sarkozy and Merkel forged a bilateral approach to tackling the crisis in the euro area. The forum has scope to take on renewed significance if Merkel wins re-election in 2013, particularly in relation to economic policy as the emphasis shifts from crisis resolution to longer term measures to promote growth and deepen European integration. During Merkel's second term, "Germany has emphasized its intention to intensify German–Polish cooperation and to place it on a similar level as its relations with France," Kai-Olaf Lang and Daniela Schwarzer wrote in a paper for the German Institute for International and Security Affairs.[15] Poland, they note, is now seen as especially important to Germany since it is following a budget and spending policy focused on financial stability. "In times of crises and turmoil it is certainly the pressing challenges of economic and financial policy where joint Weimar initiatives could be profitable for the EU," they said. At joint government consultations in Warsaw in June 2011, Merkel and Tusk drew up an ambitious agenda for cooperation, "including the idea of a German–Polish partnership for Europe."

The authors said Poland's government was upset by its exclusion as Merkel coordinated euro crisis policy with Sarkozy, especially when Poland held the rotating EU presidency for the first time in the latter half of 2011. Yet, economic and financial policy is a potentially fruitful area for cooperation at the trilateral level, they concluded. France can continue to play its role as the conduit to the southern European countries and Germany to those of the north such as Finland and the Netherlands, while Poland could fulfill a bridge function to non-euro states that are in line to join the single currency. That doesn't extend to the U.K., which is "a permanent euro bystander," in Lang and Schwarzer's view. The Weimar group could thus "help bind candidate countries more closely to the process of deepening the eurozone."

As Sikorski said in his Berlin speech, Poland today "is not the source of problems but a source of European solutions. We now have both the capacity, and the will, to contribute. We bring a recent experience of a successful transformation from dictatorship to democracy and from an economic basket case to an increasingly prosperous market economy."

Poland is trying to seize the moment. Sikorski and his German counterpart, Guido Westerwelle, wrote a joint op-ed in the *New York Times* in September 2012 outlining a "new vision for Europe," comprising a more binding economic cooperation, stronger EU oversight of national budgets and a European Monetary Fund. At its heart were plans for greater powers to be exercised at European level allied to more democratic legitimacy through, for example, a directly elected president of the European Commission, to correct the "flawed architecture" at the euro's inception that thwarted moves beyond a single monetary union toward closer political union.[16]

Europe is "standing on the edge of a precipice," Sikorski said in his Berlin speech. "Future generations will judge us by what we do, or fail to do. Whether we lay the foundations for decades of greatness, or shirk our responsibility and acquiesce in decline. As a Pole and a European, here in Berlin, I say: The time to act is now."

■ ■ ■

One week before German reunification, in October 1990, Merkel returned to her native Hamburg for the annual convention of the Christian Democratic Union, her new political home. Merkel, then virtually unknown in West Germany's wider political establishment, had a message to convey. She exhorted fellow delegates to develop contacts "with our political friends in Eastern Europe," saying they had taught East Germans much in the past few years. "Even in a united Germany, we mustn't forget that Europe doesn't end at Germany's eastern border," she said. "We can't lose sight of the problems of other peoples." Her message was to urge her fellow Easterners not to shut themselves off but to reach out. That included working through their shared history under totalitarianism "so we can learn how to actively shape democracy."

Merkel's first real experience of shaping democracy at the EU level came more than a decade later after she had risen to chair the CDU in opposition. It was summer 2004 and jockeying had begun for the post of president of the European Commission to succeed Romano Prodi. Gerhard Schröder, the Social Democratic chancellor, and French President Jacques Chirac, a member of the conservative UMP, both favored the Belgian Prime Minister Guy Verhofstadt, a Liberal who had joined

Germany and France in opposing the U.S.-led invasion of Iraq. The *Frankfurter Allgemeine Zeitung* later reported that Merkel wanted to stop Verhofstadt's appointment, so joined with the U.K. Conservative Party, then in opposition, to field Chris Patten, the last British governor of Hong Kong who was by then EU commissioner for external relations, for the top commission job. The goal was never to get Patten into the post, merely to divide support for Verhofstadt's candidacy. It worked, and at Merkel's instigation, José Barroso, the serving prime minister of Portugal who had backed George W. Bush and Tony Blair on the war in the Iraq, was put forward as the compromise candidate. He was appointed commission president in November that year.[17]

The elaborate dance of forging European alliances and navigating the backrooms of EU policy making has become Merkel's stock in trade. During the euro-area crisis, she used it to beat off demands made of Germany and to get her way. After she woke up to the threat of contagion in August 2011, quietly acceding to ECB bond buying and embracing Greece, she decided that Europe had to be rebuilt if it was to be saved in the longer term. For all concerned, the race would be to the top not the bottom. And yet those in the southern arc of hardship complain they cannot all be Germans. Part of the beauty of Europe, they say, is that everyone is not German. Europe's blessing is its regional diversity, the same attribute that Merkel praised in Gdansk.

For Romano Prodi, the two-time Italian prime minister who led the European Commission from 1999 to 2004, overseeing EU enlargement to the east and the euro's introduction, Germany will always need to compromise to take Europe with it. "I think we need Germany, but Germany needs Europe more than we need Germany," he said.[18]

By electing to strike deals with Sarkozy and impose them on the rest of the continent, Merkel has presided over a "very bad period" for Europe, stoking resentment among other countries. In addition, the Franco–German relationship is no longer the one of equal partners it once was, meaning that Germany has been solely in charge throughout the crisis, dominating. With Germany enjoying superior political and economic strength, Merkel was able to dictate events using the shelter of Sarkozy's backing, leading to "these strange summits" where Merkel laid down the rules and Sarkozy explained them to the press, said Prodi. "Kohl was pro-European for choice. Angela Merkel is pro-European for necessity."

Yet with a battle looming over her plans to transfer powers to EU institutions, Merkel has no choice but to take up the cry of Europe and lead from the front – and has now come to that conclusion, "because she needs time to adjust," he said. "Now it's clear that the long-term interests of Germany are inside Europe."

Kohl too has criticized Merkel's European path. In a rare intervention in September 2011, the former chancellor said that Germany had overturned its postwar ethos of predictability and had become an unreliable partner under his one-time protege. Without the return of a political "compass" guiding Germany's actions in relation to her foreign partners, "the consequences would be catastrophic: the basis of trust would be lost, insecurity would spread, and in the end Germany would be isolated," he said in an interview with the journal *Internationale Politik*. Europe is not "an end in itself for naive dreamers," he said. "Europe remains without alternative for Germany." Leaders must allow that they will be measured by history, he said. "That shouldn't scare us; quite the opposite, it should give us courage and optimism for the way ahead. We all have chances, we only have to grasp them." Therein lies the greatest foreign policy priority of present times, in Kohl's view: "that Germany and Europe finally resume their responsibility for the world as a whole."[19]

Merkel was once asked about her vision and passion for Europe in front of the assembled Berlin press corps. The reporter had to remind her to answer the question. "That's right, yes . . . passion," she said. The room erupted with laughter and Merkel joined in. Then she explained the "Merkelian type of passion," which she said was strong. "I've always been a passionate European," she dead-panned. "Most of all, I'm passionately in favor of dealing with problems by tackling them at the root." She explained why Europe had to take its cue from the strongest economies or risk losing its status as a "global player of international importance." Emerging economies were closing the gap and Europe couldn't rest on its laurels. "This is my credo and this is what motivates me," she said. "I have a very clear vision of what Europe should undertake, and must undertake, so the people in Europe can continue living in prosperity."[20]

Merkel was among the European leaders who traveled to Oslo in December 2012 for the awarding of the Nobel Peace Prize to the EU, which she placed into the same context. In an interview with German television's RTL Aktuell six months earlier, she made clear that her drive is toward a Europe that will progress at different speeds of integration, with the euro countries leading the way and those that refuse to join in consigned to the periphery. The euro means a multi-speed Europe already exists, with the U.K. and Denmark saying from the outset they want nothing to do with the single currency. That trend "will be compounded," Merkel said. "Because whoever is in a currency union together must close ranks. We must always be open to allowing everyone to join in, but we can't stand still as a result of one or the other not yet wanting to come along."[21]

Cameron meanwhile turned Britain about and took the country in the opposite direction, with no clear destination in sight. In January 2013, he yielded to the euro-skeptics in his Conservative Party and announced a referendum on the U.K.'s membership of the European Union to be held by 2017, assuming he were to win the next election due in 2015. Describing public and political acceptance in the U.K. of the EU in its current form as "wafer thin," he pledged to renegotiate the terms of British membership to repatriate unspecified powers from Brussels and put the result to a public vote. The EU ought to focus on the common market, bolster competitiveness and nurture free trade, he said. Cameron won cheers from his parliamentary group for his stance, but the opposition Labour Party accused him of sowing uncertainty among businesses over the U.K.'s future status in Europe. In Scotland, which is historically less prone to anti-European sentiment than England, the prime minister's gamble risked inflaming the already bitter campaign for a referendum on independence to be held in 2014. German Foreign Minister Guido Westerwelle responded to Cameron's speech by warning that the U.K. couldn't expect to "cherry pick" the choicest pieces of the EU and reject the rest. Merkel, however, went out of her way not to add to the fire. She welcomed Cameron's emphasis on competitiveness, a focus she shared, while stressing that Germany wanted Britain to remain in the EU. Germany "is certainly prepared to talk" about British interests, although other countries will want a say and a compromise is what's needed at EU level, she said.[22] Privately, German officials inculcated with the postwar ethos of deepening and broadening Europe were bemused at Cameron's attempt to reduce it to a common trading bloc. Still, stressing their shared interests, they signaled a readiness to stand by their British cousins, unlike some in Europe more willing to let them go. After all, it was the Germans who put the Saxon in Anglo-Saxon. Some of the questions Cameron asked of Europe were valid; Britain stands for an openness to the world, for free trade and entrepreneurship, values that are less evident in other parts of Europe, such as France. Germany wants Britain in, all the more so because some are happy to see them out, but that doesn't detract from the fact that his referendum plan is seen in Berlin as a dangerous gamble. Yes, the Germans say they will listen when Cameron attempts to renegotiate the terms of Britain's EU membership. But he shouldn't expect much of a deal.

When it comes to European integration, Merkel is again playing hardball. Having decided to save the euro, she has determined to go further and remold Europe in Germany's image. Her mantra is that Europe must seize the chance created by the crisis and emerge stronger on the other side. Rather than being blamed for the euro's demise, she has moved on Kohl-like to grasp the potential opportunity to go down in history as the chancellor who forged Europe anew for the globalized era. Unlike Kohl, she has signaled there are clear limits to German munificence and that she won't balk at risking isolation. Those like Poland that agree with her are welcome to come along; those such as the U.K. that do not and will never agree can do as they please, but don't expect Germany to wait for them.

Geography and the tide of history may be with the German chancellor. The 2004 wave of EU enlargement to include immediate German neighbors Poland and the Czech Republic among 10 new members shifted the center of European gravity to the east. When the union had 12 members, its geographical midpoint was in France – the village of Saint-André-le-Coq in the Auvergne. That center has moved eastward with each phase of accession. Unsurprisingly, the exact center is up for debate, the answer depending on how the EU's outer edges are defined, whether to include its outlying archipelagos and its dependent territories. Calculations made by France's Institut Géographique National found that with 15 members, the center shifted from France to Belgium, and subsequently across the Rhine into Germany. After the 2007 accession of

Bulgaria and Romania brought the EU to 27 members, the geographical center moved squarely within German territory: to a wheat field outside Gelnhausen in Hessen, to be precise.[23] With Croatia slated to join the EU on July 1, 2013, Europe's pivotal point is shifting further east, and so closer to Berlin.

Notes

1. Ana Palacio, "The Peril's of Europe's Navel Gazing," *Project Syndicate*, January 11, 2012: http://www.project-syndicate.org/commentary/the-perils-of-europe-s-navel-gazing.

2. "Bagehot blog," *The Economist*, December 9, 2011: http://www.economist.com/blogs/bagehot/2011/12/britain-and-eu-0.

3. Merkel, Brussels press conference: http://www.bundeskanzlerin.de/Content/DE/Mitschrift/Pressekonferenzen/2011/12/2011-12-09-pk-bruessel.html?nn=74446.

4. Sikorski speech to German Council on Foreign Relations in Berlin, November 28, 2011: https://dgap.org/sites/default/files/event_downloads/radoslaw_sikorski_poland_and_the_future_of_the_eu_0.pdf.

5. Norman Davies interview with Malgorzata Bos-Karczewska, editor-in-chief of Polonia.nl: http://polonia.nl/?p=6815.

6. Merkel speech to the Christian Democratic Union in Karlsruhe, November 15, 2010: http://www.karlsruhe2010.cdu.de/images/stories/docs/101115-Rede-Merkel.pdf.

7. Charlemagne Prize speech, May 13, 2010: http://www.bundeskanzlerin.de/Content/DE/Rede/2010/05/2010-05-13-karlspreis.html.

8. "Deutsch muss man lernen," *Die Zeit*, September 30, 2004.

9. Telephone interview, January 4, 2013.

10. German Federal Statistics Office: https://www.destatis.de/DE/PresseService/Presse/Pressemitteilungen/2012/09/PD12_326_122.html.

11. EU Commission, February 2013 outlook, Table 1: http://ec.europa.eu/economy_finance/eu/forecasts/2013_winter/overview_en.pdf.

12. EU Commission, February 2013 outlook, Table 1: http://ec.europa.eu/economy_finance/eu/forecasts/2013_winter/overview_en.pdf.

13. German Foreign Ministry website: http://www.auswaertiges-amt.de/DE/Aussenpolitik/Laender/Laenderinfos/Polen/Bilateral_node.html.

14. Merkel speech in honor of Tusk, May 31, 2012: http://www.bundesregierung.de/Content/DE/Rede/2012/05/2012-05-31-merkel-rathenau-preis.html.

15. Kai-Olaf Lang and Daniela Schwarzer, "Consolidating the Weimar Triangle," The German Institute for International and Security Affairs: http://www.swp-berlin.org/fileadmin/contents/products/comments/2011C30_lng_swd_ks.pdf.

16. Sikorski and Westerwelle article for *New York Times* website, September 17, 2012: http://www.auswaertiges-amt.de/sid_E742DDF3889E8F769455BDF572 E84B76/EN/Infoservice/Presse/Interview/2012/120917-BM-Sikorski-VisionEurope.html?nn=626352.

17. "Angela Merkel: A Rational European," *Frankfurter Allgemeine Zeitung*, October 13, 2012: http://www.faz.net/aktuell/politik/europaeische-union/angela-merkel-europaeerin-aus-vernunft-11924570.html.

18. Interview in Berlin on October 23, 2012.

19. Kohl interview published in *Internationale Politik*, May 2011: https://zeitsch rift-ip.dgap.org/de/ip-die-zeitschrift/archiv/jahrgang-2011/september-oktober/wir-müssen-wieder-zuversicht-geben.

20. Merkel press conference, July 22, 2011: http://www.bundeskanzlerin.de/Content/DE/Mitschrift/Pressekonferenzen/2011/07/2011-07-22-som merpk-merkel.html.

21. Merkel interview with RTL Aktuell, June 6, 2012: http://www.bundeskanz lerin.de/Content/DE/Interview/2012/06/2012-06-07-merkel-ard.html?nn=385694.

22. Gonzalo Vina, Robert Hutton and Kitty Donaldson, "Cameron Promises Referendum by 2017 on U.K. Leaving EU," *Bloomberg News*, January 23, 2013: http://www.bloomberg.com/news/2013-01-23/cameron-to-promise-referendum-by-2017-on-u-k-leaving-eu.html.

23. See: http://www.center-of-eu.com/index.php?mach=english.htm.

Chapter 12

Chronicles

Jean-Claude Trichet, who led the ECB during the crisis until Mario Draghi took over on November 1, 2011, recalls going to New York in early 1998 and telling Wall Street investors about the impending introduction of the euro on January 1 the following year. They told him he was talking nonsense. "Too bold, too strange, never done – absolutely impossible," he said. "And I knew myself of course that it was totally prepared and it will be done. You had a strategic political commitment, not to speak of the technicalities of it, that was there. I told them that for the most important marketplace in the world it's better to be in tune with reality." He sees the crisis from the U.S. subprime calamity through to the sovereign debt turmoil as one continuous thread throughout which the euro never dipped below $1.17, thus remaining above its entry value. He chuckled at the thought of the number of hedge funds that "lost their culottes, as we say in French" in betting against the euro. "The euro, as a currency, has demonstrated a remarkable stability in the crisis. And the euro area has proved a capacity to correct its own weaknesses: don't bet on the belief that the euro area will change in its nature with countries leaving it," he said. "The euro is there, it will be there, there is no doubt."[1]

Merkel defeated the doomsayers in 2012, when betting against the 17-nation currency turned out to be the wrong call. While it was Draghi, the Goldman Sachs alumnus, who fought contagion with the threat of unlimited ECB bond buying, investors consistently underestimated or failed to understand the political will in Europe to keep the euro together. John Paulson, the Wall Street investor who manages $19 billion in hedge funds, said the euro would fall apart because it was "structurally flawed" and wagered against European sovereign bonds. Citigroup Inc. economists led by Willem Buiter in London said in July there was a 90 percent chance that Greece would leave the euro. They assumed an exit by January 1, 2013. Instead, Greek bonds surged the most worldwide and the country stayed in the euro as no one, Merkel included, wanted to take the risk of severing its financial lifeline. She remains on record as wanting to see as many countries as possible adopt the euro.

Her battle for elected politicians' supremacy over financial markets was waning as the debt crisis entered a relative lull in late 2012, yet she wasn't about to declare a truce. Having preached worldwide financial regulation, she also agreed to start EU talks on setting up a Europe-wide banking supervisor, a step along the way to a so-called banking union that signals deeper integration and will open the door to the region's permanent rescue fund – with Germany as the biggest capital provider – to aid blighted banks.

When she took office in November 2005, Merkel gave a speech to the Bundestag setting out her policy on Europe, saying she would fight for German interests while pushing for alliances and cooperation. "I know that our partners have great expectations of us," she said. "The expectations are so great because Europe finds itself in the midst of a deep crisis. At its root, I believe this crisis is about a lack of mutual trust." Having made the decision to defend the euro, she has turned the grand European project into a test of whether the currency union's other countries have faith in Germany to follow her rules to save it. While arguing like a dispassionate scientist, her aim is to show that core European values such as democracy and human rights are better guides for globalization than systems of countries such as China.

Merkel began her 2013 diplomacy by receiving Antonis Samaras, the Greek prime minister who finally delivered on austerity commitments, at the Chancellery in Berlin for a demonstration of common purpose, saying Germany has to work to secure economic growth and jobs no less than Greece does. She spelled out her election-year agenda a few days before, mixing homespun truths about the power of hard work and the need to beat global economic rivals. Wearing a festive silver jacket and with the Reichstag as her backdrop, she used her New Year's address from the Chancellery to deliver a blunt message to the nation: that 2013 will be harder economically than the previous year. Germans must focus on their core strengths of research and innovation to create jobs and stay ahead, she said. "When we can do what others can't, then we retain and create wealth," she said. As her goals for 2013 she listed addressing the challenges of Germany's energy transformation, demographic change, and bringing the state's finances under control. As much of Europe embarks on a course of structural overhaul, "the reforms that we've introduced will require a whole lot of patience to work. The crisis is not over by a long way," she said. In particular, much still needs to be done at international level to better oversee the financial markets. "The world has still not fully learned the lessons of the devastating financial crisis of 2008. Never again can such irresponsibility as happened then be allowed to repeat itself. In the social-market economy, the state is the guardian of order. People must be able to have faith in that."[2]

It was a seven-minute manifesto that encapsulated Merkel's almost religious ethos of work, perseverance, and ultimate redemption. In terms of content, most of it could just as easily come from her Social Democratic Party opponents. Going into 2013, a year that would determine whether she exceeded her SPD predecessor Gerhard Schröder's two terms and won a third, Merkel appeared at her most presidential. She began the year with support for her Christian Democratic bloc edging above 41 percent in polls, the highest of her chancellorship.[3] She extended her lead as Germany's most popular politician in a monthly poll for ZDF television, with her crisis lieutenant, Finance Minister Wolfgang Schäuble, in second spot. Voters were happier with her government than at any time during her second term and said their personal economic situation was rosier than at any time since the question was first asked by pollster Forschungsgruppe Wahlen in January 2004. Eight weeks previously, in early November, she warned the times of crisis would continue and put a date on its duration: at least five more years, and even then only if accompanied by "a bit of strictness" in attacking Europe's problems. That would conveniently take her to the end of a third term – which according to one senior party insider is as long as she intends to serve.

Even if the sovereign debt crisis were starting to ease, a number of long-term challenges stood between Merkel and her goal of serving out a third term. Her decision to shut off Germany's nuclear capacity means the government must seek to more than triple the share of renewables in the energy mix by 2050. Targets were already being missed in 2012 as plans to develop some 25,000 megawatts of offshore wind power by 2030 were delayed amid technical and financing difficulties.[4] The government attempted to elevate the "energy overhaul" to a matter of national importance above mere electioneering. Merkel, speaking in December 2012 at the inauguration of a 380-kilovolt smart grid in Schwerin, state capital of Mecklenburg-Western Pomerania in Germany's northeast, stressed the experimental nature of the technology and financing needed to bring offshore wind power from the north coast to the industrial centers in the south. "This is absolute virgin territory for all investors," she said. "When you look at the number of projects that still have to be realized, then you know that a lot of work lies ahead."[5] Rather than the risks associated with developing grand projects, the danger for the government lies in the price consumers will be asked to pay for power, already among the highest in Europe. The government has announced plans to curb subsidies for solar, biomass and wind power, but that couldn't stop the four grid companies from raising the surcharge consumers pay for funding renewable energy for 2013 to a record.

Merkel's constant warnings about the threat to Germany's economic standing, notably from China, are backed by an OECD forecasting model for growth and prosperity. The OECD estimates that China will overtake the euro area by one measure of GDP around the end of 2013 and the U.S. a few years later, becoming the world's biggest economy. India is projected to surpass the euro area around 2032, while rising productivity and relatively young populations will also drive gains by countries such as Indonesia and Brazil. While China and the euro region each accounted for 17 percent of world GDP in 2011, China's share will jump to 27.9 percent in 2030 as the euro area's shrinks to 11.7 percent. That's a steeper decline than projected for the U.S., whose share will fall from 22.7 percent to 17.8 percent, according to the OECD's extrapolations. China's contribution to GDP will be little changed in 2060, while the euro area's share will decline further to 8.8 percent, again more quickly than the U.S.[6] Germany's economy is projected to expand at an average of 1 percent per year through 2060, the lowest rate among the 42 countries in the study, which sees the fastest growth in India, Indonesia, China, Saudi Arabia, South Africa, and Mexico. Even so, emerging countries will close only part of the gap in living standards with advanced nations. The paper also provides fodder for Merkel's concern about the rest of the euro area. Productivity is projected to increase more quickly in Germany than in the U.K., France and Italy. Using the U.S. standard of living as the baseline, while aging populations and low birth rates hold back growth in much of Western Europe in the decades ahead, Germany will maintain its living standard relative to the U.S., according to the study. Countries such as France, Spain, Italy, Austria and Ireland are projected to fall behind, while eastern EU members – most of them currently outside the euro – will increasingly close the gap.

Back in 1980, Günter Grass wrote a fictionalized account of a reading tour he made of China entitled *Headbirths: Or, the Germans are Dying Out.* Germany's perennially low birth rate, among the lowest in the world, saw about 200,000 fewer births than deaths in 2012, according to official projections. However, the population rose by about the same number to 82 million as a result of immigration, the second year in a row of a population increase after eight years of decline. While other European countries in the crosswires of the crisis suffer recession and record unemployment, in relatively unscathed Germany immigration was set to outstrip outward migration by 340,000, the most since at least 1995.[7]

European officials from Commission President José Barroso to Luxembourg's Jean-Claude Juncker started 2013 by sounding the all-clear as a measure of investor confidence returned to the euro area. While austerity fatigue and European countries' willingness to transfer sovereignty as a condition of closer integration remain potential stumbling blocks, the difference this time was that the ECB had turned into the euro area's backstop when governments couldn't agree on what to do. Draghi's unprecedented pledge to defend the currency signaled an expansion of the ECB's powers, which will only increase when it takes on Europe-wide tasks of banking supervision. The central bank's move became necessary after the euro area's 17 governments squabbled and haggled for more than two years over every measure to stem the debt crisis. Investors – the financial markets that Merkel said she was battling for control over the euro area's destiny – were increasingly betting on the currency union's breakup. That sovereign-bond spreads reflected this speculation was a crucial reason Draghi cited in making his conditional offer of unlimited ECB bond buying. A log of U.S. Treasury Secretary Timothy Geithner's calls and meetings in the debt crisis showed that his main European contacts were Draghi and his predecessor Trichet. Next most frequent was Germany's Schäuble, followed by the French finance ministry.[8] The compilation by Bruegel, the Brussels-based think tank, based on Geithner's publicly available schedule, underscores the Obama administration's concern throughout the debt crisis. The Frankfurt-based ECB also is a place where Germany doesn't have a veto. When Bundesbank chief Jens Weidmann dissented on the ECB's bond-buying vote, Merkel faced a quandary. She solved it by voicing support for Weidmann as well as Draghi. It's an indication that the euro area and the ECB, whose anti-inflation mandate was modeled on the Bundesbank, may be up for grabs between a German-led northern tier and the southern euro-area countries that look to France as an ally. The Banque de France was created in 1800 by Napoleon Bonaparte to spur economic growth after a recession during the period of the French Revolution. Its task was "to issue bank notes payable to the bearer on sight in exchange for discounted commercial bills." The French national bank, headquartered a block from the old Royal Palace Gardens in Paris's stately First Arrondissement, changed its statute to become independent of the state only in 1993.[9] The Bundesbank, housed in a 1960s concrete high-rise near a sports complex and an autobahn ramp in Frankfurt, was founded in 1957 with the express aim of keeping West Germany's deutsche mark stable after the nation's disastrous experience with hyperinflation during the 1920s. Until the ECB took over monetary policy from national central banks in the euro area and afterwards as part of the euro system, the Bundesbank says it "fulfilled this mandate for half a century with greater determination and success than almost any other monetary institution in the world."

The righteous pride on the other side of the Rhine has always grated on French policy makers, who view the ECB's natural role as more activist, closer to the Federal Reserve's. Letting the ECB help level the economic and fiscal differences within the euro area rather than relying primarily on the German recipe of austerity to boost the competitiveness of the weaker countries fits with the French view of the ECB as "a real federal institution" for the euro area, as Musca puts it. At that point, joint euro-area debt issuance becomes less urgent. That view, and Merkel's ambiguity, don't jibe with the Bundesbank's self-image as the protector of German savers from inflation. Weidmann, who was Merkel's economic adviser in the Chancellery until she chose him as Bundesbank head, sees the central bank on the cusp of a slippery slope toward breaching its mandate by financing national debts and deficits. By covering for euro-area governments, the ECB in his view risks becoming the tool of elected politicians too weak or unwilling to administer painful economic therapy in their countries. If the ECB rolls over once, it will roll over again. Weidmann, whose post gives him a seat on the ECB policy-making Governing Council, says the central bank didn't need to make its bond-buying offer. "Then policy makers would have had to act," he told the *Frankfurter Allgemeine Sonntagszeitung*, which elevated to him "resistance" leader in the purported battle for the ECB's direction. "I certainly know that these decisions are difficult for policy makers. But it's the task of policy makers, not the central bank, to decide about a redistribution of solvency risks in Europe."[10]

True to the deal between her and Sarkozy in late 2011, Merkel hasn't stood in the ECB's way. As the ECB's policy shifts and the Federal Reserve's "quantitative easing" alleviated the immediate crisis, her poll ratings and those of her party climbed at the end of 2012. She may face pressure to take a stand if Europe's debt crisis returns. When the ECB, then led by Trichet, agreed in 2009 to buy 60 billion euros of covered bonds to counter recession in the euro area, Merkel spoke up to warn that the ECB's independence was at stake. She views the economic-stimulus powers of the Federal Reserve and Bank of England "with great skepticism," Merkel told an audience in Berlin that included Draghi, then head of the Bank of Italy and the Financial Stability Board, and former Bundesbank chief Hans Tietmeyer. "The European Central Bank has also bowed to international pressure a bit with its covered-bond purchases. We all have to return to an independent central-bank policy and a policy of common sense."[11]

Merkel may face even starker choices once again if efforts by vulnerable euro countries to curb borrowing and overhaul their economies falter. Boerner, the family-business lobbyist who backs Draghi's crisis response, says the risk of a north–south breakup in the euro area isn't banished yet because voters may simply reject austerity. "It's within the realm of imagination, if the southern Europeans don't carry out reforms," he says. "Do these societies have the ability to reform themselves, to become modern societies, within the democratic process?" If they don't, it's "inevitable" that a northern core euro area will split off. It would have to be a managed breakup, including orderly defaults for countries that have had enough of sacrifices in the name of European unity. "And I do believe you could manage it. Mrs. Merkel surely is capable enough to do it," Boerner says. "That said, we're not pushing for it. I also don't think it's going to happen."

A glimpse of how a northern euro might look was on show in Merkel's Stralsund constituency in May 2012, when Germany chaired the 11-nation Baltic Sea Council. With representatives from the Nordic countries to the Baltic states, Poland, Russia and the European Commission, it is a forum in which Germany, and Merkel, feels completely at ease. Merkel hosted her fellow leaders at "Zur Fähre," a pub dating back to 1332 whose name evokes the nearby ferry dock. She toasted her guests with white wine as they sat by candlelight around a varnished wooden table, a ship's wheel decorating the wall behind her. To her right sat the EU's José Barroso while on her left was Norwegian Prime Minister Jens Stoltenberg, wielding a schooner of beer.[12] Most of the countries represented share a philosophy of economic stability that mirrors the German view, whereas the 17-member eurozone is made up predominantly of countries that do not think like Germany. If the Baltic Council countries were Europe, then Europe would not have a problem, she might say. The trouble is that the Baltic Sea Council has no unified view on Europe. Indeed, of the best performers, Norway isn't even in the EU, the Swedes are EU members but shy away from the euro, while Poland, committed to join the single currency, isn't there yet. Until that time, Merkel is happy for every Baltic state that joins the euro since they bring a way of thinking that is in tune with German sensibilities.

Merkel has come a long way since she told the Bundestag in March 2010 that countries might have to be kicked out of the eurozone if they didn't hold to the rules. Yet for all her subsequent talk of political union in Europe, the topic didn't merit a mention in her goals for 2013. Furthering integration may even now be at an impasse, with fellow European countries having swallowed as much as they can stomach of Merkel's medicine and Merkel herself unwilling to risk upsetting German voters before the fall election. Her call for a European competitiveness pact to follow on from the fiscal compact and steps made toward a banking union ran into resistance days after she put it at the core of her address to the 2013 World Economic Forum in Davos, as Swedish Prime Minister Fredrik Reinfeldt said he opposed shifting more powers to Brussels.[13]

All the same, the German chancellor has a track record of getting her way and proving outside observers wrong. Constanze Stelzenmüller, head of the Berlin office of the German Marshall Fund, writing in the *Financial Times* in 2005 the day after Merkel's party and Schröder's SPD wrapped up three weeks of negotiations to form a government, noted that the only historic precedent for a grand coalition lasted just three years, from 1966 to 1969. The new coalition, with Merkel as chancellor and Steinbrück her finance minister, was an "interregnum arrangement" and would last two years, if that. As Stelzenmüller also noted, however, Merkel "is a canny, cool-headed operator who has built a political career on being underestimated."[14]

Key for now is that Merkel remains in tune with voters, having dragged them along with her through the years of crisis. Many small steps is her axiom, and it concurs with the German electorate: in times of crisis, Merkel rids Germans of their inner angst. "Germans are a very nervous people, bowing to hysteria, very quickly becoming afraid," said Boerner. "Merkel alleviates that."

After seven years in power, she's cobbled together a view of the financial crisis that's unlikely to change if she stays in charge. She fended off waves of calls from her fellow European leaders to agree to pool the euro area's debt, including a proposal by her own council of economic advisers. Anyone who wanted to pacify markets with an easy way out "has no clue about the economy," the physicist-turned-crisis-manager said.[15] By mid-2012, the new Socialist government in Paris gave up on joint euro-area bonds, acknowledging they were a line Merkel wouldn't cross. Amid polls that consistently show German voters refuse to agree to underwrite the debts of their fellow Europeans, the SPD has quietly backed away from its prior support for euro bonds. Her statement that euro bonds wouldn't happen in her lifetime, reportedly made behind closed doors to lawmakers in Berlin, was named Quote of the Year by the *Frankfurter Allgemeine Zeitung*, Germany's newspaper of record.[16]

Samaras complained about the "cacophony" of opinion in Germany about how to deal with Greece, including within Merkel's coalition. The record shows that Merkel's voice is the one that counts. She won every parliamentary vote related to the debt crisis, though not without dissent. She saw off an anti-Europe groundswell among the Free Democrats, her second-term coalition ally. She has headed the CDU since 2000, outlasting several male rivals for top posts. She has held sway in two governing coalitions of different constellations, and would doubtless succeed in dominating a third. More than three years after the debt crisis began, her policies have changed the face of Europe and underscored her endurance. She is one of the last pre-crisis government leaders still standing – her euro-area peers in France, Italy, Spain, Greece, Ireland, Portugal, Slovakia, and Slovenia all fell. Cyprus, which sought a bailout in mid-2012, voted for a change of president in February 2013, electing a candidate whom Merkel backed. Italy's legislative elections the same month didn't go Merkel's way, after a comeback by Berlusconi and a surge in support for the anti-austerity movement of Beppe Grillo produced a stalemate.

Investors, economists and other political leaders criticize her as cautious and slow off the mark, qualities she showed in abundance before Greece's first bailout, the first big decision point in the debt crisis. Merkel doesn't see that as a drawback and polls suggest voters trust her because of it. Going slow and imposing tough conditions on aid also helps her balance Germans' desire to be seen as good Europeans with voters' anger at bailouts for weaker euro-area countries. This is a country that loves stability: the iconic VW Golf, Volkswagen's best-selling car, has been on the market since 1974 always under the same name. Even policy makers in other countries exasperated with her approach express understanding for legislative and constitutional hurdles she has to navigate in Germany and admiration for her effort to keep Germans from turning against the euro. Economic growth in the middle of the debt crisis is a feel-good factor that benefits Merkel, while her modest lifestyle doesn't make waves. In Merkel's battle with the markets, she may not have imposed the primacy of politics, but the two sides have fought to a standstill. Her agenda for Europe is utilitarian. It is conservative in the sense of preserving Europe's strengths – Germany's economy, and the welfare states that prevent the kind of social conflict that led to war in the 20th century. "Europe may be at a fateful crossroads," she said at a German–Portuguese business forum in Lisbon in November 2012. "The next few years will decide whether or not we can keep up with the rising emerging countries and the best industrial countries in the world. I believe we have to tell people in our countries again and again: If we don't do it ourselves, nobody on the outside will step in to help us maintain or increase our prosperity."[17] That's a message Merkel has made her own, as she exhorts Europeans to raise their collective performance to compete in a globalized world. For all her many detractors, Merkel has ensured it is one Europe is no longer able to sit back and ignore.

Notes

1. Trichet comments in e-mail to authors, January 2013.
2. Merkel's New Year's message, video: http://www.bundeskanzlerin.de/Content/DE/Artikel/2011/12/2011–12–31-neujahresansprache.html.
3. Poll trends: http://www.wahlrecht.de/umfragen/forsa.htm.
4. Stefan Nicola and Brian Parkin, "Merkel's Offshore Windpower Dream for Germany Stalls," *Bloomberg News*, January 17, 2013: http://www.bloomberg.com/news/2013–01–16/merkel-s-offshore-wind-power-dream-for-germany-stalls.html.
5. Merkel speech to open power grid line, December 18, 2012: http://www.bundeskanzlerin.de/Content/DE/Rede/2012/12/2012–12–18-merkel-nordleitung.html.
6. "Looking to 2060: A Global Vision of Long-Term Growth," OECD Economics Department Policy Notes, No. 15, November 2012.
7. German Federal Statistic Office release, January 15, 2013: https://www.destatis.de/DE/PresseService/Presse/Pressemitteilungen/2013/01/PD13_013_12411.html;jsessionid=F3B1626AD08E9FD33316878ED60C4B8A.cae1.
8. Jean Pisani-Ferry, "Tim Geithner and Europe's Phone Number," Bruegel, November 4, 2012: http://www.bruegel.org/nc/blog/detail/article/934-tim-geithner-and-europes-phone-number.
9. Banque de France history: http://www.banque-france.fr/en/banque-de-france/history/the-milestones/1800-creation-of-the-banque-de-france.html.
10. Article on Bundesbank website: http://www.bundesbank.de/Redaktion/DE/Interviews/2012_12_30_weidmann_fas.html.

11. Official Merkel transcript: http://archiv.bundesregierung.de/Content/DE/Rede/2009/06/2009–06–02-merkel-insm.html?nn=273438.

12. "Prost! In dieser Hafenkneipe tagt Kanzlerin Merkel," *Bild*, May 31, 2012.

13. Handelsblatt interview, January 27, 2013: http://www.handelsblatt.com/poli tik/international/fredrik-reinfeldt-schwedens-premierminister-stellt-sich-ge gen-merkel/7694610.html.

14. Constanze Stelzenmüller "Merkel's Coalition Will be Lucky to Survive Two Years," *FT opinion*, October 10, 2005: http://www.ft.com/intl/cms/s/2/fd7112da-39b6–11da-806e-00000e2511c8.html#axzz2I8ycUekQ.

15. Tony Czuczka, "Merkel Says Those Demanding Endgame to Europe's Debt Crisis Have 'No Clue'," *Bloomberg News*, October 4, 2011: http://www.bloomberg.com/news/2011–10–04/merkel-says-she-remains-opposed-to-joint-euro-area-bonds.html.

16. http://www.faz.net/aktuell/gesellschaft/menschen/zitate-des-jahres-2012-solange-ich-lebe-12012004.html.

17. Official transcript of Merkel comments: http://www.bundesregierung.de/Content/DE/Rede/2012/11/2012–11–12-merkel-lissabon.html.

Appendix – Photo credits

Photo 1
Ullstein Bild – P.S.I. Bonn

Photo 2
CDU – Michael Ebner/Meldepress – Creative Commons

Photo 3
J.H. Darchinger/Friedrich Ebert-Stiftung

Photo 4
Ullstein Bild – Ebner

Photo 5
German Government Press Office/Christian Stutterheim

Photo 6
picturealliance-dpa–dpaweb/Peter Kneffel

Photo 7
Bloomberg photographs supplied by Bloomberg Photo Service:
www.bloomberg.com/contentlicensing/photos
All Rights Reserved, Copyright 2013 Bloomberg LP.
Guido Krzikowski/Bloomberg

Photo 8
German Government Press Office/Jürgen Gebhardt

Photo 9
German Government Press Office/Guido Bergmann

Photo 10
German Government Press Office/Guido Bergmann

Photo 11
Bloomberg photographs supplied by Bloomberg Photo Service:
www.bloomberg.com/contentlicensing/photos
All Rights Reserved, Copyright 2013 Bloomberg LP.
Antoine Antoniol/Bloomberg

Photo 12
Philippe Wojazer/AFP/Getty Images

Photo 13
Bloomberg photographs supplied by Bloomberg Photo Service:
www.bloomberg.com/contentlicensing/photos
All Rights Reserved, Copyright 2013 Bloomberg LP.
Kostas Tsironis/Bloomberg

Photo 14
Bloomberg photographs supplied by Bloomberg Photo Service:
www.bloomberg.com/contentlicensing/photos
All Rights Reserved, Copyright 2013 Bloomberg LP.
Andrew Harrer/Bloomberg

Photo 15
Bloomberg photographs supplied by Bloomberg Photo Service:
www.bloomberg.com/contentlicensing/photos
All Rights Reserved, Copyright 2013 Bloomberg LP.
Mario Proenca/Bloomberg

Photo 16
German Government Press Office/Jesco Denzel

Photo 17
Bloomberg photographs supplied by Bloomberg Photo Service:
www.bloomberg.com/contentlicensing/photos
All Rights Reserved, Copyright 2013 Bloomberg LP.
Hannelore Foerster/Bloomberg

Photo 18
German Government Press Office/Guido Bergmann

Photo 19
German Government Press Office/Guido Bergmann

Bibliography

Amott, James (2011) Agricole May Lose EU10.4b on Greek Euro Exit, Natixis Says, *Bloomberg News*, November 2.

Bagehot's notebook (2011) Britain, not leaving but falling out of the EU, *The Economist*, December 9.

Bayer, Wolfgang (2000) Geheimoperation Fürstenberg, *Der Spiegel*, January 17.

Boyd, Sebastian and Shenn, Jody (2008) Hank the Great? Paulson Copies Frederick With Bonds, *Bloomberg News*, August 7.

Buergin, Rainer (2008) Merkel Converts to Bank-Bashing, *Bloomberg News*, November 7.

Buergin, Rainer (2009) Hypo Rescue Was Needed as World Faced 'Abyss', *Bloomberg News*, August 20.

Bush, George W. (2010) *Decision Points*, Broadway Paperbacks, pp. 412–13.

Chrepa, Eleni (2012) Greek President Papoulias Slams German 'Insults' as Aid Discussions Stall, *Bloomberg News*, February 15.

Christie, Rebecca (2010) Geithner Says Europeans 'Acting Forcefully,' Need to Revamp Fiscal Policy, *Bloomberg News*, May 25.

Christie, Rebecca (2011) Geithner Warning of 'Catastrophic Risk' Highlights Gap With EU, *Bloomberg News*, September 17.

Cremer, Andreas (2007) G-8 Communique to Stress Improved Economy Outlook, Germany Says, *Bloomberg News*, June 5.

Cremer, Andreas (2007) Merkel Quarrels With Bono, Geldof Over African Aid, *Bloomberg News*, June 7.

Cremer, Andreas (2007) Merkel Says German Wage Disparities Threaten Social Cohesion, *Bloomberg News*, December 11.

Croft, Catherine (2004) *Concrete Architecture*, Gibbs Smith.

Czuczka, Tony (2011) Germany Would Back Greece Debt Restructuring, Hoyer Says, *Bloomberg News*, April 15.

Czuczka, Tony (2011) Merkel Says Those Demanding Endgame to Europe's Debt Crisis Have 'No Clue', *Bloomberg News*, October 4.

Czuczka, Tony (2013) Germany is not bent on dominating Europe, President Gauck Says, *Bloomberg News*, February 22.

Czuczka, Tony and Donahue, Patrick (2011) Merkel's Nuclear Policy Under Fire as Greens Surge in Elections, *Bloomberg News*, March 28.

Czuczka, Tony and Fouquet, Helene (2011) Sarkozy Temper Boils, Banks Yield in Six-Day War Saving the Euro, *Bloomberg News*, November 2.

Czuczka, Tony and Parkin, Brian (2010) Merkel Tells Her Party Europe Can't Afford to Let the Euro Fail Over Debt, *Bloomberg News*, November 15.

Donahue, Patrick and Parkin, Brian (2010) German Lawmakers Back Greek Aid Package, *Bloomberg News*, May 7.

Erlanger, Steven (2002) Germans Vote in a Tight Election in Which Bush, Hitler and Israel Became Key Issues, *New York Times*, September 22.

Fitzgerald, Alison and Faler, Brian (2008) Congress Sends $168 Billion Economic Stimulus to Bush, *Bloomberg News*, February 8.

Goldfarb, Zachary A. (2012) Can Obama Save Manufacturing? *Washington Post*, July 13.

Groendahl, Boris (2011) German Banks Top French With $23 Billion in Greek Debt, BIS Report Shows, *Bloomberg News*, June 6.

Gutschker, Thomas and Lohse, Eckart (2012) Angela Merkel: A Rational European, *Frankfurter Allgemeine Zeitung*, October 13.

Guynn, Randall D. (2010) The Financial Panic of 2008 and Financial Regulatory Reform, Harvard Law School Forum on Corporate Governance and Financial Regulation, November 20.

Hayden, Jones and Weeks, Natalie (2010) Greece Gets First Installment of Emergency Loans, *Bloomberg News*, May 18.

Hertling, James (2012) Greek Crisis Timeline from Maastricht Treat to ECB Bond-Buying, *Bloomberg News*, September 5.

Kade, Claudia (2010) Merkels Abstieg in die zweite Liga, *Financial Times Deutschland*, April 14.

Kennedy, Simon and Meier, Simone (2010) G-7 Pledges to Keep Stimulus Even Amid Budget Stress, *Bloomberg News*, February 6.

Kirchfeld, Aaron and Sirletti Sonia, (2011) Commerzbank Plans to Repay $20 Billion in State Aid Using Capital Increase, *Bloomberg News*, April 4.

Krauel, Torsten (2012) The EU Today is Angela Merkel's GDR, *Die Welt*, May 2.

Krugman, Paul (2010) Kurzarbeit, *New York Times* website, September 2.

Krugman, Paul (2012) Ich Bin Ein Berliner, Or Something, *New York Times*, November 28.

Kurbjuweit, Dirk (2009) Angela the Great or Just Mom?, *Der Spiegel*, November 3.

Langguth, Gerd (2005) *Angela Merkel: Rise to Power*, Deutscher Taschenbuch Verlag, Munich, pp. 157–8.

Lévy, Bernard-Henri (2012) Reforms are not enough to save Europe, *Frankfurter Allgemeine Zeitung*, November 20.

Liefgreen, Dan and Kenna, Armorel (2011) Italians Obsessed by 'Lo Spread' as Advance in Bond Yields Makes Headlines, *Bloomberg News*, November 14.

Mandelbrot, Benoit B. and Hudson, Richard L. (2008) *The (Mis)Behavior of Markets: A Fractal View of Risk, Ruin, and Reward*, Profile Books.

Mangasarian, Leon and Czuczka, Tony (2009) Merkel's Bargain with Ackermann Signaled Re-Election, *Bloomberg News*, August 24.

Matussek, Karin (2010) Ex-IKB CEO Convicted of Misleading Investors About Bank's Subprime Risks, *Bloomberg News*, July 14.

Merkel, Angela (1993) Der Marsch zur Macht, *Emma*, May–June.

Merkel, Angela and Müller-Vogg, Hugo (2005) *Angela Merkel – My Way*, Hoffmann und Campe Verlag, Hamburg, pp. 55, 68 and 121.

Müller-Vogg, Hugo (2012) How Angela Merkel Comforted Samaras With a Story of Her Father's Eye Complaint, *Bild*, August 24.

Nichols, Hans and Dorning, Mike (2011) Obama Says Europe Crisis 'Severe Strain' on World Economy, *Bloomberg Businessweek*, October 6.

Nicola, Stefan and Parkin, Brian (2013) Merkel's Offshore Windpower Dream for Germany Stalls, *Bloomberg News*, January 17.

Osang, Alexander (2009) Die deutsche Queen, *Der Spiegel*, May 11.

Palacio, Ana (2012) The Peril's of Europe's Navel Gazing, *Project Syndicate*, January 11.

Parkin, Brian and Bensasson, Marcus (2012) Merkel Urges Greece to Maintain Austerity to Stay in Euro, *Bloomberg News*, October 9.

Petrakis, Maria and Kennedy, Simon (2012) Papademos to Ministers: Back Bailout or Quit, *Bloomberg News*, February 10.

Petrakis, Maria, Weeks, Natalie and Bensasson, Marcus (2011) Papandreou Grip on Power Weakens, *Bloomberg News*, November 14.

Pisani-Ferry, Jean (2012) Tim Geithner and Europe's Phone Number, *Bruegel*, November 4.

Rach, Claudia (2006) Bush Walks in Communist Leaders' Footsteps in Germany, *Bloomberg News*, June 13.

Rogoff, Kenneth (2010) The Euro at Mid-Crisis, *Project Syndicate*, December 2.

Stelzenmüller, Constanze (2005) Merkel's Coalition Will be Lucky to Survive Two Years, *FT opinion*, October 10.

Thesing, Gabi (2012) Germans Still Favor Cash Over Cards for Payment, Bundesbank Says, *Bloomberg News*, October 17.

Tomlinson, Richard and Suess, Oliver (2009) Merkel Makes Like Obama With German Stimulus Excluding Europe, *Bloomberg News*, March 25.

Vits, Christian and Crawford, Alan (2010) Former East Germany Beats California on Jobs: Chart of the Day, *Bloomberg News*, October 6.

Weiss, Richard (2012) Kuka Robots Invade China as Wage Gains Put Machines Over Workers, *Bloomberg News*, April 13.

Westbrook, Jesse (2008) Obama Picks Site of Berlin Speech After Brandenburg Gate Flap, *Bloomberg News*, July 20.

Wise, Michael Z. (1998) *Capital Dilemma: Germany's Search for a New Architecture of Democracy*, Princeton Architectural Press.

Wolf, Martin (2010) Germans are Wrong: The Eurozone is Good for Them, *Financial Times*, September 7.

Index

Index compiled by Annette Musker